The Clarity of God's Existence

The Clarity of God's Existence

The Ethics of Belief after the Enlightenment

OWEN ANDERSON

WIPF & STOCK · Eugene, Oregon

THE CLARITY OF GOD'S EXISTENCE
The Ethics of Belief after the Enlightenment

www.wipfandstock.com

ISBN 13: 978-1-55635-695-7

Manufactured in the U.S.A.

Contents

Foreword

I MUST ADMIT THAT I was a bit skeptical when Owen sent me this manu-
script. I have known Owen for several years, and have followed his writing that has appeared as reviews and longer pieces in *Reviews in Religion
and Theology*. He has become a regular contributor to that journal (of
which I am the associate editor), and he covers a remarkable range of
material and subjects, always with an impeccable writing style and crisp
clear prose. But I tend not to be a big fan of works on apologetics, because
I tend to think that the truth of Christianity is proven in the trenches, so
to speak, in arguments over specific issues, rather than in general debates
about what apologetics should be.

I was wrong. This is an exciting book that advances the status of
apologetics by analyzing and probing some fundamental issues in contemporary philosophy and theology. The emphasis on clarity is, to me, new and
fresh and provocative. First of all, it provides an alternative to the idea that
arguments for God must be primarily analyzed as true or false, right or
wrong, and instead provides a method for testing their meaning. Second,
it connects in fundamental and creative ways with our notions of moral
responsibility. I am currently teaching a course on philosophy and religion
to undergraduates at Wabash College, and when we do the proofs, a re-
curring concern of the students is the problem of responsibility. At what
point do we hold people responsible for things they should or could know?
Conversely, how clear must God be in order to expect general revelation to
have any authority in our lives? And what is clarity anyway?

In sum, the issue of clarity links epistemology and moral philosophy
in a creative and constructive fashion. But that is only part of this book's
strengths. It is also a nice combination of historical criticism and contemporary analysis. I think Owen is able to pull this off due to the elegance
and simplicity of his focus. The question of excusability lies at the heart of
several theological doctrines and plays a role in any discussion of God's
judgment or the afterlife. Owen focuses on the connection of inexcus-

ability and redemption, which I found intriguing. I'm really surprised that the constellation of clarity, responsibility, and inexcusability has not been examined in detail before.

I truly believe that Owen's introduction of a new principle into philosophy of religion—the principle of clarity—will gain attention and analysis from many other philosophers and theologians and could very well become a standard trope in the field of philosophy of religion.

A final trait that I like about this book is its ability to economically and effectively delve into and characterize traditional or historic Christianity for the purposes of adjudicating among competing philosophical attempts to obscure the importance of clarity. Owen defends his thesis with the clearest exposition.

Stephen H. Webb
Wabash College
Oct 2007

Preface

PHILOSOPHICALLY, THE ENLIGHTENMENT BEGAN when Descartes made a search for clear and distinct ideas to serve as a foundation for knowledge. Currently, both secular and religious thinkers agree that the Enlightenment program failed. For instance, Alvin Plantinga denies that attempts to find such a foundation can succeed,[1] and Kelly James Clark asserts that the Enlightenment had an overly stringent conception of rationality that should be abandoned for intuitive and common sense religious belief.[2] Similarly, Graham Oppy argues that while there are no successful proofs for a divine being, there are also no successful proofs against the existence of a divine being.[3] The only irrational position, according to Oppy, is to maintain that reason can prove anything about God's existence one way or the other.[4] Even a recent edited volume which claims to be a defense of natural theology against the skepticism of David Hume concedes that there is no argument from natural theology that *proves* the existence of God such that it is irrational to maintain the opposite conclusion.[5] The book goes so far as to maintain that it is unlikely that any metaphysical claim can be proven in this manner.[6] The skepticism of Hume seems to have prevailed even in a book claiming to defend against Hume.

So what happened to the search for clear and distinct ideas on which to build a foundation for knowledge? It seems to have been abandoned in a two-fold process: first, inadequate candidates for clear and distinct ideas were used as foundations, and second these were shown to be insufficient by philosophers such as Hume and Kant. The important challenge from

---

1. Plantinga, *Warranted Christian Belief*, 68.
2. Clark, *Return to Reason*, 158.
3. Oppy, *Arguing*, 413.
4. Ibid., 425.
5. Sennett and Groothuis, *In Defense*, 16.
6. Ibid.

Hume and Kant is not their particular arguments against specific religious beliefs, such as miracles or scripture or the resurrection of the dead, but their critique of reason. It is the denial of the human ability to use reason to know about reality that is devastating and pervasive. As noted above, even those who defend religious beliefs against Hume have swallowed this pill of skepticism. The acceptance of the critique of reason is not incidental—the challenge from Hume and Kant is incisive and devastating to previous attempts to attain certainty about reality.

If nothing is clear, what are the implications? Specifically, if nothing is clear about basic features of reality, such as what has existed from eternity, can humans be held responsible or accountable for believing anything? There is a relationship between responsibility and clarity such that if a person is responsible to believe something, it must be clear, and if it is not clear then there can be no responsibility for belief. Or, if one wishes to admit of degrees of responsibility and clarity, then it can be affirmed that there is a relationship between the degree to which something is clear and the degree to which a person is responsible for belief. This means that the highest level of responsibility, such as everlasting punishment in hell, requires the highest level of clarity.

For something to be clear in this sense is for it to be based on clear distinctions, such as between *a* and *non-a*, or *being* and *non-being*. The denial of clarity involves the denial that there are clear distinctions—the opposite of what is clear is impossible because it denies the very distinction necessary for intelligibility. In such a case there would be no excuse for believing the opposite; one would be responsible for believing what is clear. Realizing that not everything is clear in this way, Enlightenment thinkers sought for a foundation of clarity. If the foundation is not clear then nothing else will be clear; alternative structures for belief such as coherentism still require that there are clear principles to guide belief (such as the law of non-contradiction). For Christianity the most basic belief on which the rest of the Christian worldview is founded is the existence of God. Furthermore, Christianity maintains that the failure to believe in God is inexcusable (the highest level of responsibility).[7]

The following is not a proof for the existence of God. It is one step removed from that. The following is an examination of why it is important for Christianity to demonstrate the clarity of God's existence. This

7. Romans 1:20. All Bible verses are from the New King James Version.

will include needing to wade through numerous attempts by Christians to avoid the need for clarity, and insufficient alternatives to clarity such as plausibility, probability, warrant, or intuition and common sense. It will also require focusing as sharply as possible on the challenge to reason from Hume and Kant, and how previous theistic arguments have failed. While the topic of God's existence always gets significant attention in philosophical literature, the need for clarity to establish inexcusability is conspicuously absent.

Acknowledgments

I WOULD LIKE TO thank Surrendra Gangadean for his help and mentor-ship over the years. His influence is obvious on every page, although any mistakes are my own. My hope is that this book will help illuminate the need for clarity about God's existence, and encourage people to read and carefully interact with the arguments that Surrendra Gangadean has presented in his book *Philosophical Foundation: A Critical Analysis of Basic Beliefs.*

I greatly appreciate the assistance of Arturo, Roger, and Val in help-ing me edit and proofread. This is the second book of mine that my Grandfather has proofed and his help and suggestions were very impor-tant to me. A special thanks should be given to Brian for all the careful work he did and in his help with formatting.

I would like to especially thank my wife Sherry, who has been with me through the many stages of work that it has taken to write this book, and who has been a source of encouragement.

Inexcusability, Redemption, and the Need for Clarity

What are the implications for Christianity if God's existence cannot be proven? The central message of Christianity involves a call to repentance from sin and the need for redemption. What is sin, and how does the failure to know God factor into sin? The Enlightenment has been criticized by contemporary Christian philosophers as relying too heavily on reason, but what are the implications if reason cannot be used to know God? In this chapter we will consider the relationship between clarity, inexcusability, and the need for redemption.

THE CHRISTIAN GOSPEL DOES not make sense apart from an understanding of sin. For this reason the Apostle Paul begins the book of Romans with a description of sin, with a special focus on the sin of failing to know what is clear about God (Romans 1:20). But what makes sin so bad that it requires redemption through Christ? Why is failing to know God a problem? Skeptics have noted that if we cannot know then we cannot be held accountable. Consider the subtle yet devastating manner in which David Hume challenges Christian belief. After arguing against the possibility of miracles, he says:

> Our most holy religion is founded on *Faith*, not on reason; and it is a sure method of exposing it to put it to such a trial as it is, by no means, fitted to endure. . . . we may conclude, that the *Christian Religion* not only was at first attended with miracles, but even at this day cannot be believed by any reasonable person without one. Mere reason is insufficient to convince us of its veracity: And whoever is moved by *Faith* to assent to it, is conscious of a continued miracle in his own person, which subverts all the principles of his

understanding, and gives him a determination to believe what is most contrary to custom and experience.[1]

For Hume the term "faith" means "blind faith" and perhaps even that which is contrary to reason. And yet the Christian religion claims that all persons should believe in God, and that the failure to do so is one of the sins (perhaps the central sin of "not understanding" that Paul identifies in Romans 3:11) for which Christ died. The following will ask if the claim that all humans ought to know God can be defended if it is not clear that God exists. Is the failure to know God culpable ignorance? Historic Christianity has maintained that unbelief is a sin.[2] However, after the challenges to theistic belief raised during the Enlightenment (especially by David Hume and Immanuel Kant), many have concluded that God's existence cannot be proven. If this is true then it follows that humans cannot be held accountable for not believing in God. And yet this would be a serious challenge to the claims of Historic Christianity.

The purpose of this work will be to argue for a principle called "the principle of clarity." This principle states that if the failure to know God (unbelief) is inexcusable (culpable ignorance), then it must be clear (readily knowable) that God exists. This means that it is necessary for God's existence to be clear (readily knowable) in order to make sense of the Christian claim that unbelief is culpable ignorance and requires redemption. Here, the term "God" will be used as conceived of in theism where God is said to be a spirit who is infinite, eternal, and unchanging in power, knowledge, and goodness. This is distinguished from all forms of non-theism, including deism, pantheism, panentheism, and polytheism. It is also distinguished from a vague "higher power" or "higher being." To establish that there is no excuse for failing to know God requires showing that the alternatives are not rational.

For there to be clarity there must be clear distinctions. Formally, this is stated as the distinction between *a* and *non-a*. At the most basic level, there must be a clear distinction between *being* and *non-being*. In asking about God's existence, we are asking if there is a clear distinction between what is eternal and what is temporal, and if "eternality" can be applied to the material world, the self, or anything else, or if it only can be applied to God. Clarity is required for inexcusability. One is inexcusable if:

1. Hume, *Enquiries*, 100.

2. Packer, *Concise Theology*, 11.

1. One holds to self-contradictory beliefs.

2. One does not have integrity—does not live according to the principles one teaches.

3. One does not know what is clear—since thinking is presuppositional (the less basic assumes the more basic), if anything is clear, the basic things are clear. Thus, one is inexcusable if one does not know what is basic.

4. One denies that there are clear distinctions. Clarity requires distinguishing between *a* and *non-a*. An example of a basic belief that is clear is the distinction between *being* and *non-being*. There is no excuse for failing to distinguish these because their distinction is the foundation of all thought—to give an excuse requires this distinction.

To challenge the claim that unbelief is inexcusable, the critics of Christianity need only to show that God is difficult to know, or not knowable.[3] This would provide an excuse for unbelief. Such an excuse would undermine the claim that the unbelievers are guilty for their unbelief, and thus take away any grounds of the need for redemption.[4] It is therefore necessary for Historic Christianity to establish that there is a need for redemption by showing that unbelief is inexcusable. This must be done before other parts of the Christian message can be understood, such as atonement through a representative, the deity of Christ, total depravity and the effectual calling, or the resurrection of the dead.

The purpose here is not to prove whether God does or does not exist, although the last chapters will consider what steps would be necessary in giving a proof. The purpose here is to consider a question that is part of the ethics of belief: What should I believe? If Historic Christianity claims that all persons should believe that God exists and that he has a specific nature, then all persons must be able to know God. Contemporary thinkers who have attempted to address the challenge that theistic belief should not be held because it is intellectually inadequate (the *de jure* objection), such as Alvin Plantinga and Nicholas Wolterstorff, have pointed out that

3. J. L. Schellenberg, *The Hiddenness of God.*

4. This is one aspect of *mens rea*, which asserts that a person is guilty both if they intended a wrong act, and also if they could have known an act was wrong but didn't actually know (culpable ignorance). To assert that a person is guilty, this knowledge must have been available to them through a reasonable amount of effort (see the entry on *mens rea* in "The Cambridge Dictionary of Philosophy" 2nd ed.).

theistic belief is analogical to beliefs that the materialist holds, such as belief in other minds or the reality of the physical world. The present work addresses a different aspect of the question. If all humans are held responsible for knowing God so that one is guilty for unbelief, then God must be knowable by all humans. This work will consider whether or not such a standard can be held after the challenges of the Enlightenment by thinkers like David Hume and Immanuel Kant.

Since the purpose is not to prove or disprove the existence of God, but to consider if such a strong claim as inexcusability can be made about unbelief, the following will not attempt to look at all individual expressions of theistic arguments. Instead, it will consider the basic kinds of arguments—the ontological, cosmological, and teleological—and how they came to be expressed by notable thinkers such as Aquinas and Locke. While fine-tuning of the arguments has been the response in the twentieth century by thinkers like William Lane Craig or Alvin Plantinga, the following will point out that the challenge given by Hume and Kant is aimed at the capacity to know anything about God by reason, and therefore a response must go beyond fine-tuning of the arguments.

The requirement for the clarity of God's existence is not imposed on Christianity from without, but is maintained by Christianity itself as well as being asked for by critics of theism. Defeaters have been raised to all of the traditional arguments for the existence of God. Skepticism about belief in God, both in terms of the actual existence of God, and the ability to know God, is common. This means that if Christianity is to continue to hold that it is clear that God exists, then it must respond to these defeaters. There is a difference between being personally certain or persuaded that God exists, and being able to show objectively that it is certain that God exists (objective certainty requires showing that the opposite is impossible). Skeptics of theism are asking for objective certainty, and given the statements about inexcusability made by the Apostle Paul, this appears to be a fair demand given both what the skeptic wants and what Christianity maintains.

The need for redemption posited by Historic Christianity assumes objective clarity which in turn establishes inexcusability and a basis for asserting that unbelief is sin. Terrence Penelhum sees this need for clarity when he says: "I see the role of natural theology as that of addressing this multiple ambiguity in our world; and if it is a role that cannot be discharged, Christians (and indeed all theists) have a problem in the very fact of ambiguity itself."[5] If the world is ambiguous, unclear, then there is not a clear distinction between being and non-being, between good and evil, or between true and false, and there can be no basis for making any claims whatsoever.

The claim that humans need redemption asserts that they need to be forgiven by God for something. Exactly how (under what conditions) this forgiveness is given is of central importance to the three theistic religions and is one of the main differences dividing them. To say that unbelief deserves just punishment is to say that a person in unbelief is guilty (morally culpable) for having unbelief, hence deserves just punishment for that reason, and requires the forgiveness of God if this punishment is to be avoided. One implication of asserting that unbelief requires forgiveness is that it must be clear that unbelief is wrong. This implies that the source of the knowledge of God and the source of the explanation of how to be forgiven for unbelief cannot be the same; there must be a distinction between general and special revelation.

General revelation refers to what can be known of God at all times by all persons. It is distinct from special revelation which is given through transmission and has not been accessible to all persons. J. I. Packer describes general revelation in the following way:

> General revelation is so called because everyone receives it, just by virtue of being alive in God's world. This has been so from the start of human history. God actively discloses these aspects of himself to all human beings, so that in every case failure to thank and serve the Creator in righteousness is sin against knowledge, and denials of having received this knowledge should not be taken seriously. God's universal revelation of his power, praiseworthiness, and moral claim is the basis of Paul's indictment of the whole human race as sinful and guilty before God for failing to serve him as we should (Romans 1:18–3:19).[6]

The content of special revelation is a description of the nature of, and the need for, redemption, and also a description of redemptive history. This means that it assumes that the reader can know God from general revelation and can know that there is a need for redemption. The assertion that a person is guilty for unbelief requires that the knowledge of God is available to that person apart from the revelation about how to be

5. Penelhum et al., *Faith,* 166.

6. Packer, *Concise Theology,* 9.

forgiven for not knowing God (special revelation). In other words, there is a logical (if not historical) order between these revelations: God must first be revealed to all persons, and this revelation must be ignored, in order for the need of a divine revelation about how to be forgiven for failing to know God to make sense. Because special revelation is not available to all persons at all times, and because special revelation (as revelation about redemption) presupposes that the reader knows who God is, it must be the case that there is a clear general revelation of God if the unbeliever is to be held guilty. Special revelation is not sufficient to establish the guilt of unbelief.

It is worth noting now that the claim that there is a clear general revelation of God also provides a framework for determining which books that claim to be special revelation are in fact special revelation. A book that claims divine origin, or a prophet who claims to have special revelation, and yet communicates a message that contradicts what is known of God from general revelation, cannot actually be special revelation or from God. Much has been made about the Nag Hammadi texts, or Gnostic Gospel. Yet these are not theistic works, and so it should not be a surprise that they are not part of the canon. Thus, while it might be the case that the particular content of special revelation cannot be deduced from general revelation, many "impostors" can be ruled out if God is known from general revelation.

The principle of clarity is a necessary presupposition of the redemptive claims of Christianity. If unbelief is inexcusable, then it must be clear that God exists. This does not mean that every specific Christian thinker expressly stated, or even thought about, the consequence of this if/then statement. The argument is that this has not been sustained as it should be, particularly after challenges to belief in God given during the Enlightenment. Many Christians have taken the knowledge of general revelation to be an immediate, intuitive knowledge and so have not seen the need for proofs. And yet the antecedent (that unbelief is inexcusable) is asserted by Christians and is an important part of the redemptive claims of Christianity. In fact, it will be argued here that there is a relationship between this principle and the way in which redemptive claims are held. When a given thinker holds that unbelief is inexcusable, that thinker is necessarily committed to also holding this principle. It would be unjust to punish someone for unbelief unless it was clear that he had an epistemic obligation to believe. But where this principle is thought to be impossible to hold, or too strict, then the inexcusability of unbelief will also be abandoned in favor of some kind of inclusivism, pluralism, or universalism.

1.1. CHRISTIAN SCRIPTURES AND CLARITY

J. I. Packer notes that the Christian scriptures affirm that God can be known through general revelation:

> God's world is not a shield hiding the Creator's power and majesty. From the natural order it is evident that a mighty and majestic Creator is there. Paul says this in Romans 1:19–21, and in Acts 17:28 he calls a Greek poet as witness that humans are divinely created. Paul also affirms that the goodness of this Creator becomes evident from kindly providences (Acts 14:17; cf. Romans 2:4), and that some at least of the demands of his holy law are known to every human conscience (Romans 2:14–15), along with the uncomfortable certainty of eventual retributive judgment (Romans 1:32). These evident certainties constitute the content of general revelation.[7]

The clarity of God's existence is affirmed in the Christian scriptures. In the Old Testament, David asserts, "The fool has said in his heart, 'There is no God'" (Psalm 14:1). Only that person who is negligent or unreasonable can fail to know God. It is this passage that inspired Anselm to look for a proof that could be used by all persons to know God. Anselm is an example of a Christian thinker who affirms that it is clear that God exists, apart from questions about whether or not his ontological argument does what he would like it to do. In Psalm 19 David says, "The heavens declare the glory of God, and the firmament displays His handiwork" (Psalm 19:1). The heavens are accessible to all humans, and so the implication is that all humans can know God, his glory, and his handiwork. The Prophet Isaiah also affirms the principle of clarity when he says, "The whole earth is full of His glory" (Isaiah 6:3). The implication is that since the whole earth is full of the glory of God, humans everywhere can know God.

Both the Ten Commandments and the Apostle Paul begin with the sin of unbelief. The first two commandments are against any failure to know God, or replacing God with something else. In Romans 1:20 Paul states, "For since the creation of the world His invisible attributes are clearly seen, being understood by the things that are made, even His eternal power and Godhead, so that they are without excuse." Although they

---

7. Packer, *Concise Theology*, 9.

knew God, their minds became darkened and they exchanged this for idols. In verses 21–27 Paul then describes how the failure to know God as one should results in numerous other sins. Clearly, Paul believes that God can be, and should be, known by all humans and it is the failure to do so that leads to other sins and requires redemption. When Paul spoke to the philosophers in Athens he affirmed that God has made it possible for all persons to know him:

> He has made from one blood every nation of men to dwell on all the face of the earth, and has determined their preappointed times and the boundaries of their dwellings, so that they should seek the Lord, in the hope that they might grope for Him and find Him, though He is not far from each one of us; for in Him we live and move and have our being (Acts 17:26–28).

According to Paul, the Greek philosophers, and all humans who dwell on the face of the earth, can and should know God. In Hebrews 11:1 faith is defined as the *evidence* of things not seen. Faith is contrasted with sight—what is seen—and not with reason or proof. Proof can be of what is not seen, and therefore it requires faith to be committed to reason and accept the conclusion without visible verification. In verse 6 it says that God is the rewarder of those that diligently seek him, reminder of what was said in Romans 3:11–14, that sin is the failure to seek, to understand, and to do what is right.

This can also be seen in the Lord's Prayer. It begins "Our Father in heaven, Hallowed be Your name" (Matthew 6:9). God's name is to be hallowed (glorified). However, if God cannot be known, then his name cannot be glorified. It is therefore a necessary presupposition that God can be known, and that he can be known by fishermen and tax collectors, not only by philosophers.

1.2. HISTORIC CHRISTIAN THINKERS AND CLARITY

In this book, "Historic Christianity" will take the process found in Acts 15 as the model and refer to what the best minds have agreed upon after much discussion. Acts 15 recounts the Council of Jerusalem in 50 A.D., after which there have been other formative councils, such as Nicea dealing with the Trinity, and Chalcedon dealing with Christology. The basis for "much discussion" is the scriptures, and so these councils are not taken to be infallible. But here it will be maintained that there is a "Historic

Christianity" that is based on a worldview which is being developed over time through working out implications and growing in consistency. This occurs in the context of a challenge to the faith, and requires the pastor/teachers to respond to the challenge. The most recent example is the Westminster Confession of Faith, which resulted after the challenges of the Reformation concerning the nature of justification, atonement, sacraments, sovereignty of God, the place of scripture and role of the church.

This view of Historic Christianity is in contrast to a view, expressed by Bart Ehrman in his *Lost Christianities*, that there are only Christianities, and that what decides which of them comes to be called "Christianity" is a power struggle mainly at the political level. There is no doubt that there are power struggles and political intrigues. But it is also true that there is rational consistency between ideas, so that we can speak of systems of ideas (worldviews), and that people argue in favor of these worldviews because they are convinced they are true. Texts such as the Gnostic Gospels were not rejected simply due to power struggles, but because they contradict basic ideas in the rest of scripture, such as theistic belief. This is called Historic Christianity not necessarily because it has been held by the majority at any one time (although throughout the centuries it is the majority position), but because it is the most consistent with the scriptures and the presuppositions of Christianity from general revelation.

Thus, we can speak about Historic Christianity which is based on theism, holds to the Trinity and the dual nature of Christ, and claims that sin is the failure to seek, understand and do what is right. Furthermore, it asserts that redemption is required, and that redemption can only be attained through the death and resurrection of Christ. There is much more to the Christian worldview, but in this book we are considering its assumptions—specifically the assumption of theism.

The Westminster Confession of Faith (as well as the Larger and Shorter Catechism) affirms the principle of clarity. The Confession itself begins by saying, "The light of nature, and the works of creation and providence do so far manifest the goodness, wisdom, and power of God, as to leave men inexcusable."[8] In his commentary on the Confession, A.A. Hodge affirms that the Confession begins this way in order to maintain that there is no excuse for unbelief: "That the light of nature and the works of creation and providence are sufficient to make known the fact that

---

8. *The Westminster Confession*, 1:1.

there is a God, and somewhat of his nature and character, so as to leave the disobedience of men without excuse."[9] G. I. Williamson also notes that the Confession affirms inexcusability:

> It has long been the habit among Christians (even of Reformed persuasion) to speak of the insufficiency of natural revelation, as if there were something defective in the revelation it makes of God. This may be seen in the traditional use of the 'theistic proofs'... After these, and similar arguments, were developed and brought together, it was hoped that unbelievers might be convinced that (a) 'a god' probably exists; and (b) that if he does exist, he might possibly be the God of the Bible. Only when the possibility of the existence of 'God' was thus 'proved' was it expected that the unbeliever would admit further evidence that might confirm the fact that God really does exist... What is wrong with this approach? Simply this: every fact (and the sum total of all facts) *proves* the existence of the God of the Bible. And there is good reason. This God is. He always was. He existed before anything was made. And the whole universe exists only because he planned it. Every detail of the related aspects of existence has the precise character and purpose that God intended. It therefore has meaning that is God-given.... Everything in heaven and earth says that the true God is, that he is glorious, that he is creator and ruler of all, and that we are his creatures.[10]

It is important to note that Williamson is opposed to simply showing that God probably exists. Rather, he wants to affirm that God is readily knowable, and this is the basis for inexcusability. If this is what is affirmed in the Westminster Confession of Faith, then it is a significant position within Christianity, and has had major influence. What will be argued here is that it has not been developed as it should be, and that most Christian apologists have not maintained the important relationship between clarity and inexcusability.

The Westminster Larger and Shorter Catechisms both begin by asking, "What is the chief and highest end of man?" The answer given is that "Man's chief and highest end is to glorify God, and fully to enjoy him forever."[11] This cannot be done if God is not knowable. In its consideration of the Ten Commandments, the Larger Catechism says that what is required of all men in the first commandment is "the knowing

9. Hodge, *Westminster Confession* 1.1
10. Williamson, *The Westminster*, 1.
11. Westminster *Larger Catechism* Q.1.

and acknowledging of God to be the only true God, and our God; and to worship and glorify him accordingly."[12] Again, here it is affirmed that all humans can and should know God. This is a, if not the, major confession of the Reformation, and is still held to as a doctrinal standard by many Protestant denominations. Benjamin Warfield says, "No Catechism begins on a higher plane than the Westminster 'Shorter Catechism.'"[13] This is because it points humans to the right relation with God:

> The Westminster Catechism cuts itself free at once from this entanglement with lower things and begins, as it centers and ends, under the illumination of the vision of God in His glory, to subserve which it finds to be the proper end of human as of all other existence, of salvation as of all other achievements. To it all things exist for God, unto whom as well as from whom all things are; and the great question for each of us accordingly is, How can I glorify God and enjoy Him forever?[14]

The claim made in this catechism is that God should be known and glorified by all humans (not only those with access to special revelation). Warfield then traces the source of this question and answer in the catechism to the influence of John Calvin. Warfield argues that in Calvin's *Institutes*, "the knowledge of God is presented as the chief end and highest good of man."[15]

The second question of the Larger Catechism is, "How doeth it appear that there is a God?" The answer given is, "The very light of nature in man, and the works of God, declare plainly that there is a God."[16] Furthermore, in his commentary on the Larger Catechism, J.G. Vos says, "This 'light of nature' is common to all mankind. The heathen who have never received God's special revelation, the Bible, have a certain knowledge of God by nature, and a certain consciousness of the moral law in their own hearts (Romans 2:14–16). To believe in God is natural to mankind; only 'the fool' says in his heart that there is no God."[17] Concerning what the light of nature reveals about God, Vos says:

---

12. *Larger Catechism* Q. 104.

13. Warfield, "The Westminster Assembly and Its Work," 379.

14. Ibid.

15. Ibid., 382.

16. Larger Catechism Q. 2.

17. Vos, *The Westminster*, 5.

> The light of nature and the works of God bring to mankind a message concerning the existence of God, his eternal power and deity (Romans 1:19–20), his glory (Psalm 19:1), and his moral law (Romans 2:14–16). This natural revelation of God and of his will is sufficient to leave men *without excuse* for their sins (Romans 1:20–21).[18]

Stephen Charnock's work on the existence and nature of God is one of, if not the, most comprehensive works on the subject by a Christian thinker. He begins, as does Anselm, with a consideration of the fool in Psalm 14:

> For the first, every atheist is a grand fool. If he were not a fool, he would not imagine a thing so contrary to the stream of the universal reason of the world, contrary to the rational dictates of his own soul, and contrary to the testimony of every creature, and link in the chain of creation: if he were not a fool, he would not strip himself of humanity, and degrade himself lower than the most despicable brute. It is a folly; for though God be so inaccessible that we cannot know him perfectly, yet he is so much in the light, that we cannot be totally ignorant of him. . . . the demonstrations reason furnisheth us with for the existence of God, will be evidences of the atheist's folly.[19]

Charnock then continues to give what he thinks are arguments that establish the existence and nature of God in a way that is accessible by all humans, and is only denied by the fool (in other words, only the unreasonable deny God). This is very much in contrast to contemporary apologists who mainly aim at showing "plausibility" of belief.

But what I would like to argue is that Charnock expresses the attitude about the existence of God that is most prevalent in Christianity, and has become a block to giving a successful response. That attitude is that God's existence is the foundation of Christianity and is so obvious it need not be argued for:

> The existence of God is the foundation of all religion. The whole building totters if the foundation be out of course: if we have not deliberate and right notions of it, we shall perform no worship, no service, yield no affection to him. If there be not a God, it is impossible there can be one, for eternity is essential to the notion

18. Ibid., 6. Emphasis mine.
19. Charnock, *The Existence*, 25.

of a God; so all religion would be vain, and unreasonable to pay homage to that which is not in being, nor can ever be. We must first believe that he is, and that he declares himself to be, before we can seek him, adore him, and devote our affections to him. We cannot pay God a due and regular homage, unless we understand him in his perfections what he is; and we can pay him no homage at all, unless we believe that he is.[20]

However, there must be some sense in which Charnock thinks that arguments are necessary because he gives us 500 pages of text doing so. This also helps illustrate my point. He does so in response to the challenge of the atheist. It is in response to a challenge that Christianity begins to work out its doctrines. This can be seen from the earliest times of Christianity, when the challenge of Arianism required a more complete statement on the Trinity and nature of Christ; in questions of the freedom of the will in contrast to Pelagianism; in questions of the nature of grace and faith in contrast to indulgences. And so what this work will look at is the challenge to the very existence of God given by some of the most notable thinkers of the Enlightenment. It is not the case that there were no atheists before the Enlightenment. But the philosophies of Hume and Kant give a more pointed challenge to belief in God than has ever been given before.[21] Christian thinkers can no longer assume that everyone believes in God, or that God's existence is so obvious it need not be argued for, or that only an elite few need or can understand the arguments.

1.3. OVERVIEW OF ENLIGHTENMENT CHALLENGES TO GOD'S EXISTENCE

The Enlightenment challenge raised an important question to the very essence of Christianity: Can God be known by all persons apart from special revelation? This question leads to many other important questions, including: How do we know if there is scripture, which interpretation of scripture is correct, and why should we accept Christianity as opposed to some other religion or naturalism? Rejecting appeals to scripture or

20. Charnock, *The Existence*, 26.

21. Hume believed that the problem of evil was a significant challenge to belief in God, but he allowed that, for all we know, there is a simple solution to the problem of evil—in other words, for all we know God exists, and if so there is an unknown solution to the problem of evil. It is interesting that Hume allowed for this, although he did not believe it to be the case or see how it could be.

tradition as divisive and question-begging, the Enlightenment looked for an answer that could be accepted by all. The Enlightenment asserted that the answer must be found by reason. Reason as the laws of thought is universal, the same in all, and subjective and divisive (because unable to be confirmed publicly) like religious experience. While the optimism of the Enlightenment has largely been abandoned in favor of skepticism, its challenge to belief in God remains. The need for reason to show that God exists, and questions about reason's capacity to do so, is a helpful challenge and should be welcomed as a potential for further development. However, the pattern mentioned above has also happened in the case of this challenge. In response to the challenge some have abandoned Christianity for naturalism, pantheism, deism, and others. Of those who remained in Christianity, some refused to offer a response to the challenge, and instead rejected reason and the Enlightenment as the source of the problem. Others attempted to offer a response. We will see that these responses have not been successful to date.

It might be pointed out that the Wars of Religion are what brought this question to the forefront. Religion, and appeals to special revelation and tradition, began to be viewed as divisive and harmful. The search was made for something that was universal. At first this was said to be found in the religion of humanity, but as this was found lacking it was rejected in favor of skepticism or naturalism. The Enlightenment increasingly rejected a divine Christ, and instead focused on his moral/ethical teachings; this led to deism and eventually naturalism. If Christianity cannot show that it is clear that God exists, then the most consistent response is to abandon it for another worldview. However, if it can be shown that it is clear that God exists, then the failure to believe is inexcusable and the question arises as to whether this unbelief requires redemption. While deism asserts that God is not concerned with unbelief, theism asserts that unbelief requires redemption and that God gives special revelation to explain how this redemption will take place.

Growth in understanding occurs in the process of challenges and responses. There is a common pattern of response in each new challenge. The challenge causes some to abandon the worldview while others hold firm. Of those that continue to maintain the worldview a response is required to meet the challenge. Some offer responses and some do not. Of those that offer a response, some are successful and some are not. Since the goal of the challenge is to show that at some point Christianity is inconsistent, a successful response must be an intellectual response that deepens the understanding of Christianity and shows that there is not a contradiction (consider the eventual framing of the doctrine of the Trinity: one God, three persons). Herein is the debate and discussion.

This pattern will become more specific in that there is a predictable causal relationship in how persons either abandon Historic Christianity or respond inadequately to these challenges. Those thinkers who maintain that God cannot be known by humans through the use of reason will also adapt the claim that unbelief is inexcusable and modify the means of redemption. For instance, contemporary theologians (beginning in the nineteenth century) who believe either that God is not knowable or that God (in the theistic sense) does not exist, abandon the exclusivist claims of Historic Christianity and instead adopt some form of inclusivism or pluralism. This is entirely consistent with the claim that God is not knowable. A similar example is found in the Medieval period with its doctrines of purgatory, implicit faith, sale of indulgences, and its exalted view of the best of the Greek and Roman world (for instance, Cato's role in Dante's *Divine Comedy*).

There is a logical relationship operating between these beliefs. If humans cannot know God, then to be consistent one must adopt some form of inclusivism or pluralism and deny that unbelief is inexcusable. However, if one wishes to defend a form of exclusivism as found in Historic Christianity, one must hold that it is clear that God exists. The pattern we will see is that those who accept that it is not clear that God exists also abandon Historic Christianity and its exclusivist claims about redemption, while those in Historic Christianity who refuse to show that it is clear that God exists are unable to offer an adequate response to the Enlightenment challenge.

1.4. BOOK OVERVIEW

And yet Christianity cannot abandon the inexcusability of unbelief without also abandoning much else that has been held as central to the faith. The clarity of God's existence is a necessary presupposition to the Christian claims about redemption. If unbelief is inexcusable, then God's existence must be clear. If God's existence is not clear, then it cannot be inexcusable to fail to believe in God. Whichever conclusion one draws (either it is clear that God exists, or it is not and unbelief is not inexcusable) is momentous. The next three chapters will be spent arguing that the principle of clarity is a necessary presupposition of the Christian claims of redemption and that Christianity cannot avoid it without changing those claims. Additionally, notable thinkers and the arguments they offer in relationship to the principle of clarity will be examined.

There have been multiple attempts to get around the requirement of clarity. These were present both before and after the challenges of Hume and Kant. The tension arises between the claim that unbelief is inexcusable and requires redemption and the commonly held view that it is difficult to know God. Any worldview that wishes to maintain that unbelief is inexcusable and requires redemption must also maintain the principle of clarity. Attempts by Christianity to get around the need for the clarity of the knowledge of God fail because they undermine the claim of the need for redemption. Indeed, apart from claims about redemption, if there is no clarity there can be no meaningful distinctions and therefore intelligibility is lost. If there is not a clear distinction between *true* and *false*, then nothing can be affirmed or denied. If there is not a clear distinction between *being* and *non-being*, then nothing can be said to be or not be. If there is not a clear distinction between *good* and *evil*, then no values can be maintained and no choices made. This is true for any worldview. However, Historic Christianity has laid emphasis on these and therefore the clarity of God's existence is a necessary presupposition to its claims about redemption.

In pursuing this line of argument the following will, of necessity, respond to objections from non-Christians to the Historic Christian claim that all humans need redemption through Christ for inexcusable unbelief. It will also require responding to Christians who have either departed from Historic Christianity or have not thought through the implications of their beliefs about redemption. Often non-Christians are responding to the deficiencies in the belief system of Christians and are doing so in a consistent and thoughtful manner. The problem with the non-Christian response is not that they are inconsistent but they are assuming that there is not a clear general revelation of God's existence. Unfortunately, they are often joined in this assumption with the very Christians who claim that all humans need redemption. As such, I will address both what is necessary within the Christian worldview to justify its claims about redemption and what is necessary on the part of the Christian worldview to respond to external challenges. The term "Historic Christianity" will be used to refer to that worldview expressed in such creeds as the Apostles' Creed, the Nicean Creed, and the Chalcedon Creed. Historic Christianity is theistic, holds that scripture is divinely inspired, and that salvation is necessary for all persons and is available only through the atoning work of Christ. Since the message of redemption and inexcusability is essential to Christianity, the question herein will be whether contemporary Christians can develop a response to the Enlightenment challenges without abandoning its claims about redemption.

Chapter 2 will consider attempts to avoid the requirement of the principle of clarity. Each attempt to avoid clarity will end up without grounds for the inexcusability of unbelief and therefore be unable to logically maintain that all humans need redemption for unbelief. This means that such attempts are inconsistent with Historic Christianity and its redemptive claims. It will also be shown that those Christians who have adopted some means of denying clarity, have also generally abandoned claims about the need for redemption in favor of forms of inclusivism or pluralism. Such a move is consistent with the denial of clarity, but should be viewed as an abandonment of Historic Christianity.

Chapter 3 considers attempts to avoid the need for arguments to know God, and Chapter 4 will examine the traditional arguments for God's existence. The arguments as given by Aquinas and Locke will be the focus. Attention will be paid to the arguments themselves, and to whether or not each thinker believes that it is clear that God exists. The goal here is not to argue for or against the existence of God, but to examine whether or not it has been shown by the traditional arguments that it is clear that God exists.

Aquinas will be looked at because he stands as the first and most notable attempt to systematize proofs for God's existence. His proofs are *a posteriori*. For many, God's existence must be accepted by faith (appeal to authority) rather than as knowledge, because the proofs can only be understood by a few. He does not think that it can be proven that the material world is not eternal apart from special revelation. Aquinas does not think that it is clear that God exists and because of this he does not stress the inexcusability of unbelief. Instead, he makes allowances for the masses who are unable to think through the proofs. The question is whether God, as perfectly just, can hold people accountable for unbelief if they could not have known him, and what accommodations will be made, such as the sale of indulgences or second chances after death.

Locke's views will be examined because of his position in the Enlightenment and the approach he takes to God's existence, which is very different from that of Aquinas's position. Locke asserted that it is clear that God exists. He gave a combination of *a priori* and *a posteriori* arguments. The problem for Locke is that his argument has many weak points so that while he does assert the clarity of God's existence, he does not prove it. Further, he does not see that clarity entails inexcusability and consequently he fails to see the need for redemption and special revelation. Locke's empiricism is the central source of his inability to establish the clarity of God's existence.

Chapter 5 examines the criticisms given by David Hume and Immanuel Kant in order to identify the crux of their challenge and how this affects the principle of the clarity of God's existence. David Hume offered significant objections to the theistic arguments. It is reported that he told Boswell that he was never an atheist until he read Locke and Clarke.[22] He offers significant challenges to both *a priori* and *a posteriori* arguments. He denies that it is clear that God exists. Perhaps the most important point of his critique is his challenge to reason. Because of his empiricism he ends in a skepticism which serves as the motivating point for Kant.

Immanuel Kant attempted to respond to Hume's skepticism. However, he ends by denying that reason can know being in itself. While he believes that God must be posited for morality, he does not think that God's existence is clear or can be proven by reason. He categorizes all theistic arguments into three kinds, and argues that each of these is based on the ontological argument. He believes that this argument fails, and therefore all theistic arguments fail. His legacy is conspicuous in both the nineteenth and twentieth centuries, and is the basis for many of the strongest attacks on theism. If Hume and Kant cannot be answered then it would seem that theistic proofs are not possible and, therefore, the claim that unbelief is inexcusable is indefensible.

Chapter 6 examines the legacy of Kant in some of the major critics of theism and theistic proofs. In doing this, the presuppositions behind the Humean and Kantian criticism will come into sharper focus. If a solution can be found that will support the principle of clarity, it will be in identifying the central challenge and seeing how this can be refuted.

---

22. Copleston, *A History of Philosophy*, 309.

Chapter 7 considers the major responses to these challenges and why they have come short. These responses are largely the product of the twentieth century, and many are still being attempted today. However, it will be shown that they do not adequately respond to the challenges of Hume and Kant, and that they are not sufficient to demonstrate the clarity of God's existence, or the inexcusability of unbelief and the need for redemption. As such they are inadequate and counterproductive.

Chapter 8 considers the necessary conditions for clarity and the steps needed to show that it is clear that God exists. The first of these is that there is no being from non-being, or its equivalent expression that there are no uncaused events. Arguing that the impossibility of being from non-being is a necessary assumption for all intelligibility, this chapter establishes this as the first step in the process of showing the clarity of God's existence. This chapter, as well as the next, also begins to frame the response to the critique of reason given by Hume and Kant.

Chapter 9 gives an overview of philosophers who attempt to posit uncaused events or being from non-being, from Sextus Empiricus to Quantum Physics, including Eastern thinkers like Lao-Tzu and Chuang-Tzu. The argument given is that none of these succeed in showing that there could be being from non-being, and any attempt to hold that there is becomes unintelligible.

Chapter 10 concludes the book with a look at what must be done from here to show that it is clear that God exists. Arguing that something has existed from eternity, and that only God can be eternal (in contrast to the material world or finite self), this chapter is a conceptual response to the criticisms of Hume and Kant. This final chapter argues that there are obvious steps that must be taken, and can be taken, to show that it is clear that God exists. Leaving a full development of these for another book,[23] these steps are given and briefly defended.

The argument presented in this book can be summarized as saying: Clarity is necessary for inexcusability, the traditional proofs did not establish clarity, Hume and Kant challenged the ability of reason itself to know God, responses to Hume and Kant have not established clarity, and if Historic Christianity is to continue to claim that unbelief is a sin, then it must show the clarity of God's existence.

---

23. See Surrendra Gangadean's *Philosophical Foundation: A Critical Analysis of Basic Beliefs.*

The inexcusability of unbelief must be demonstrated or the redemptive claim of Christianity is unintelligible. What if Bertrand Russell is correct when he says: "The whole conception of God is a conception derived from the ancient Oriental despotism. It is a conception quite unworthy of free men. When you hear people in church debasing themselves and saying that they are miserable sinners, and all the rest of it, it seems contemptible and not worthy of self-respecting human beings."[24] Or, consider Graham Oppy's claim that there is no successful proof for the existence of God.[25] If this is true then should I believe in God, and can unbelief be said to be inexcusable? The goal of this work is primarily to establish the principle of the inexcusability of unbelief and its necessary position as a presupposition to the redemptive claims of Christianity. If the Christian can show this principle to be true, and that it is, in fact, clear that God exists, then unbelief is inexcusable. However, if this cannot be shown, then the Christian claim about the need for redemption from unbelief becomes unintelligible. This hints that a great deal is at stake in this discussion, both for the Christian and the non-Christian.

---

24. Russell, *Why I Am Not A Christian*, 23.
25. Oppy, *Arguing*, 425.

2

Attempts to Avoid the Need for Clarity

While it may seem that it is non-Christians, or atheists, who mainly reject the idea of the clarity of God's existence, it is also Christians who often attempt to avoid this requirement. Such a requirement is said to be too strict, or out of the reach of most people, or not what God wants. In this chapter we will consider some of the most popular attempts to avoid the clarity of God's existence.

THE CLAIM THAT ALL humans need redemption is central to Christianity. It is this that its many divisions share in common. Historic Christianity has been exclusivist on this point, asserting that redemption can be achieved only through the atoning work of Christ. It asserts that the need for redemption is universal among humans, that all have sinned. In its early years this set Christianity in contrast to religions based on heredity, the inclusivist/pluralist polytheism of Rome, or secret knowledge available only to a few initiates.

The Christian claim is that all humans need redemption from sin. Redemption and sin are necessarily joined. Redemption does not mean simply growth or maturing. Growth does not require redemption—it does not require payment and forgiveness. Nor is redemption merely an escape from suffering. Redemption is a purchasing out of a position of guilt by another. Persons in the state of sin and guilt cannot redeem themselves. Another is required to act as redeemer. Hence, any discussion of redemption must include a discussion of sin and guilt.

In Christianity, sin has been defined as any want of conformity to or transgression of God's law. The first act of non-conformity would be to deny that there is a God or a law of God. This is unbelief. Unbelief as the first sin is the originator of all other sins. A decree against unbelief is implicit in the first commandment. Jesus summarizes all of the commandments in "You shall love the Lord your God with all your heart, with all your soul, and with all your mind" (Matthew 22:37). Paul asserts that "He who comes to God must believe that He is, and that He is a rewarder of those who diligently seek Him" (Hebrews 11:6). Christianity affirms that unbelief is sin and requires redemption.

To conform to God's law requires that one can know God and the law. If God is unknowable then the claim that all humans need redemption from unbelief becomes indefensible. Redemption assumes that there is sin and guilt. But if humans cannot know God, then they cannot be guilty in failing to know God. It may be the case that there is a need for help from God, but not redemption. If humans have an excuse, such as that God is unknowable or very difficult to know, then there is not guilt for unbelief. Paul sees this and asserts, "For since the creation of the world His invisible attributes are clearly seen, being understood by the things that are made, even His eternal power and Godhead, so that they are without excuse" (Romans 1:20). According to Paul and Historic Christianity, God is knowable by all and consequently unbelief is inexcusable. To say that there is no excuse for failing to know God is to say that the alternatives are not rationally acceptable (for instance, are contradictory). Christianity must be able to prove that there is a God in order for its message to be meaningful.

It could be asserted that unbelief is not what matters, but rather that actions like theft and sexual immorality are what incur guilt and require redemption. Paul certainly does not hold this, but rather asserts that unbelief is the beginning of all other transgressions. This is the darkening of the mind; it is not seeking and not understanding that results in not doing what is right. And it is worth noting that the Ten Commandments begin with two commands about knowing God. The theistic traditions all affirm that unbelief is in fact a sin. More generally, if it is clear that God exists and humans have the capacity to know this but do not, then they are failing in their responsibility to use reason to know the truth. This failure to know the truth bears a certain kind of blame that makes unbelief a kind of sin.

Historic Christianity presupposes the principle of clarity. Historic Christianity affirms that unbelief is culpable ignorance. Traditionally, the clarity of God's existence is spoken of as being known through general revelation. General revelation is what all persons can know about God at all times, in contrast to special revelation (scriptures).

General revelation is so called because everyone received it, just by virtue of being alive in God's world.... God has now supplemented general revelation with the further revelation of himself as Savior of sinners through Jesus Christ. This revelation, given in history, and embodied in Scripture, and opening the door of salvation to the lost, is usually called special or specific revelation.[1]

Historic Christianity presupposes that there is a clear revelation of God. It is the failure to know God through general revelation that requires redemption and the message found in special revelation. "Scripture *assumes*, and experience confirms, that human beings are naturally inclined to some form of religion, yet they fail to worship their Creator whose general revelation of himself makes him *universally known*."[2] To deny the clarity of God's existence is to render the message of redemption unintelligible, and to undermine the basis for needing special revelation.

The debate between exclusivists (only one path to God), inclusivists (multiple paths to God), and pluralists (God is only one form of the ultimate) rests on whether general revelation is clear.

Exclusivists hold that salvation is available only in Jesus Christ to the extent that those who have never heard the gospel are eternally lost.... For *pluralists*, other religions are legitimate means of salvation. Pluralism involves a positive and a negative element: Negatively, pluralism categorically rejects exclusivism (and often also inclusivism); positively, it affirms that people can find salvation in various religions and in many ways ... *inclusivists* hold that while salvation is ontologically founded on the person of Christ, its benefits have been made universally available by the revelation of God.[3]

The exclusivist can consistently maintain that unbelief is inexcusable and requires redemption because there is a clear general revelation for all humans. However, exclusivists have generally not held that it is clear that God exists from general revelation. Consequently, inclusivists and pluralists have pointed out that it would be unjust for persons to be condemned for unbelief when there was no way for them to overcome their unbelief. For the exclusivist to assert that God will condemn whom he will is inadequate because it separates God's condemnation from that

1. Packer, *Concise Theology*, 9.
2. Ibid., 11. Emphasis mine.
3. Karkkainen, *An Introduction*, 24.

which is deserving of condemnation. God condemns those who are guilty. The guilt of unbelief presupposes that God could have been known. It is because of this that unbelief as sin is condemned.

The modern trend in academia has been toward inclusivism and pluralism. "Exclusivism seems so unrealistic in the light of our knowledge of the wider religious life of mankind."[4] The awareness of the variety and sincerity of the world's religions make either inclusivism or pluralism appear to be more consistent than exclusivism. To the inclusivist and pluralist the claims of Historic Christianity to exclusive redemption through Christ are unintelligible. Exclusivism is said to contradict the justice of God due to the fact that some are unfairly condemned because they did not know God and yet could not have known God.

> With regard to a more positive and tolerant attitude toward other religions, we should not ignore the radical transformation of intellectual climate brought about by the Enlightenment. Before the Enlightenment and the rise of classical liberalism that followed, most people took it for granted that an exclusive claim to the superiority of Christianity needed no extensive justification. The Enlightenment eradicated major pillars of orthodoxy, however, and left theology and the church to rethink major doctrines and convictions. Even those who followed orthodoxy could not go back to the pre-Enlightenment homogenous culture but had to give their testimonies in an intellectually more tolerant and permissive cultural milieu. There was a shift from dogmatic definitions to a new appreciation of the ethical life and love of neighbor as the essence of religion.[5]

However, it is also true that Historic Christianity is neither pluralistic nor inclusivistic. Consequently, for those interested in Historic Christianity the question of the clarity of general revelation must be viewed as important, indeed essential.

Exclusivists must show that there is a clear general revelation of God to all humans. It is circular to try to establish an exclusivist position by appeals to tradition or the Bible. Such attempts have been ineffectual. However, if it is established that there is a clear general revelation of God, then unbelief is inexcusable and is sin. This sin and the accompanying

---

4. Hick, "A Philosophy of Religious Pluralism," 425.
5. Karkkainen, *An Introduction*, 19.

guilt deserve everlasting condemnation. This makes sense of the exclusivists' claim and is consistent with the justice of God.

The current challenge for Historic Christianity is to give justification for its claim that all humans need redemption through Christ, by showing that there is no excuse for not knowing God—that unbelief is culpable. In order to establish this, the clarity of general revelation must be shown. In order to highlight this need, seven attempts to avoid clarity will be considered and shown to contradict the Christian claim about redemption. While the point is to show that such attempts are inconsistent with clarity and therefore with the inexcusability of unbelief, it will also be relevant to show that they are not insurmountable problems for establishing the principle of clarity.

2.1. SKEPTICISM

Clarity conflicts with skepticism. Skepticism as a universal claim says that knowledge is impossible. Some skeptics might say that some knowledge is possible but God is unknowable. If this claim is true then unbelief, as ignorance, is not culpable. Both forms of skepticism are often the result of continuing divisions between humans. As the skeptic views these divisions, and the lack of progress made in the realm of knowledge, he concludes that knowledge must be impossible. One reason given for skepticism is that philosophy appears to have made little progress in natural theology or metaphysics:

> I will therefore conclude with pointing to two most important features of the higher life which stand in the same position. First, Philosophy: in spite of the arduous and unwearied efforts of men of the highest intellectual power it cannot be affirmed that the last three centuries have provided us with a philosophy of acknowledged supremacy, in relation to which all others can be set in place as historical stages superseded by a consummating system. Neither in Germany nor in France, nor in the British world, taking them separately, has this been achieved: much less has it been accomplished in Europe as a whole. And, secondly, in Christian Theology as the dogmatic exposition of the contents of the Gospel, the Reformation has caused a bisection, and has not brought uniformity even on the Protestant side of the line; while in the application to Church government and modes of worship the situation is still more varied and diversified. If this is so for Philosophy on the one hand and for Christian Theology on the other, ought we be surprised that variety

has prevailed, and still prevails, in the region of Natural Theology,
where these have a certain extent of common interest?[6]

However, the reality of continuing divisions does not prove that we cannot know but only that some, in fact, many do not know. The skeptic assumes that humans are seeking to know and yet failing to know. If this
were true then it would also be true that God's existence is not clear. The
alternative possibility is that humans are not seeking to know God, so
that even though God's existence is clear the result is that none know
God. It is often the case that those who are not seeking think they are
seeking. Therefore, the mere reality of persons who claim to be seeking
and yet do not know is insufficient to disprove clarity. In fact, the reality
that persons do not know God could be taken as an argument in favor of
the need for redemption. Natural theology, as the study of God as known
through general revelation, stands in contrast to skepticism and fideism.
The former says that God is not knowable, the latter that belief should be
placed blindly (without proof or justification) in the absence of the ability
to know God.

Apart from determining its accuracy, skepticism can be shown here
to be inconsistent with the need for clarity presupposed by the claim that
all humans need redemption. If we cannot know then we cannot be held
responsible. Whether knowledge is not possible in general, or God is unknowable, such claims are incompatible with Historic Christianity since
redemption requires guilt and guilt in this case requires knowledge.

Skepticism provides an excuse for unbelief. An example is expressed
by Hans Kung: "It is possible to deny God. Atheism cannot be eliminated
rationally. It is irrefutable."[7] If such a view as this is true, then the unbeliever has an excuse. The lack of proof or evidence constitutes an excuse
in this case because one cannot be said to be guilty for failing to believe
what one has no reason to believe. As rational beings, nothing more can
be expected from us but to hold beliefs that are rational. It should not be
surprising that one who holds a view like Kung's will also abandon the
redemptive claims of Historic Christianity and instead explore inclusivism and pluralism.

6. Caldecott, *The Philosophy*, 421.
7. Kung, *Does God Exist?*, 568.

2.2. FIDEISM

Clarity conflicts with fideism. Fideism claims that we should believe even in the absence of proof. The fideist agrees with the skeptic that knowledge is not possible. However, where the skeptic refrains from belief, the fideist asserts a leap should be made. Belief should be held without proof, or in spite of the lack of proof. For some fideists this is a regrettable concession and it is admitted that knowledge would be superior. For others a blind leap is superior to reason and knowledge and should be made boldly. If fideism is true, then unbelief, as ignorance, is not culpable.

Fideism often rests on an appeal to authority. The fideist defers to another person or text that is said to know. This knowledge is transferred to the believer, even though the believer lacks proof. The essential question is whether the sources are reliable, and which (if any) of the many books that claim to be special revelation actually are from God. Perhaps the objects of religious activity are products of the imagination:

> Our natural incredulity in these matters is increased by our study of history. Educated people are well aware of the way in which, in ancient Greece, men continued to talk confidently about the lives and characters of the Olympian gods long after they were reasonably sure that these were fictitious beings. Perhaps we are in a similar situation. Perhaps millions who flock to church on Sundays in order to pray are only exercising their own imaginations in a world in which there are many to pray, but nowhere One who can listen or care to respond. It is conceivable that the entire evolutionary process, involving millions of years, is purely meaningless, in the sense that it involves no purpose and reflects no mind. It is possible that the only example of consciousness in the entire universe is that which we know in our little lives on one particular planet, and that, beyond the surface of our earth, there is neither life nor consciousness nor understanding anywhere, but only space and planets and stars. To say that we know better by the light of faith is not a convincing answer; the early Greeks had faith, but their faith was centered on nonexistent objects.[8]

The fideist is unable to explain why the leap should be made to one belief system rather than another. As soon as proof is offered in support of the leap (say, to Christianity instead of Buddhism), the leap is no longer fideistic.

8. Trueblood, *Philosophy of Religion*, 18.

Fideism faces the same contradiction with the claim that humans need redemption as does skepticism. Also, in asking humans to believe without proof, fideism is contrary to human nature as rational. It asks humans to accept a story about the world apart from rational proof:

> The contemporary fideist tries to support his position by developing a story about reason's limitations and by contending that this story deserves general acceptance. Inquiry into the ground for this view is important because any claims about the capacities and scope of reason have vast significance for philosophy. It is not the fact that fideists place religion in the sphere of the non-rational that bothers me, but that the Irrelevancy Thesis has implications for our understanding of the promise of reason and of the philosophic life. Thus, in arguing a position that is sympathetic to the possibility of a religion based on reason, I aim to save reason, not religion, from diminution.[9]

How do we know what to believe without proof? Fideism undermines itself. In offering an argument for why one ought to make the blind leap to a specific religious system, fideism is recognizing that arguments are necessary. The question of what to believe is settled by searching for justification. Even the appeal to one's heart or emotions is an attempt at justification. It should be expected that those who accept fideism will also abandon exclusivism and the historic claims of Christianity about redemption in favor of some form of inclusivism or pluralism. This emphasizes the incompatibility of fideism and the claim that unbelief is inexcusable. Attempts to resolve this incompatibility by asserting that belief in God needs no justification because it is properly basic will be considered later.

2.3. PROBABILITY AND PLAUSIBILITY

Clarity conflicts with the view that God's existence is only probable. Such a position concedes that it is possible that God exists and possible that God does not exist. A given argument might make it appear more or less probable that God exists. William Lane Craig takes this approach in his assessment of the truth of Christianity. The standards that he uses for the truth of a worldview are internal consistency and accordance with the known facts of experience. It is unclear how probability applies to selecting a worldview:

9. King, "Fideism and Rationality," 432.

Notice that such a test does not guarantee the truth of a world-view. For more than one view could be consistent and fit all the facts yet known by experience; or again, a view which is systematically consistent with all that we now know could turn out to be falsified by future discoveries. Systematic consistency thus underdetermines worldviews, and so, as in the case of inductive reasoning, we must be content with plausibility or likelihood, rather than rational certainty.[10]

However, this approach mistakes the probability of outcome with plausibility. The claim that God's existence is highly probable because the speaker finds that various considerations lean in that direction, is really a statement about the speaker. Another person might hear the same considerations and still be convinced of atheism. What is plausible to one is not so to another; plausibility is subjective.

Some outcomes can be known probabilistically. Past outcomes can be calculated statistically to give a probabilistic prediction of what might happen. This approach assumes that the future will be like the past, which is an assumption that cannot be calculated probabilistically without circularity. For something to be known probabilistically there must be a limited number of possible outcomes. If the possible outcomes are infinite then the probability cannot be calculated because probability requires a ratio. In relation to what is the given belief probable?

Pascal's Wager is susceptible to the "many gods" objection. It is not clear which worldview should be chosen or upon which to be wagered. Multiple worldviews include an afterlife and transcendent being. It is far from clear that Historic Christianity should be wagered on, and if all that is available to humans is "the wager," then Historic Christianity should not be wagered on because its redemptive claims become incoherent—due to the fact that this probabilistic approach provides the unbeliever with an excuse. Unbelief cannot be ruled out and as such is a viable option. Therefore, it is not inexcusable, and does not carry with it guilt or the need for redemption. The probabilistic approach is inconsistent with the inexcusability of unbelief. It cannot support the claim that unbelief is culpable.

10. Craig, *Reasonable Faith*, 40.

2.4. MYSTICISM AND RELIGIOUS EXPERIENCE

Clarity conflicts with mysticism. Mysticism relies on inner experience as proof for belief. This inner experience is described in similar ways by mystics in various and contradictory religious systems. Consequently, it cannot be used to support the claim that unbelief is inexcusable. The relevant question is not whether or not there was an experience, but how to interpret the experience. The mystical experiences are interpreted in many different ways and as support for contradictory systems, some of which are not theistic.

Appeals to religious experience as valid in supporting Christian belief have become popular in the past number of decades due to the work of William Alston. In his book *Perceiving God*, Alston argues that religious experiences can confirm belief in God because they presuppose that there is a God.[11] However, there is not a distinction drawn between the experience and the interpretation of the experience. Thus, Alston speaks of the experience of being sustained by God. But what should be distinguished is the experience, and the person's interpretation of this experience as an experience of being sustained by God. This same experience can be had by others who give it a contrary interpretation. Thus, to use these experiences as confirmation of belief in God is circular because they import belief in God into their interpretive premise, and therefore beg the question.

To establish the inexcusability of unbelief it must be clear which interpretation is correct. No experience is meaningful without interpretation. A person might see a tree or a hill, but what does this mean? Is it an idea or a material object? A person might feel at one with the universe, but what does this mean? Should it be interpreted in light of brain chemistry or Advaita Vedanta?

William James, in describing the mystical state, quotes Saint Teresa in saying:

> The soul is fully awake as regards God, but wholly asleep as regards things of this world and in respect of herself. During the short time the union lasts, she is as it were deprived of every feeling, and even if she would, she could not think of any single thing. . . . Thus does God, when he raises a soul to union with himself, suspend

11. Alston, *Perceiving God*, 1.

the natural action of all her faculties. She neither sees, hears, nor understands, so long as she is united with God.[12]

But in the same work James considers the mystical experiences of the Hindus, Buddhists, Muslims, and Christians. All use their particular experiences to support contrary religious claims about the nature of reality. Or, perhaps they all describe the same kind of reality and it is a reality that is contrary to the theistic worldview:

> This overcoming of all the usual barriers between the individual and the Absolute is the great mystic achievement. In mystic states we both become one with the Absolute and we become aware of our oneness. This is the everlasting and triumphant mystical tradition, hardly altered by differences of clime or creed. In Hinduism, in Neoplatonism, in Sufism, in Christian Mysticism, in Whitmanism, we find the same recurring note, so that there is about mystical utterances an eternal unanimity which ought to make a critic stop and think.[13]

To claim that the self is one with God is contrary to the central distinction in theism between God as eternal, infinite, and unchanging, and the creation as temporal, finite, and changeable. Therefore, the problem with mysticism as far as clarity is concerned, is that either the mystical experience can be interpreted to fit multiple and contrary worldviews, or it tends toward the claim that "all is one" which is contrary to theism. Either way, mystical experiences cannot be used as the basis for inexcusability. James affirms this when he says: "Mystics have no right to claim that we ought to accept the deliverance of their peculiar experiences, if we are ourselves outsiders and feel no private call thereto."[14]

The Hindu mystics affirm that there is more than the life of sense data and the material world, but they have a very different view than does the theist. Their view is monistic and spiritual. Ultimate reality is pure consciousness where all is one:

> Brahman is indivisible and pure;
> Realize Brahman and go beyond all change.
> He is immanent and transcendent.
> Realizing him, sages attain freedom

---

12. James, *Varieties*, 316.
13. Ibid., 324.
14. Ibid., 328.

And declare there are no separate minds.
They have but realized what they always are.
Waking, sleeping, dreaming, the Self is one.
Transcend these three and go beyond rebirth.
There is only one Self in all creatures.[15]

Mysticism cannot provide a basis for accepting theism and rejecting Hinduism. It cannot provide an answer to the question "Why should I believe?" posed by the ethics of belief.

Not all persons have religious experiences, and yet all are said to be responsible. Historic Christianity claims that the existence of God can be known from the things that are made. This is an inference and not a mystical experience. Unbelief can be inexcusable only if theism is the only rational position to hold. Mysticism does not establish this.

Mysticism often is asserted in the context of assuming that there is not a clear general revelation. It may allow that there are multiple ways to know God while asserting that only a mystical experience can give direct knowledge of God. It is an alternative to the hopelessness of skepticism. However, if skepticism has already been rejected in favor of a clear general revelation, then mysticism need not be invoked. At this point, mysticism becomes an attempt to avoid having to use reason to understand general revelation, and as such can contribute to the problem of unbelief.

The claim that God, or anything, can be known directly is problematic. If God is known then he is known as he reveals himself, through the works of creation, providence, and redemption. The mystic seeks to bypass these for a direct vision of God, but in so doing ignores the ways that God reveals himself. Contemporary appeals to religious experience to confirm Christian belief are attempts to know God directly, rather than through the use of the mind to draw inferences and reach sound conclusions. Sometimes an inner experience is claimed to be the work of the Holy Spirit, and that other religions who make similar claims are counterfeits that do not change the value of what is real. But the question for the individual is: How do I interpret this experience (is it the Holy Spirit), and are there other interpretations?

15. "Easwaran, *The Upanishads*, 243.

2.5. SCRIPTURE ALONE

Clarity conflicts with the claim that God can only be known through scripture. This claim is often related to fideism because scripture is used as the authority appealed to as the ground for belief. An example of such a position is found in Gordon Clark. He states: "Therefore I wish to suggest that we neither abandon reason nor use it unaided, but—on pain of skepticism—acknowledge a verbal, propositional revelation of fixed truth from God. Only by accepting rationally comprehensible information on God's authority can we hope to have a sound philosophy and a true religion."[16] This approach fails to establish the need for redemption through the inexcusability of unbelief. It often views any attempt to prove God's existence by reason as a form of rationalism and argues that rationalism fails in all of its forms. In rejecting rationalism some Christians reject the ability to know apart from special revelation:

> Christianity depicts itself—essentially theological though it be—not as a supremely constructed metaphysical theory, but as a revelation, differing in kind from secular philosophies grounded in rational reflection ... Its basic premise is that the living God should be allowed to speak for himself and to define the abiding role of reason and the meaning of revelation ... The rationalistic approach subordinates the truth of revelation to its own alternatives and has speculated itself into exhaustion.[17]

It is true that those calling themselves rationalists have argued for contradictory and competing views, and not all have been theists. However, the problem might be that they did not use reason critically enough rather than that reason in itself (as opposed to human reasoning) is inadequate. Specifically, rationalists have always constructed their theory on presuppositions, and then worked to coherently deduce implications from these. However, their presuppositions are assumed in a fideistic manner, and their system can only be as strong as these presuppositions. Notice that Clark, in positing scripture as the starting point, is fideistically accepting it as authority in the same way that non-Christians accept their ultimate authority (as soon as Clark offers an argument in favor of starting with scripture then he is relying on something besides scripture as a standard of proof). The question becomes: Which presuppositions should I accept?

16. Clark, *Religion*, 86.
17. Henry, *God*, 95.

If this cannot be known, and one might as well accept non-theistic pre-suppositions as theistic ones, then non-theism is a rational option and unbelief is excusable. What must be found is a way to determine which presuppositions to accept. How can we know which book that claims to be of divine origin actually is of divine origin? John Bunyan, the author of *Pilgrim's Progress*, wrestled with this question:

> How can you tell but that the Turks had as good Scriptures to prove their Mahomet the Saviour, as we have to prove our Jesus is; and could I think that so many ten thousands in so many Countreys and Kingdoms, should be without the knowledge of the right way to Heaven . . . and that we only, who live but in a corner of the Earth, should alone be blessed therewith? Everyone doth think his own Religion rightest, both Jews, and Moors, and Pagans; and how if all our Faith, and Christ, and Scriptures, should be but a thinks-so too?[18]

Scripture, as redemptive revelation, *assumes* that humans need to be redeemed. It claims to be God's word. To use it as proof that God exists, or that humans need redemption, is circular. Scripture assumes that humans are fallen and stand in need of redemption. Christian scripture begins by speaking about God who created the heavens and the earth, about the Fall, and about the seed of the woman who will crush the head of the serpent. It speaks about the Messiah as the Redeemer who is to come, and then of how Jesus of Nazareth fulfills the requirements of the Messiah. All of this must assume that there is a clear general revelation of God that humans have rejected to make sense of the redemptive message of Historic Christianity.

It cannot be that ignorance of scripture is that for which humans need to be redeemed. Redemptive revelation is needed *only* because there is a need for redemption. Redemption presupposes guilt and inexcusability. Therefore redemptive revelation presupposes the inexcusability of unbelief. This is precisely the point at which Paul begins his systematic theology expressed in the book of Romans.

Scriptures are inadequate to establish inexcusability because not all persons have had access to scripture, and yet all are responsible (according to Historic Christianity). Many of those in Historic Christianity have asserted that scripture is the only source of our knowledge of God, and

18. John Bunyan, quoted in Veli-Matti Karkkainen, *An Introduction to the Theology of Religions*, 18.

this has made the exclusivist position appear unfair. The inclusivists and pluralists are correct to point to this problem. And yet there is no problem if God is knowable by all through a clear general revelation. Scripture is necessary to communicate how redemption will be accomplished and applied. Redemption need not be given to all. Justice requires only that the guilty are condemned equally, it does not require that all be forgiven. Grace can be given to some without compromising justice. The limited access to special revelation is not inconsistent with the justice of God when it is understood in connection with a clear general revelation given to all. It is important to consider that general revelation provides guidelines for determining what is special revelation and what is a fraud, in the simple standard that whatever contradicts what is known from general revelation about God cannot be from God. For instance, when applied to the Gnostic Gospels which are not consistent with prior special revelation, and are not consistent with the nature of God as known from general revelation.

To say that scripture is necessary for redemption is consistent with the claim that all humans are responsible for unbelief. Many thinkers confuse soteriological issues with the necessary presuppositions behind the redemptive claims of Historic Christianity. It could be true that God effectually calls some and leaves others in unbelief. And yet it is also true that this unbelief is inexcusable because it is rationally unjustifiable. This means that it is both true that there can be a clear general revelation of God to all humans, and that redemption can only be achieved through the enlivening work of the Holy Spirit to enable a person to accept the Gospel as communicated in scripture.

Many modern discussions of natural law, general revelation, and common grace have made the mistake of relying on a false antinomy: Either God is knowable through general revelation or salvation can only be found in scripture. But both could be true by asserting a third option: While God is knowable through general revelation, all humans have rejected this knowledge and are therefore in need of redemption which is communicated through special revelation. The Westminster Confession of Faith begins with this relationship (1.1). In order to prove that special revelation is necessary, the principle of clarity must be established and the clarity of God's existence shown through general revelation. Apart from doing so, the need for special revelation is merely a conjecture, and its claims about redemption become inconsistent when the inexcusability of unbelief cannot be established.

2.6. NO FREE WILL, OR FREE WILL AND PREDESTINATION ARE INCOMPATIBLE[19]

Clarity conflicts with the claim that humans do not have free will. The denial of free will could be taken as following from the claim that God predestines all that comes to pass. Christianity does assert that God brings all things to pass according to his will for the praise of his glory, and it also asserts that humans are responsible before God.[20] The relevant issue here is that if humans do not have free will then they are not responsible. It is therefore in the interest of Christian theism to show that humans are responsible and do have free will. In the history of Christianity the discussion has been among the Augustinians/Calvinists, the Pelagians/ Semi-Pelagians, and the Hyper-Calvinists. Again, the relevant issue here is that Christianity must preserve human responsibility and the ability to know God. Any view that denies or undermines human responsibility is contrary to the Christian claim that humans are responsible for knowing God. However, this need not necessitate a Pelagian, or libertarian, view of freedom and responsibility. A compatibilist view such as Augustine or Calvin presented is also consistent with responsibility and may in fact avoid some significant problems associated with the Pelagian, or libertarian, view. The problem arises when a position such as Hyper-Calvinism is maintained, which denies the relevant kind of causal responsibility to the human agent.

Pelagius was known for his piety and he asserted that Christian teaching should encourage people to live a pious life. He was offended by Augustine's *Confessions* because he thought Augustine blamed his impious lifestyle on a weakness or inability, and affirmed that he could only do good when God allowed him to do so. Pelagius thought this undermined the purpose of moral teaching.

---

19. Some of this section appeared as the article "Augustine's Ethics of Belief and Avoiding Violence in Religious Disputes" in *New Blackfriars*.

20. *The Westminster Confession of Faith*, Chapter 5.4, Of Providence:

"The almighty power, unsearchable wisdom, and infinite goodness of God so far manifest themselves in his providence, that it extendeth itself even to the first fall, and all other sins of angels and men; and that not by a bare permission, but such as hath joined with it a most wise and powerful bounding, and otherwise ordering, and governing of them, in a manifold dispensation, to his own holy ends; yet so, as the sinfulness thereof proceeded only from the creature, and not from God, who, being most holy and righteous, neither is nor can be the author or approver of sin."

> The phrase 'Command what you will, O God, and give what you command' was felt to be particularly objectionable. For Pelagius, this hopelessly confused the assistance God gave to the disciple with the moral power that God expected the disciple to supply (to reform and accept discipline). Pelagius thought that if a disciple persevered in strong discipline and prayer he or she would reach a state of stability where even the desire for sin would fade away."[21]

Notice that what bothers Pelagius is precisely what is at issue here: If the human cannot do what he should, then he cannot be held accountable.

The problem with Pelagianism is that it leaves some areas of life outside the sovereignty of God. In contrast, Augustine affirmed the sovereignty of God in all that comes to pass, including the ability for a disciple to do good. Calvin also stressed the sovereignty of God.

> It is certainly easy to prove that the commencement of good is only with God, and that none but the elect have a will inclined to good. But the cause of election must be sought out of man; and hence it follows that a right will is derived not from man himself, but from the same good pleasure by which we were chosen before the creation of the world."[22]

Many in the Augustinian/Calvinist tradition affirm that predestination is compatible with responsibility. Augustine distinguished between liberty and ability, and discussed the four-fold state of man: *posse pecare* (possible to sin), and *non-posse non-pecare* (not possible not to sin), *posse non-pecare* (possible to not sin), *non-posse pecare* (not possible to sin). While ability changes in each of these, liberty does not. At each state man is free to do as he pleases, but his ability to do good or evil changes. Consider the Westminster Confession:

> God from all eternity did by the most wise and holy counsel of his own will, freely and unchangeably ordain whatsoever comes to pass; yet so as thereby neither is God the author of sin; nor is violence offered to the will of the creatures, nor is the liberty or contingency of second causes taken away, but rather established.[23]

In contrast, Hyper-Calvinists have denied that there is freedom of the will in any sense, instead asserting a kind of hard determinism. However,

21. McGuckin, *The Westminster*, 256.
22. Calvin, *The Institutes*, 257.
23. Westminster Confession 3.1.

it would be a mistake to confuse all of Augustinianism/Calvinism with Hyper-Calvinism.

In order to make sense of this responsibility it is worth taking some time to consider the relationship between human *ability* to know and human *desire* to know. Can I know God if I want to? Am I free to do as I please? Here I maintain that at the basic level of liberty to use reason, liberty and ability are directly connected so that if I want to use reason I can use reason.

It may be helpful to distinguish between *levels* of freedom. Much discussion about freedom takes place at a less basic level, while what is important is freedom at the most basic level. Levels of freedom are: The *political* level, the *practical* level, the *psychological* level, the *worldview* level, the *presuppositional* level, and the *rational* level. Each level is progressively more relevant to freedom and overrides the previous level in the sense that if there is not freedom at the more basic level, then there is not freedom at the less basic levels. I may be politically free to buy a soda, but not practically free because I have no money. I may be practically free to buy a soda but not psychologically free due to a deep aversion to soda. I may be psychologically free to buy a soda but not do so because my worldview rules it out. It is true that if I am psychologically free to buy a soda but do not have any money, then I cannot buy a soda. However, lack of money does not take away freedom to want a soda. Once we get to the worldview level of freedom we are speaking about my freedom to select a belief. Many of my beliefs are determined by my worldview due to the requirements of consistency. Hence, by selecting a given worldview, I am not free to believe just anything with regards to God or the afterlife. Specifically, my freedom to choose a worldview is affected by my choice of axioms, or presuppositions. The presuppositions I begin with will affect, or even determine, the worldview I select. Finally, the most basic level is the freedom to use reason. Not all presuppositions are rational (survive scrutiny by the laws of thought). Some may be self-contradictory. The most basic level of freedom is the freedom to use or not use reason. It is at this level that a person is *always* responsible and *always* free.

Many objections about freedom miss the point because they address a less basic level without getting to the freedom to use reason. A person may have strong psychological urges to use drugs that override his practical freedom to refrain from using drugs. But the psychological urges are less basic than his worldview, presuppositional, and rational freedom.

Different worldviews will respond to strong psychological urges differently. By selecting a given worldview the person is also determining how he will respond to such urges. The same is true of his selection of presuppositions, and of his willingness to use reason. Thus, strong psychological urges cannot be said to override one's willingness to use reason, but rather the extent to which one has used reason will determine one's presuppositions and worldview, and this will affect how one responds to strong psychological urges.

There is some question as to whether belief in God (or anything) is voluntary. Without settling the matter we can proceed by noting that it is necessary to presuppose that belief in God is voluntary to make the claim that unbelief is inexcusable. However, there is good reason to think that belief is voluntary, or at least the willingness to use reason critically to arrive at true, justified belief is voluntary. This can be supported by distinguishing between appearances and belief about appearances, and between initial impressions and critical reflection. Appearances, such as what I am now seeing, are involuntary (except that I can look away). However, my belief about the nature of what is appearing to me is, or can be, voluntary. I say "can be" because it might be the case that I am not aware of my cultural baggage and therefore I make judgments about the nature of appearances without critical reflection. However, once questions are raised about my judgments, by myself or others, my certainty is questioned and I must defend my belief or abandon it. Belief may not be voluntary in the sense that I must obey the demands of reason and believe the conclusion that I think is the most reasonable. However, what is voluntary is the extent to which I am willing to critically reflect. Many persons close their ears to objections. The willingness to use reason is voluntary, even if appearances and believing a sound conclusion are not—this is the most basic freedom. The claim that unbelief is inexcusable presupposes that belief in God is voluntary in this sense—you *can* if you *want* to, and blame for not doing so cannot be transferred to anyone else.

This is also relevant to the discussion of fideism and Reformed Epistemology because a person might claim that he is appeared to as if God exists, or as if he is forgiven by God. He might claim to be more certain of this than of anything else. However, such certainty disappears, or is called into question, when challenges (defeaters) arise. One need not wait for defeaters to be raised by others; potential defeaters should be considered with the goal of knowing the truth. To avoid all defeaters is to live the unexamined life, and that life is not worth living.

2.7. THE FALL PROVIDES AN EXCUSE

Clarity conflicts with the claim that since humanity was corrupted in the Fall, people have an excuse for their unbelief. This objection to clarity combines elements of the objection that humans do not have free will with the idea that humans are now inclined toward evil. As was true with the free will objection to clarity, it is outside the scope of this work to solve the problem of evil and free will. However, it is possible to make the point that the principle of clarity can be upheld against this objection. Historic Christianity affirms the effects of the Fall and also that after the Fall humans remain responsible for their sin. The sovereignty of God in predestinating, the effects of the Fall to make humans will what is evil, and the continued freedom and responsibility of wrong decisions, are able to be consistently maintained in a compatibilist system. Again, consider the Confession:

> I. God from all eternity, did, by the most wise and holy counsel of His own will, freely, and unchangeably ordain whatsoever comes to pass; yet so, as thereby neither is God the author of sin, nor is violence offered to the will of the creatures; nor is the liberty or contingency of second causes taken away, but rather established.

> II. Although God knows whatsoever may or can come to pass upon all supposed conditions; yet has He not decreed anything because He foresaw it as future, or as that which would come to pass upon such conditions.[24]

It is important to keep in mind the four-fold state of man mentioned above. Before the Fall, man is in the state of the possibility to sin (*posse pecare*). After the Fall, man is in the state of no possibility of not sinning (*non-posse non-pecare*). For those who are justified in Christ there is the state of possibility to not sin (*posse non-pecare*), and then in the glorified state not possible to sin (*non-posse pecure*). Augustine discusses these, and they are part of the Westminster Confession's chapter on free will. They are helpful because they avoid mistaking liberty and ability which is done in so much contemporary discussion, particularly by those who favor a

---

24. *The Westminster Confession of Faith*, Chapter 3.1–2 Of God's Eternal Decree.

libertarian view of free will, and the middle-knowledge solution to the problem of evil and divine foreknowledge.

This attempt to avoid clarity sometimes claims that while there was a clear general revelation of God before the Fall, the Fall corrupted this revelation so that now knowing God requires special revelation. The claim is that humans after the Fall cannot use their mind to conclude that God exists through the use of reason: "It should be clear by now that from Berkouwer's perspective the existence of God cannot be proved, and the reality of God cannot be known by rational reflection on the created order. Natural man is incapable of drawing right conclusions from the cosmos, since his thinking and judgments are controlled by sin."[25] However, general revelation as an objective reality cannot be corrupted; rather, it is human willingness to see what is clear that can be corrupted (I cannot use my own unwillingness as an excuse). Rational reflection on the created order would bring the knowledge of God, but the fallen human is *unwilling* to so reflect.

Some might attempt to use this unwillingness as an excuse. This excuse says: "I cannot know God because I am fallen and unwilling, but being fallen and unwilling is outside of my control and is therefore not my fault." At first this looks like a very promising excuse. However, upon closer examination, it is unsuccessful. The problem is that it speaks as if being fallen is something *outside* of the person, forcing him to act in a certain way. Rather, to be fallen is a description of a person who is *not willing* to know God. The person's unbelief (intellect), failure to seek God (desires), and failure to act righteously (will) reflect the true character of that person.

Historically, both the Pelagians and the Augustinians/Calvinists have affirmed that the Fall does not remove human responsibility. The Pelagians have done so by denying that the effects of the Fall are total:

> Pelagius believed that God gave grace to human beings, certainly, but his primary grace was the freedom to choose and respond. Those who chose the path of goodness would be given further encouragement by God to progress in the spiritual life.... [Augustine] believed the human race's capacity for free moral choice was so damaged by the ancient (and continuing) fall from grace and enlightenment that even the desire to return to God has first to be

---

25. Demarest, *General Revelation*, 144.

supplied by God's prevenient grace. All desire for, and movement toward, the Good was the gift of God.[26]

Augustine affirmed the sovereignty of God over all aspects of human life, while Pelagius seems to leave human choice outside of God's sovereignty.

Calvin also affirmed that all aspects of human life and history are under the sovereignty of God, including the Fall and its effects. The corruption of sin is extended to reason itself, as if reason were unable to reveal God. The distinction between the corruption of mankind's willingness to use reason and the corruption of reason itself can become blurred:

> I feel pleased with the well-known saying which has been borrowed from the writings of Augustine, that man's natural gifts were corrupted by sin, and his supernatural gifts withdrawn; meaning by supernatural gifts the light of faith and righteousness, which would have been sufficient for the attainment of heavenly life and everlasting felicity. Man, when he withdrew his allegiance to God, was deprived of the spiritual gifts by which he had been raised to the hope of eternal salvation. Hence it follows, that he is now an exile from the kingdom of God.[27]

This view can be maintained in a manner that affirms the compatibility of the Fall and human responsibility, or a manner that denies human responsibility. It is often maintained that "human reason" is corrupt, or is different from God's reason. This is true if by "reason" it is meant "reasoning," or "thinking process." But here "reason" refers to the laws of thought which cannot be corrupt (as if a is a—the law of identity—were changed after the Fall), and they are universal for all thinkers.

The consideration of the Fall as an excuse should be focused on whether I can use reason to choose what to believe (remember the levels of freedom). If I cannot use reason when I want to, then I am not responsible. But if I can use reason when I want to, and I do not, then I deserve the consequences of failing to use reason to know God. This failure itself is sin, rather than being the result of sin. And it is this sin that results in all other kinds of sin. It could be called the "root sin." It might even be called the "original sin" in the sense of "first sin." In eating the fruit, Adam and Eve believed the serpent, that they could know good and evil in the way that God knows good and evil. It is a fundamental contradiction to think

---

26. McGuckin, *The Westminster,* 257.

27. Calvin, *The Institutes,* 233.

that a temporal, finite being could know good and evil in the way that God, who is an eternal, infinite being, does.

In this sense all unbelievers commit the original sin (if it is clear that God exists). All believe something about God and themselves that is a fundamental contradiction. And yet it is they who believe it, and so it is they who are responsible. Furthermore, they are free at the present time to change their minds and believe in God. If they do not want to do so because of various considerations, then they should be content because they are doing what they want.

To use the Fall, or predestination, as an excuse becomes absurd: "I want to believe in God but I cannot because my fallen nature keeps me from doing so," or "I want to believe in God but I cannot because God predestined me to unbelief." Both assume the truth of what they claim to not be able to believe in: "I believe that unbelief is a sin, and it is therefore false that God does not exist, and I believe that it is true that God does not exist," or "I believe that God exists and that he is keeping me from believing that God exists."

2.8. CONCLUSION: CLARITY AS A PRECONDITION TO REDEMPTIVE CLAIMS

Some of the discussion above has raised soteriological questions about the nature of salvation, the Fall, and free will. However, much of the discussion in soteriology is irrelevant to whether or not Christianity must presuppose the clarity of God's existence and is therefore outside the scope of this work. Soteriology assumes that humans need redemption and seeks to explain how this occurs. The present purpose is to seek proof for the claim that humans need redemption by arguing that the clarity of God's existence is a necessary presupposition to the Christian claim about the need for redemption and forgiveness. Paul, in Romans, speaks about redemption, whereas the present work is looking at whether redemption is necessary. Augustine and Calvin should be understood as assuming that humans need redemption and then explaining how redemption operates. The present work is looking at *why* and *whether* humans need redemption and is therefore a different topic. How redemption is applied to humans (say, through the regenerating work of the Holy Spirit) presupposes that humans need redemption; Christians who claim to be regenerated should be able to show that God exists and that unbelief is inexcusable. Christians have been restored from not seeking to seeking and so all the more they should be able to show what is clear.

However, the last three contrasts to clarity (scripture alone, no free will, the Fall as an excuse) are helpful because they highlight the fact that the principle of clarity need not assume a libertarian view of free will. In fact, this view of free will may be incompatible with the principle of clarity. This view of free will requires uncaused or indeterministically caused events, whereas responsibility requires that my beliefs cause my actions for which I am responsible. Responsibility requires clarity and it requires that my actions are caused by my wants, which are the result of my rational deliberation (or failure thereof). Uncaused or indeterministically caused events leave open an excuse, and this is contrary to the claim that unbelief is inexcusable. The possibility of an excuse might be part of the attractiveness of the libertarian view. However, the following will proceed with the assumption that Historic Christian soteriology as found in Paul, Augustine, Calvin, and the Westminster Confession of Faith is consistent with the principle of clarity.

Attempts to avoid the need for clarity about God's existence have largely been proposed by Christians, demonstrating the general lack of awareness about the principle of clarity. If the need for clarity cannot be avoided without undermining the redemptive claims of Historic Christianity, then the next issue to address is how it can be shown to be clear that God exists. *Maximal responsibility*, the kind Historic Christianity maintains to be the case for unbelief, requires maximal clarity. *Maximal clarity* requires proving the impossibility of the alternatives, thus leaving no rational excuse for believing them. Clarity at this level requires giving an argument, and yet, as will be seen in the next chapter, there are numerous attempts to avoid the need for arguments.

3

Attempts to Avoid the Need for Arguments

Having addressed the most popular attempts to avoid the need for clarity, there is
still a question as to whether an argument is necessary to come to know God. Can't
God be known in other ways, for instance, through direct perception—religious
experience? Isn't this demand for an argument to attain knowledge a secular impo-
sition from Greek, or Enlightenment, philosophy? In this chapter we will consider
some notable thinkers who attempted to avoid the need for arguments.

"GOOD GOD!" CRIED DEMEA, interrupting him, where are we?
Zealous defenders of religion allow that the proofs of a Deity fall
short of perfect evidence!"[1] Why should we expect perfect evidence, evidence that demonstrates the impossibility of the contrary? Why should
we expect it to be clear that God exists? We don't have clarity in many
areas of life, so why should we expect it in matters pertaining to belief in
God? The need for proof depends on the consequences. Where there are
little or no consequences then proof (in the sense of certainty, or showing
the impossibility of the opposite) will not be as important. But where the
consequences are serious, a matter of eternal life or eternal death, then
proof becomes necessary. Skeptics point out, correctly, that if we cannot
know then we cannot be held accountable. If we cannot know, and are
asked by God why we did not believe, then we can reply "not enough
evidence!"[2]

---

1. Hume, *Dialogues*, 19.
2. Bertrand Russell is reported to have said this would be his reply if it turns out that
God does exist and asks why Russell did not believe.

There has been a long tradition of denying the necessity and efficacy of proofs. For example, Pascal denied the need for proofs. "Proofs
are excluded not because they are false but because they are useless and
dangerous: the God to whom they lead is in fact an idol."[3] The common
reason for this rejection is the conviction that arguments cannot persuade, but instead something else is needed. This might be true, and is a
separate subject than what is being addressed here. Christianity need not
give an argument for God's existence in order to persuade, but must give
an argument to show that unbelief is inexcusable because God's existence
is clear.

An argument is necessary to show clarity, and clarity is necessary
to support the claim that ignorance of God is culpable. This is because
immediate perception is insufficient and because challenges must be addressed. Immediate perception of a chair is not an inference or an argument. However, perceiving a chair is not a conclusion either. "I am being
appeared to 'chair-ly'" might be immediate, but "I see an external object
that exists apart from minds" is an interpretation of the perception. All
experience and perception must be interpreted. But this is where differences arise. Is the chair a material object that exists apart from minds? Is
the chair an idea in the mind of God? Is the chair part of maya (illusion)
that is due to avidya (ignorance) which must be overcome through mok-
sha (enlightenment)? The same can be said for immediate perceptions of
God. Is God an existing being? Is God an idea in a mind? Is God the result
of brain chemistry? The immediate perception is insufficient and requires
interpretation which means an argument is necessary. Clarity requires
that the correct interpretation be clear to reason so that accepting some
other interpretation is inexcusable.

Arguments are also necessary because there are opposing views
which raise relevant and important challenges to theistic belief and
Historic Christianity. If these cannot be responded to through rational
argumentation then unbelief has an excuse. It is therefore an important
feature of Historic Christianity that it must respond to challenges in order
to make sense of its claim that humans need redemption from unbelief.

There are various attempts to get around giving an argument. Before
looking at specific theistic arguments and challenges to these, it will be
helpful to consider those who attempt to get around the need for argu-

---

3. Armogathe, *Proofs*, 307.

mentation. To some extent positions such as fideism, skepticism, and mysticism are attempts to get around giving an argument and they have already been considered. But the following will consider embodied forms of these in particular thinkers who are still quoted today in order to avoid the need to give an argument. The views to be considered are the view that human rationality is deficient (expressed here by Thomas Aquinas), the view that philosophy is irrelevant, and even perhaps harmful, (expressed here by Tertullian), the view that all persons know God directly through a *sensus divinitatis* (expressed here by Calvin), the view that belief in God can be warranted apart from an argument (expressed here by Reformed Epistemology), and the view that rational people can disagree about the existence of God because there are no rationally persuasive arguments (expressed here by Graham Oppy).

3.1. THOMAS AQUINAS[4]

Thomas Aquinas expresses a common view that human reason is deficient and faith (as acceptance of a belief on authority without rational proof) above reason is necessary for certitude, speed of knowing, making God known widely, and because of the deficiencies of reason:

> It is necessary for man to receive by faith not only things which are above reason, but also those which can be known by reason; and this is for three motives. First, in order that man may arrive more quickly at the knowledge of divine truth. For the science to whose province it belongs to prove the existence of God and many other such truths is the last of all to offer itself to human inquiry, since it presupposes many other sciences; so that it would be far along in life that man would arrive at the knowledge of God. The second reason is, in order that the knowledge of God may be more widespread. For many are unable to make progress in the study of science, either through dullness of ability or through having a number of occupations and temporal needs, or even through laziness in learning and all these persons would be altogether deprived of the knowledge of God, unless divine things were brought to their knowledge by way of faith. The third reason is for the sake of certitude. For human reason is very deficient in things concerning God.[5]

---

4. Some of this section appeared as the article "Augustine's Ethics of Belief and Avoiding Violence in Religious Disputes" in *New Blackfriars*.

5. Aquinas, *Summa Theologica*, II q. 2.a 4.

If certitude is not possible through reason then there can be no responsibility. The problem is that to deny the efficacy of reason includes denying reason's ability to decide what authority or worldview in which to place one's faith. Aquinas affirms that more than one view can be rational and has argued in favor of pluralism. This conclusion is consistent with the view that reason cannot tell us which view to accept. However, it is inconsistent with the exclusivist position of Historic Christianity and therefore requires an abandonment of the redemptive claims of Christianity. Aquinas does abandon these claims. He does not believe that unbelief is inexcusable. As such, he is a wonderful example to highlight the principle of clarity. If God's existence is not clear then unbelief is excusable and redemption through Christ is not necessary.

If God is not easily knowable then there is not inexcusability. This is a further and more stringent requirement than simply asserting that God is knowable through reason. God could be knowable through reason but only by those with an I.Q. of over 250. This would mean that unbelief is excusable for most people. Rather, if unbelief is inexcusable for all humans as rational beings, then God must be easily knowable to all. This is what it means to say that God's existence must be clear. If it is not clear, then unbelief has an excuse. As we will see, some argue for God's existence but deny clarity, while others argue for God's existence and affirm clarity.

If God cannot be known by everyone, then the need for redemption does not make sense. This is the foundation on which the need for inexcusability rests. If everyone is inexcusable, then everyone must be able to know. Aquinas's four points contradict this. If faith apart from or above reason is necessary for certitude, speed of knowing, widespread knowledge of God, and is due to the deficiency of reason, then not everyone can know God and unbelief is excusable. Faith resting on authority is not available to everyone. Not everyone has had access to scripture or church history and therefore they do not know in what to put their faith. Aquinas attempts to provide a solution to this problem with his pluralism, which is a result of his belief that the world is ambiguous. Historic Christianity must solve it by affirming that there is a clear general revelation to all humans, knowable through reason, so that unbelief at any time or place is inexcusable.

This consideration of Aquinas has introduced the idea of faith. Fideism has been shown to be incompatible with inexcusability. Fideism is blind belief. However, "faith" need not only mean fideism. The Apostle

Paul defines faith as the evidence of things not seen (Hebrews 11:1). Faith is contrasted with sight, not with reason. One can have rational justification for belief in something that is not seen with the eye, and this is faith. But it is not above, apart from, or against reason. This work will proceed by distinguishing between faith as proof of what is not seen, and fideism as blind belief (often based on accepting the testimony of another who is viewed as an authority).

3.2. TERTULLIAN

Tertullian did not think that philosophy was necessary and instead relied on a kind of devotion to Christ. However, he did offer many arguments on many different topics, so it is not clear how his view of Jerusalem and Athens works out in practice. It is impossible to avoid offering some kind of argument for one's position. But Tertullian represents a kind of disdain for philosophy, which he views as inherently heretical:

> He [Paul] had been at Athens, and had in his interviews (with its philosophers) become acquainted with that human wisdom which pretends to know the truth, whilst it only corrupts it, and is itself divided into its own manifold heresies, by the variety of its mutually repugnant sects. What indeed has Athens to do with Jerusalem? What concord is there between the Academy and the Church? What between heretics and Christians? Our instruction comes from 'the porch of Solomon,' who had himself taught that 'the Lord should be sought in simplicity of heart.' Away with all attempts to produce a mottled Christianity of Stoic, Platonic, and dialectic composition! We want no curious disputation after possessing Christ Jesus, no inquisition after enjoying the gospel! With our faith, we desire no further belief. For this is our palmary faith, that there is nothing which we ought to believe besides.[6]

Tertullian seems to equate philosophy with Stoicism, Platonism, and other Greek schools. If this is the extent of philosophy, then his warning is helpful but inadequate. Many problems have occurred for Christianity over the centuries in its mixing of Christian theism with non-theistic worldviews, such as Augustine's use of Platonism, and Aquinas's use of Aristotelianism, and the contemporary attempt to mix naturalist cosmology (Darwinism) with theism. These worldviews are contradictory and cannot be mixed without jettisoning major components of one or the other.

6. Tertullian, "The Prescription," 246.

However, it is the Christian's obligation to prove that the Christian worldview is the correct one as opposed to these others. Tertullian warns against them, but does he show that belief in them is inexcusable and requires redemption? It seems not. Instead, he calls persons to firm belief which requires nothing besides. But the problem with this form of fideism is the same as noted earlier. How do we know which worldview we should commit ourselves to in the fideistic fashion? Why not Roman polytheism? Tertullian has reasons (arguments) as to why Christianity is better. When he presents these reasons he leaves fideism and offers arguments. The question is: Are the arguments sound? Do they establish inexcusability and the need for redemption? The decline of Roman polytheism and the increase of Christianity were linked to the work of the Christian apologists in showing the weaknesses of polytheism.

The claim that Jerusalem has nothing to do with Athens is still used today. It comes to the forefront in questions about common ground. Is there common ground between the believer and unbeliever on which they can reason together? Some deny that there is in order to emphasize the reality of the Fall. However, fallen humans are still humans. The fallen intellect is still an intellect. The laws of thought that govern the intellect are still in that position for the fallen intellect. The difference is that the fallen intellect does not use reason to know God. The law of non-contradiction is still binding. It is common ground in that it is used by all intellects. The fallen person is still held rationally accountable for using reason, and where he does not, there are consequences for this.

Some hold the view that there is no common ground because they have tried giving arguments and the other person did not accept their conclusion. This is phrased in saying that reason is ineffectual. This is sometimes followed with the assertion that what is needed is an experience of some kind. However, the problem often lies in the actual argument that was given. Perhaps the person did not accept the argument because it was an invalid or unsound argument, and not because they are wretched and fallen. Many arguments that have been given are simply unsound and irrelevant and should be rejected. This does not prove that there is no common ground, but that more work needs to be done. An experience cannot make up for the lack of an argument, and that experience must be interpreted in order to be understood.

Even when a sound argument is given, it does not necessarily follow that the person will accept it. There is a difference between proof and persuasion. People are often persuaded by invalid arguments and not persuaded by valid arguments. What is necessary for inexcusability is proof showing that it is clear that God exists, but not necessarily persuasion. The response to a sound argument will indicate where hearers are at in their use of reason. If it is accepted, this says something about them; likewise, if it is rejected, this also says something about them. From the Christian perspective, it reveals whether the mercy or the justice of God is at work in their lives. The word "light" is used to denote understanding, as in "I see the light!" A person who "sees the light" is evidencing the mercy of God's redemptive work, while a person who does not understand is evidencing the wrath of God's justice.

It is said that while Paul plants, and Apollos waters, it is the Holy Spirit that gives the increase. But that it is the Holy Spirit who gives the increase does not imply that Paul should stop planting and Apollos stop watering.[7] While at Athens (Acts 17), Paul responded to his audience (Stoics and Epicureans) with philosophical arguments. He asserted that it is in God that we live, move, and have our being. These were issues of great concern to these Greek philosophers. Some believed Paul, others did not. However, some point out that Paul himself warns against worldly philosophy. But the qualifier "worldly" is very important. He does not say to avoid philosophy *itself*, but rather to avoid that philosophy which is founded on the *principles of the world*. And of course a Christian theist should avoid non-theistic and non-Christian principles. But Paul also encourages believers to have arguments in support of their view, as he shows by examples in Romans 1 and many other places.

3.3. JOHN CALVIN AND THE *SENSUS DIVINITATIS*

John Calvin asserts that all humans have a *sensus divinitatis*. All humans have a sense of God, a kind of immediate perception. However, he claims that this has been corrupted by the Fall. Calvin attempts to establish inexcusability with reference to the *sensus divinitatis*. "First and foremost, he wants to establish the inexcusability of unbelief. To prevent anyone from being able truthfully to say 'I didn't know,' 'God himself has implanted in all men a certain understanding of his divine majesty.'"[8] However, an immediate perception or sense of God is insufficient for reasons outlined

---

7. Warfield, "Introduction," in Francis Beattie's *Apologetics*, 25.

8. Talbot, "Is it Natural," 160.

above when considering the direct experience of mysticism; experiences must be interpreted. This formulation of the *sensus divinitatis* is insufficient in a number of other ways.

Calvin does affirm that God is knowable from general revelation:

> Towards the beginning of the *Institutes*, Calvin makes the point that all knowledge of God is revealed. Everything that man knows about God, the world, and his own self flows from the eternal Fount of knowledge ... Calvin then proceeds to argue that people possess two kinds of religious knowledge—a knowledge of God as Creator and a knowledge of God as Redeemer. God may be known as Creator by general and special revelation, whereas He is known as Redeemer only via special revelation.[9]

It can be agreed that God is only knowable as he reveals himself, and that both special and general revelations are given by God, and are the only source of the knowledge of God. This is also a helpful distinction to see that special revelation deals with the question of redemption, while general revelation is that for which humans are accountable and failure to know general revelation is what necessitates redemption and special revelation.

However, Calvin seems to confuse the ideas "infinite," "eternal," and "unchangeable," ideas that all persons have, with the theistic God:

> That there exists in the human mind, and indeed by natural instinct, some sense of Deity, we hold to be beyond dispute, since God himself, to prevent any man from pretending ignorance, has endued all men with some idea of his Godhead, the memory of which he constantly renews and occasionally enlarges, that all to a man, being aware that there is a God, and that he is their Maker, may be condemned by their own conscience when they neither worship him nor consecrate their lives to his service. Certainly, if there is any quarter where it may be supposed that God is unknown, the most likely for such an instance to exist is among the dullest tribes farthest removed from civilization. But, as a heathen tells us, there is no nation so barbarous, no race so brutish, as not to be imbued with the conviction that there is a God.[10]

That humans do not know God appears to be due to the Fall (according to Calvin):

9. Demarest, *General Revelation*, 51.
10. Calvin, *The Institutes*, 43.

But though experience testifies that a seed of religion is divinely sown in all, scarcely one in a hundred is found who cherishes it in his heart, and not one in whom it grows to maturity, so far is it from yielding fruit in its season. Moreover, while some lose themselves in superstitious observances, and others, of set purpose, wickedly revolt from God, the result is that, in regard to the true knowledge of him, all are so degenerate, that in no part of the world can genuine godliness be found.[11]

All humans are corrupt and fail to know what they should, and this leads to sinful acts. This is consistent with the principle of clarity, although the above discussion about the Fall should be considered to avoid its use as an excuse.

The problem is that it is one thing to have an idea, and another to believe that the idea is of something that exists. The way that Calvin describes the *sensus divinitatis* begs the question because it assumes that God implanted the *sensus divinitatis* whereas this is what must be proven. It also confuses the formal ideas of eternal, infinite, and unchanging, with the content-laden theistic view which says that only God is eternal, infinite, and unchanging. It is true that all humans have the idea of the eternal, but not all humans agree that God is eternal. Some humans have the idea of God, but not all do. Some of those who have the idea of God do not believe that this is an idea of an existing being. Calvin's view is insufficient to explain why we should apply the ideas of eternal, infinite, and unchanging to the theistic God. As such it does not provide a basis for inexcusability.

This sense that all humans have is ambiguous. For Calvin, the *sensus divinitatis*: "amounts to the claim that any minimally developed and psychologically healthy human being, inevitably and without having first to think about it, would trust, honor, and obey God."[12] But any student of religion knows that the term "God" is highly ambiguous. Which view of God should be accepted? It is far from obvious that the *sensus divinitatis* gives the theistic view of God, let alone the Christian view of God. What is required is an argument to establish this view of God as opposed to other views.

The doctrine of total depravity is not an excuse for unbelief. "For Calvin, this claim is partly about what each of us *would* believe, if we

11. Calvin, *The Institutes*, 46.
12. Talbot, "Is it Natural," 155.

weren't damaged by sin, and partly about what each of us still *does* believe, in spite of sin."[13] One understanding of this is that the failure to believe is not my fault and if this is so then I am not guilty and therefore do not need redemption, but merely mending or help. I am damaged and so I have an excuse. If I were not damaged I would know God. Instead, the doctrine of total depravity should be understood *in connection* with being inexcusable. What is so depraved about humans is that they are rational beings, and God's existence is clear to reason, and yet they do not believe this. Reason is not damaged or corrupted. The problem is that the fallen human does not want to use reason. For this failure there is no excuse.

Calvin's doctrine of the *sensus divinitatis* can be used to undermine inexcusability. Christians have used it to excuse themselves from needing to give proof for their position. Excusing of the self from the need to use reason to give proof can be viewed as part of the sin for which one needs redemption.

3.4. REFORMED EPISTEMOLOGY

Currently, a very popular attempt to avoid giving an argument is Reformed Epistemology. This view will be considered in more detail later as a twentieth century response to criticisms of Christian belief. However, it is worth noting its shortcomings at this point to emphasize that arguments are necessary.

Reformed Epistemology asserts that belief in God is a matter of warrant, not of proof or justification. What must be shown, according to this view, is that a person is within his epistemic rights to believe in God (is warranted), but not that God exists as opposed to other views. Its name (Reformed) should not mislead, as it makes many claims that are contrary to important aspects of the Reformed Tradition (especially as found in the Westminster Confession of Faith). Reformed Epistemology speaks of "basic beliefs," which are immediate experiences or impressions, and which justify other beliefs in a way similar to that discussed by William Alston earlier. When defeaters are raised these basic beliefs lose their warrant. But the question is: Should one wait for defeaters, or should one be critically examining one's own beliefs—is the unexamined life worth living? It should not be a matter of surprise if some adherents of this view endorse inclusivism or pluralism and in so doing reject Historic Christian

13. Talbot, "Is it Natural," 157.

claims about the need for redemption through Christ (claims central to the Reformation).

Reformed Epistemology proceeds by comparing belief in God to other beliefs that persons are not commonly (socially) required to give proof for holding. These include beliefs in other minds or the external world. One is warranted in believing in other minds, and, analogously, one is warranted in believing in God. Warrant can be challenged by "defeaters", but if these defeaters are responded to and thus defeated, the person continues to be warranted.

Warrant is grounded in proper function. According to this view, when a person is properly functioning they come to hold certain beliefs about the world, such as the belief in other minds. Similarly, this view holds that when a person is properly functioning they will come to believe in God. Belief in God is warranted because it is a result of the proper function of the mind, just like the proper functioning of the eye is to see a table. Only when the eye is damaged does this fail to happen. The Fall is just such damage, so that humans are not properly functioning and therefore do not believe in God. The only way to begin properly functioning is for the Holy Spirit to work in the person's life and repair the damage. The person who has been thus repaired is warranted in Christian belief and does not need to justify this to the unbeliever, who is still damaged and not properly functioning.

The most obvious problem is that Reformed Epistemology assumes to be true what must be proven to be true. It is one thing to say that unbelief is due to damage, it is another to prove this is the case. How can we know if this account of the Fall and the need for the Holy Spirit to restore us to proper functioning is true? One way would be to prove that it is clear that God exists so that the failure to know God is an example of improper functioning. The way to prove this would be to show that belief is the only rational option, and that unbelief violates the laws of reason and denies clear distinctions. This involves showing that all forms of non-theism are not rational options, the most obvious way being to show that they involve contradictions. Theism makes very specific claims about God that would need to be thus supported: God is eternal, infinite, and unchanging, and God is also good and concerned about the creation (in contrast to the deistic view). Reformed Epistemology is responding to the *de jure* objection which says that Christian belief is intellectually deficient. It makes a place at the "academic table of respectability" for theistic belief. This is a separate work from showing inexcusability, and some in Reformed Epistemology have offered arguments against naturalism to show it is false. But naturalism is not the only alternative worldview that is faced by Christianity. And furthermore, even if naturalism is false, perhaps all this means is that reason cannot be used to know about these sorts of matters. Another aspect of Reformed Epistemology is that it takes the knowledge of God to be immediate (which is what is meant by *basic*). We will consider problems with this approach in the next chapter.

3.5. GRAHAM OPPY

Reasonable people can disagree about many things without compromising their rationality. Graham Oppy states this in the following manner: "It seems to me to be more or less platitudinous that there are propositions that *p* such that some reasonable people believe that *p*, some reasonable people believe that not *p*, and other reasonable people are agnostic or indifferent in one way or another."[14] After considering numerous kinds of theistic proofs, he extends the claim that reasonable people can disagree to believe in God:

> I have assumed that all *reasonable* parties to the dispute about the existence of orthodoxly conceived monotheistic gods will agree with me about the way in which reason, argument, and dialectic ought to be understood (even though there is no reason why they must agree with me on the question of the existence of orthodoxly conceived monotheistic gods). So, I discriminate. On the one hand, I allow that there are reasonable believers in the existence of orthodoxly conceived monotheistic gods. On the other hand, I deny that there are reasonable believers in the existence of successful arguments for the conclusion that there are orthodoxly conceived monotheistic gods.[15]

Oppy defines a successful argument as one that brings about belief revision in a rational person.[16] His claim that there are no successful arguments means that there are no arguments that will make a rational person believe in God (changing from either "we can't know" or "there is no God").

14. Oppy, *Arguing*, 7.
15. Ibid., 425.
16. Ibid., 19.

Oppy's focus is on orthodoxly conceived monotheistic gods, which is a broader topic than Christianity. But if he is correct in his assessment of successful arguments, then there are significant implications for Christianity. Oppy holds both that reasonable people can believe in God, and reasonable people can deny God's existence.[17] If it is reasonable to deny God's existence, then one has an excuse for not believing in God. If one has an excuse for not believing in God, then the Christian claim that unbelief is sin, even the central sin that leads to all others, is false. Therefore, if Oppy is correct in his assessment of reasonableness with respect to belief in God, then Christianity's redemptive message is false.

This means that if Christianity is to defend itself, it must not simply show that there are subjectively persuasive arguments, but in fact it must show that it is *unreasonable* to deny the existence of God. Doing this removes any excuse for unbelief. Proving the inexcusability of unbelief requires using arguments; it requires proving that the alternative to belief in God (that something besides God has existed from eternity) is irrational. The way to do this is to prove that claiming something besides God being eternal is a contradiction. Therefore, the redemptive message of Christianity requires the use of arguments to show that the rejection of belief in God is irrational and contradictory.

3.6. CONCLUSION: CLARITY REQUIRES STRONG JUSTIFICATION

The above has considered both Christians and non-Christians and their attempts to minimize or deny the need for arguments. One explanation for why arguments are not seen to be important is that it is believed there have not been any successful arguments. Oppy defined success in terms of persuading rational persons. But he also recognizes that humans often are not rational.[18] Because of this, it is not possible to define success in terms of persuasion; people are often persuaded by invalid arguments, and fail to be persuaded by valid arguments. Instead, a successful argument for showing that unbelief is inexcusable must show that the alternative is impossible. This requires showing that it is a contradiction. The immediate response on the part of many is that this is too strict a standard, and for many beliefs it is. But maximal responsibility requires *maximal clarity*,

17. Oppy, *Arguing*, 456.
18. Ibid., 13.

and Historic Christianity claims that there is *maximal responsibility* to believe in God, so it *must* prove that there is maximal clarity concerning God's existence. If belief in God is maximally clear then unbelief must be inexcusable.

In the next chapter we turn to actual arguments that have been given. The non-theist will maintain that to-date no argument has shown this kind of clarity. This failure can be attributed to two sources: not seeing the need for clarity and using premises insufficient to prove that God exists (as opposed to a "highest being," "first mover," or "designer"). Most Christians who have given arguments for God's existence have done so as a side-note, rather than as a necessary presupposition to Christianity's redemptive claims. Proving that God exists becomes a topic that some philosophically-minded Christians are interested in, but is not necessary for most people. This leads to the second problem, which is that because the goal is not clarity, the arguments that are given do not consider the alternatives to belief in God and show them to be impossible. Instead, the arguments move from premises to a conclusion that is much less than the theistic God, or over-extend themselves to the theistic God. Rather than recognizing the difference between Aristotle's "unmoved mover" and God, Aquinas settles for arguments that at best prove that there is an "unmoved mover." Or traditional ontological arguments equate the "highest being" with the theistic God rather than proving this to be the case (why not *Brahman* or the *Tao*?). The best way to consider if theistic arguments have failed to show that it is clear that God exists is to consider the best examples of those arguments, which is what the next chapter will do.

4

Theistic Arguments before Hume

*If arguments are necessary, both to respond to challenges and to know God,
what is the status of the traditional arguments? What were the arguments that
Christians had given for God's existence prior to the challenge from David Hume?
In this chapter we will look at the standard types of theistic arguments and the
thinkers who worked on them. We will especially focus on Thomas Aquinas and
John Locke. Are the theistic arguments too difficult for the majority of Christians
to understand, let alone too difficult to serve as the basis for inexcusability?*

HAVING CONSIDERED A NUMBER of attempts to avoid the need for
an argument, we can now turn to consider actual arguments given
by theists. Proceeding on the assumption that an argument is necessary
to establish the clarity of God's existence, it is important to ask, "What
arguments have been given to date?" Since the following is not meant to
be an inclusive history of all theistic arguments, it will only focus on a few
examples. However, this is not a deficiency. The following will argue that
there are only a few kinds of arguments, and will focus on those thinkers
who systematized those arguments, and against whom later challenges
were raised. Hence, while the contemporary "anthropological argument"
will not be considered, this is a form of *a posteriori* argument, and this
type will be considered.

4.1. TYPES OF THEISTIC ARGUMENTS

The following will consider arguments for God's existence in light of the
principle of clarity. Skeptics have generally noted that if we cannot know,
then we cannot be held responsible. Therefore, while the various argu-

ments given historically for God's existence may have many interesting and notable aspects to consider, what will be asked here is whether they can provide a ground for certainty, and therefore clarity and inexcusability.

It is common to classify theistic arguments into three kinds, following the example of Kant. They are the *ontological, cosmological,* and *teleological* arguments. Graham Oppy also considers various other arguments that do not fit neatly into these classifications. These include minor evidential arguments, moral arguments, non-evidential arguments such as Pascal's Wager, cumulative arguments, and arguments from authority and consensus as well as religious experience.[1] Oppy's book *Arguing About Gods* is exacting in its detailed look at these arguments. The goal here is not to consider every argument that has been given, but instead to consider the most famous and popular arguments (the ontological, cosmological, and teleological) and the best expression of these by notable philosophers. These arguments are singled out because the challenges of Hume and Kant are aimed at them. However, we will encounter some of them as responses in the twentieth century on the part of Christians to the challenge of Hume and Kant, and their inadequacy will become apparent.

The ontological argument asserts that the existence of God can be proven simply based on the idea of God as a necessary being. Anselm's formulation of this will be stated below, as will Plantinga's reformatting of Anselm's argument. Anselm states his argument as follows:

> It is possible to think that something exists that cannot be thought not to exist, and such a being is greater than one that can be thought not to exist. Therefore, if that than which a greater cannot be thought can be thought not to exist, then that than which a greater cannot be thought is *not* that than which a greater cannot be thought; and this is a contradiction. So that than which a greater cannot be thought exists so truly that it cannot be thought not to exist. . . . So then why did 'the fool say in his heart, "There is no God,"' when it is so evident to the rational mind that you among all beings exist most greatly? Why indeed, except because he is stupid and a fool?[2]

In order to make the argument more explicit, Plantinga states it as follows:

1. God exists in the understanding but not in reality.

1. Oppy, *Arguing,* 2.
2. Anselm, *Monologion and Proslogion,* 101.

2. Existence in reality is greater than existence in the understanding alone.

3. God's existence in reality is conceivable.

4. If God did exist in reality, then he would be greater than he is (from 1 and 2).

5. It is conceivable that there be a being greater than God is (3 and 4).

6. It is conceivable that there be a being greater than the being than which nothing greater can be conceived (5, by the definition of 'God').

7. It is false that it is conceivable that there be a being greater than the being than which none greater can be conceived.

8. It is false that God exists in the understanding but not in reality.[3]

What is essential to the ontological argument is the move from *reason* to *being*. It assumes that *reason is ontological*—that it applies to *being* as well as *thought*. The challenge to be considered later from Hume and Kant is a challenge about the ontological use of reason, and the claim that the opposite of all matters of fact is possible. If reason is not about being as well as thought, then no form of the ontological argument can succeed.

The cosmological argument asserts that the existence of God can be proven by an argument based on cause and effect, change, or dependence. William Rowe states the cosmological argument as follows:

1. Every being (that exists or ever did exist) is either a dependent being or a self-existent being.

2. Not every being can be a dependent being.

3. Therefore, there exists a self-existent being.[4]

The essence of the cosmological argument is to argue from the reality of change, dependence, and causation to the nature of the changeless and eternal. Rowe uses the idea of dependence in his form of the arguments, others use the existence of effects or beings that require explanation. Such arguments take the experience of change, dependence, motion, etc., and argue that what is changing cannot be eternal. This applies both to the material world and the finite self. It presupposes that something must be

3. Plantinga, *The Nature*, 198.
4. Rowe, *Philosophy of Religion*, 19.

eternal (without beginning) and so presupposes some form of the ontological argument has already succeeded in showing this.

The teleological argument asserts that the existence of God can be proven by an argument based on design. William Rowe states the teleological argument as follows:

1. Machines are produced by intelligent design.

2. The universe resembles a machine.

3. Therefore, probably the universe was produced by intelligent design.[5]

Having argued that it is necessary to give an argument in order to arrive at the clarity of God's existence, the following will proceed to evaluate how notable thinkers, especially Aquinas and Locke, have conceived of the theistic arguments and the strength of their conclusions. If the theistic arguments cannot provide certainty but instead leave open the possibility that theism is false, then they are not sufficient to provide a basis for the inexcusability of unbelief.

The following will focus on Thomas Aquinas and John Locke. Aquinas systematized what had come before him in theistic thought. It is true that many thinkers before Aquinas gave theistic proofs. Two notable examples are Augustine and Anselm. A brief consideration of these will be helpful to justify focusing on Aquinas and Locke.

4.2. AUGUSTINE[6]

Augustine's development from young skeptic, to Manichean, to Christian and Church Father, involved a wrestling with ideas that has had lasting impact on the development of theology and philosophy. He developed what can be called an ethics of belief in which he maintains that there are some beliefs all humans should hold, and the failure to hold these is culpable. However, there is a tension in Augustine in terms of why he asserts these beliefs should be held. On the one hand, he offers brilliant arguments that show the absurdity of beliefs like polytheism and Greek materialism. But he also is willing to resort to force against some opponents, and has been used as a justification for the use of violence by others coming later (most nota-

---

5. Rowe, *Philosophy of Religion*, 45.

6. Some of this section appeared as the article "Augustine's Ethics of Belief and Avoiding Violence in Religious Disputes" in *New Blackfriars*.

bly in the Inquisition). Due to his emphasis on the next life and immediate knowledge of God, we can see where Augustine came short of providing a foundation for the inexcusability of unbelief. His discussion of God's existence is often limited to an intuitive/immediate knowledge of God.

Augustine's Presuppositions

Augustine operated within a Platonic worldview. This had a significant affect on how he interpreted Christianity. While he notes places that Plato came short,[7] he is in general agreement with the distinction drawn by Plato between mind and matter, and with an emphasis on an otherworldly fulfillment of life. Augustine argues that the highest good cannot be achieved in this life, and looks for a resurrection of the dead which is not a renewal of this world but a life in the heavenly world. He also emphasizes the corruption of the will,[8] and consequently focuses on unbelief as impious and vain[9] rather than as an intellectual failure. Because sin is an act of the will, there are times when intellectual engagement will be insufficient and violence is warranted.[10] These presuppositions go together and produce the resulting justification for violence: The highest good is not to be achieved in this world but is attained in the next life; the focus of sin is the will, and the will must be physically restrained rather than reasoned with (as one does with the intellect); this physical restraint justifies violence in some cases.

And yet Augustine does offer arguments, often very impressive, to demonstrate the absurdity of unbelief. Here it will be maintained that this tension is a result of mixture of beliefs in Augustine. He continues to maintain Platonic influences like those just mentioned. But he also maintains that humans are guilty before God for their unbelief, and this guilt requires that he show that unbelief is absurd. His own Platonism gets in the way of this and results in the tension that has often been influential in justifying physical violence.

The Ethics of Belief

The ethics of belief studies what should be believed by all humans. Minimally, it presupposes the *ought/can* principle. If something *ought* to

7. Augustine, *City of God*, 12.

8. Ibid., 12.

9. Augustine, *Confessions*, 2.

10. Brown, *Augustine*, 234.

be believed then it *must* be knowable. Augustine gives a very succinct statement of his ethics of belief:

> When, then, the question is asked what we are to believe in regard to religion, it is not necessary to probe into the nature of things, as was done by those whom the Greeks call *physici* . . . It is enough for the Christian to believe that the only cause of all created things, whether heavenly or earthly, whether visible or invisible, is the goodness of the Creator, the one true God; and that nothing exists but Himself that does not derive its existence from Him.[11]

Christians do not need to have an understanding of the elements,[12] the study of which so occupied the Greek philosophers. What they need to know about the world is that it was created by God.

This includes a knowledge of good and evil. "We ought to know the causes of good and evil as far as man may in this life know them, in order to avoid the mistakes and troubles of which this life is so full. For our aim must always be to reach that state of happiness in which no trouble shall distress us, and no error mislead us."[13] Furthermore, ignorance of God, and the causes of good and evil, are among the wickedness that are condemned by God.[14] The *ought/can principle* applies here: If humans *ought* to know, then they *must* be able to know. To be able to know requires that the alternative views are not possibilities. If they were possible, if they were rational options, then a rational being could not know which view to believe. By implication, all ought to know God, and the failure to know God is an epistemic and moral failure.

Augustine calls those who do not believe in God "vain" and "impious."[15] Through the arguments he gives, he believes he shows that there is no excuse for failing to believe in God. It is these same impious persons that he claims Christ must die to redeem.[16] Part One of the *City of God* is a sustained argument to show that the gods of Rome were false and should not have been worshiped. Then in Book VIII he seeks to show that

---

11. Augustine, *Enchiridion*, ix.

12. Ibid., ix.

13. Ibid., xvi.

14. Ibid., xxv.

15. Augustine, *Confessions*, VIII. ii (2).

16. Ibid., VII. ix (14).

the true philosopher is the one who loves God.[17] To do this he proposes to refute those who accept the existence of a Divinity but also worship diverse and sundry other gods.[18] Here we have belief mixed with unbelief, as opposed to the vain and impious person who does not believe at all. Both are rejected by Augustine's ethics of belief on the basis of arguments he puts forth.

Augustine considers those who believe in gods and those who believe that all things originate from matter.[19] He rejects both in favor of Platonist natural philosophy.[20] This is the view that God is the author of all things, and that besides matter there also exists the soul. First, he asserts that God exists and that he is the creator of all souls and material things.[21] Second, there is no excuse for not knowing this (vs. the Greek materialists—VIII.5; the soul is eternal—XII.21; the human race is eternal—XII.10; the world is eternal or innumerable worlds—XII.12). Third, because the failure to know God is the root of all other sins, its heinous nature requires the atoning sacrifice of Christ (no alternative atonement is possible—XXI.18; XXI.25).

These three principles go together and are foundational for Augustine's theology. His exclusivism (the third point above) requires that all persons can know God.[22] If a person could not know God, then they could not be held accountable for their ignorance (the ought/can principle). His exclusivism also requires that there is a need for redemption, that there is no excuse for failing to know God. The failure to know God must be an evil that is serious enough to need the death of the Son of God to atone. If failing to know God is not that serious, then the atoning payment need not be so significant. The magnitude of the first transgression results in eternal punishment for all who are outside the Savior's grace.[23]

The prevalence of inclusivism or pluralism in contemporary thinking is premised upon a denial of the first two principles. They assert that because it is not clear that God exists, and unbelief is not inexcusable,

---

17. Augustine, *City of God*, VIII.1.

18. Ibid., VIII.1.

19. Augustine, *City of God*, VIII.5.

20. Ibid., VIII.6.

21. Ibid., XII.28.

22. Brown, *Augustine,* 318.

23. Augustine, *City of God*, XXI.12.

it cannot be the case that Christ is required for atonement by everyone. And certainly this line of reasoning holds together, but as we have seen Augustine rejects the initial skepticism about the ability to know God. While he concedes that some things are beyond rational demonstration,[24] he clearly does not believe that this applies to the existence and nature of God, or else it could not be vain and impious to fail to believe.

Augustine's Arguments

In order to get a sense of how Augustine proceeds in proving that God exists, it is worthwhile to look at some passages. His focus is different from Anselm, Aquinas, the Enlightenment, or Modern approaches. These tend to focus on perfect beings, first causes, and design. In contrast, Augustine focuses on what is eternal (without beginning). In book 7 of his *Confessions*, Augustine distinguishes between *temporal* being and *eternal* being:

> Accordingly, whatever things exist are good, and evil into whose origins I was inquiring is not a substance, for if it were a substance, it would be good. Either it would be an incorruptible substance, a great good indeed, or a corruptible substance, which could be corrupted only if it were good. Hence I saw and it was made clear to me that you made all things good, and there are absolutely no substances which you did not make. As you did not make all things equal, all things are good in the sense that taken individually they are good, and all things taken together are very good. For our God has made 'all things very good' (Gen. 1:31).
>
> For you evil does not exist at all, and not only for you but for your created universe, because there is nothing outside it which could break in and destroy the order which you have imposed upon it. I turned my gaze on other things. I saw that to you they owe their existence, and that in you all things are finite, not in the sense that the space they occupy is bounded but in the sense that you hold all things in your hand by your truth. So all things are real insofar as they have being, and the term 'falsehood' applies only when something is thought to have being which does not. And I saw that each thing is harmonious not only with its place but with its time, **and that you alone are eternal** and did not first begin to work after innumerable periods of time.[25]

---

24. Augustine, *City of God*, XXI.5.

25. Ibid., 125. VII.xii (18)—xv (21). Emphasis mine.

I added the bold to emphasize a method behind Augustine's reasoning that can possibly be used as a key to figuring out both if God exists and if it is clear that God exists. This requires looking at whether there is anything that is eternal, and if "eternal" can be predicated of anything besides God. At least this much can be said here: If it can be shown that the claim "nothing is eternal," and the predication of "eternal" to anything besides God, involves a contradiction, then it can be said to be clear that God exists. Without developing this further here, it is important to note because Locke also adopts a similar method, and it might be that there is promise here for showing that it is in fact clear that God exists. However, to do so would require first responding to the challenge to reason given by Hume and Kant, which will be considered later.

Augustine held that only God, as an infinite, unchangeable spirit, can be eternal. All other things are corruptible and changing. The material world is corruptible, and if it had always existed it would already be in its final state of corruption. The human soul is aiming at a final end; if it is eternal, then it should already have attained this end or it can never attain this end.[26] The alternative to these is that there is an eternal spirit (nonmaterial intelligence) who created the material world and human souls.

The Problem of Evil

Perhaps the most significant objection to belief in God is the problem of evil. Certainly for Augustine this was a central consideration, and was a motivating factor in his becoming a Manichean. However, as he began to solve the problem of evil by addressing the nature of evil he moved from his Manicheanism to Christian theism. His solution was to deny that evil has any real existence, and instead that it is a corruption of the nature of what exists—this is a rejection of the dualism of Manicheanism.

Credo Ut Intelligam

A final issue worth addressing in Augustine is his use of the phrase "Believe in order to understand, because unless you believe, you will not understand." Commonly stated in its Latin form, *credo ut intelligam*, this has become a motto for many Christians in their approach to apologetics and the ethics of belief. It will be shown here that Augustine's use of this phrase is not similar to Anselm's, and is in contrast to a phrase used by

26. Augustine, *City of God*, XII.21.

Tertullian. If broadly applied, *credo ut intelligam* appears to undermine the need for arguments to establish the clarity of God's existence.

If one must first believe in order to understand, then it is not clear which religion/worldview one should believe to understand. The Roman polytheist or Greek materialist can reply to Augustine's arguments: You must first believe our position in order to understand it. If it is not clear which worldview to believe in order to understand (and every worldview can make this claim), then the failure to believe in God cannot be inexcusable (or vain and impious).

Furthermore, it is hard to understand what this phrase means. If you do not understand something, then it is difficult to see how you could believe it. What is it that is being believed? One could believe anything by this standard, with the hope of understanding it later. It undermines the possibility of an ethics of belief.

Instead, it seems that the phrase should be: "I believe because I understand," or "I believe to the extent that I understand." Consider how Augustine proceeds in the *City of God*. As a person comes to understand that the gods of Rome were ineffectual, one comes to place their belief in God the Creator. Or as one sees the absurdity of Greek materialism, or the absurdity of believing in eternal cycles or innumerable worlds, one comes to believe in God. This is the way that the understanding operates. *Credo ut intelligam* calls for blind belief (fideism), but Augustine does not approach God's existence in that manner.

This does not explain Augustine's use of the phrase. It occurs in one of his sermons in the context of a discussion about the Trinity. He does not apply it to all aspects of Christianity or all areas of belief. It seems to be a contrast with Tertullian's approach. Tertullian said: *credo quia absurdum est*, "I believe because it is absurd." This was also a phrase about the Trinity. Where Tertullian is willing to believe in the absurd, Augustine was not. If he, like Tertullian, had been willing to accept absurdities, what would happen when he argued against the gods of Rome? After having shown that belief in the gods of Rome is absurd, he would then have to believe it himself or accept those who do. When Tertullian was discussed above, it was mentioned that he was himself a notable apologist who offered many arguments against opposing views. His claim about absurdity seems to be best understood as an affirmation of the strength of his belief. If taken literally and applied, it would require that he accepts those worldviews he had argued were absurd.

Augustine's claim is that the Trinity is not an absurdity, and as one explores this doctrine, one will come to understand it. One cannot understand an absurdity, it remains forever beyond comprehension. But according to Augustine, the doctrine of the Trinity is not like this. Believing in God the Creator, the divinity of the Son of God, and the Holy Spirit as sent by the Father and Son, one must believe in the Trinity. Greater understanding comes with time as this doctrine is studied. The formation of this doctrine in the Nicean Creed avoids contradiction and absurdity: One God, Three Persons (not One God and Three Gods, or One Person and Three Persons). Augustine is encouraging rational inquiry where Tertullian's phrase would shut it down. But Augustine's phrase is not applied to all areas of belief, but is based on having shown the clarity of God's existence and done intricate exegetical work in the Scriptures to support the doctrine of the Trinity. In this limited application he differs from Anselm, who is more famous in his use of *credo ut intelligam* and seems to have given it a broader application.

Augustine and the Ethics of Belief

Augustine's ethics of belief *presupposes* the inexcusability thesis. He believes that it is clear that God exists, and gives arguments to show that alternative views are not possible. He especially focuses on the inadequacy of the Roman gods, the Greek materialists, and those who believe in God but also worship other gods. Of special concern are the problem of evil, and his reconciliation of God's predestination, free will, and human responsibility. Attempts to avoid the need for arguments, by thinkers like Thomas Aquinas, Tertullian, John Calvin, and the Reformed Epistemologists, fail to uphold the clarity of God's existence and therefore cannot support the inexcusability of unbelief. Augustine's ethics of belief is a necessary presupposition to exclusivist claims by Christianity; if Christ is *necessary* for redemption, then the sin that needs redemption *must* be inexcusable. This sin begins with the failure to know God, and the implication is that the failure to know God is inexcusable because it is clear that God exists. Augustine's work to show that it is inexcusable to hold to the alternative religions/worldviews of his day, provides a model that can be utilized to address the challenges that have arisen since his time. Certainly there have been significant challenges to arguments for God's existence and the knowledge of God after Augustine. Augustine continues to contribute to this discussion by providing a method in the inexcusability thesis that serves as the basis for a robust approach to the clarity of God's existence. Yet there is also a tension within Augustine that has come down to the present day which can only be relieved by critically examining the presuppositions that limited Augustine's analysis of unbelief as sin, and therefore limited his ability to show the clarity of God's existence.

4.3. ANSELM

A second notable thinker who is often discussed in contemporary discussion of theistic arguments is Anselm. Anselm gave both *a posteriori* and *a priori* arguments, but is best known for the latter. He asserted that the idea of God tells us that God exists so that *only* the fool denies God. This argument attempts to show that the denial of God's existence involves a contradiction. As was seen earlier, what is especially important for our considerations here is that Anselm believed that unbelief was inexcusable, something *only* the fool would do. Yet it is one thing to assert this and quite another to prove it.

The argument formulated by Anselm has assumptions about what it is to be perfect. "Naturally, Anselm's argument is valid only within the framework of certain presuppositions that are not universally accepted. Thus, for instance, it presupposes that existence is a perfection, that perfection can be conceived, and that the structures of reality correspond to the structures of thought."[27] This form of the ontological argument makes a mistake similar to one mentioned earlier about Calvin. It argues from the idea of perfection, or an eternal being, to the existence of God. It could be true that all humans have the idea of the perfect, eternal, and that this idea involves the corresponding belief that the eternal exists. However, there are many different views as to just what is eternal. Matter is believed by some to be eternal, others that ultimate reality is consciousness (Brahman). To prove that it is clear that God exists, the Christian must show that only God is eternal, that all other claims about the eternal involve a contradiction, and Anselm does not do this. However, he gives a methodology for arguing that something must be eternal, which we will explore later.

---

27. González, *A History of Christian Thought*, 163.

4.4. THOMAS AQUINAS

Aquinas rejected *a priori* proofs and instead focused on *a posteriori* proofs. He stands as the great systematizer in the tradition and as such is an obvious thinker on which to focus. His arguments are still considered today, and are often modified to attempt to reply to the challenges from the centuries after Aquinas.

Aquinas begins with the claim that God is known through his actions. This is a denial of the *a priori* approach and an affirmation that only the *a posteriori* will be fruitful. "Everything is knowable according as it is in act, God, Who is pure act without any admixture of potency, is in Himself supremely knowable. But what is supremely knowable in itself, is not knowable to some other intellect, on account of the excess of the intelligible object above the intellect; as, for example, the sun, which is supremely visible, cannot be seen by the bat by reason of its excess of light."[28]

Aquinas asserts that all knowledge begins with the senses:

> Our natural knowledge takes its beginning from sense. Hence our natural knowledge can go as far as it can be led by sensible things. But our mind cannot be led by sense so far as to see the essence of God, because the sensible effects of God do not equal the power of God as their cause. Hence from the knowledge of sensible things the whole power of God cannot be known; nor therefore can His essence be seen. But because they are his effects and depend on their cause, we can be led from them so far as to know of God whether He exists, and to know of Him what must necessarily belong to Him as the first cause of all things, exceeding all things caused by Him.[29]

This approach creates significant problems for knowing God which are seen by Hume. Infinitude cannot be known through the senses. Yet God is infinite. The implication is that if we are to know this aspect of God it must be apart from the senses. But in this life all of our knowledge is mediated through the senses. Therefore, in this life we cannot have knowledge of God's infinitude, we must wait for the next life. Aquinas's assumptions lead to the doctrine of the beatific vision. However, this undermines inexcusability because the unbeliever can blame his unbelief on his body. In addition, Aquinas's empiricism tends toward views of grace and

28. Aquinas, *Summa Theologica*, 49. I q. 12, a 1.
29. Ibid., 58. I q. 12, a 12.

faith where these are said to work apart from the intellect and knowing God. The masses are unable to understand the proofs and so must accept God's existence on authority. In the twentieth century this doctrine was extended to non-Christians in Vatican II (1962–1965), which affirmed that they can be implicit believers.

Aquinas does affirm that proofs are possible. He quotes Paul in Romans 1 to affirm this. "The Apostle says: *The invisible things of Him are clearly seen, being understood by the things that are made* (Romans 1:20). But this would not be unless the existence of God could be demonstrated through the things that are made. For the first thing we must know of anything is whether it exists."[30] But again, he thinks the knowledge of God is minimal while in the body. God's essence cannot be known while in the body:

> God cannot be seen in His essence by a mere human being, unless he be separated from this mortal life. The reason is, because, as was said above, the mode of knowledge follows the mode of the nature of the knowing thing. But our soul, as long as we live in this life, has its being in corporeal matter; hence naturally it knows only what has a form in matter, or what can be known in this way. Now it is evident that the divine essence cannot be known through the natures of material things. For it was shown above that the knowledge of God by means of any created likeness is not the vision of His essence. Hence it is impossible for the soul of man in this life to see the essence of God.[31]

However, Aquinas does affirm that knowing God is eternal life. "But life everlasting consists in the vision of the divine essence, according to the words: *This is eternal life, that they may know Thee the only true God. (John 17:3).*"[32] The divine essence cannot be known in this life while in the body. Therefore eternal life is not possible in the body. The unbeliever has an excuse.

Aquinas's arguments proceed from experience to God. He gives his famous "five ways" to prove that God exists. His arguments are *a posteriori*. He argues from aspects of human experience that are common to everybody, and then concludes with God. He considers the reality of motion and concludes with a first mover. He considers the reality of degrees of greatness and concludes with a greatest being. He considers change and

30. Aquinas, *Summa Theologica*, 12. I q. 2, a. 2.

31. Ibid., 57. I q. 12, a. 11.

32. Ibid., 51. I q. 12, a. 4.

the appearance of governance and concludes with a first cause of change and a governor. Perhaps his third way can be construed as an *a priori* argument from the ideas of contingency and necessity, although these could also be thought of as coming from the experience of dependence to the idea of an independent being.

We can anticipate problems in these arguments, although we will look at Hume and Kant in detail later. None of the conclusions of these arguments resembles the God of theism. These same arguments could be used to support any number of non-theistic worldviews, such as Greek dualism. As such, they are insufficient both as proofs and as a ground for clarity. In addition, Aquinas's empirical epistemology will also present significant problems. Hume will take this epistemology to its logical conclusion of skepticism. If a solution to the criticism of Hume is to be found, it will require rethinking empiricism. This means that Aquinas's arguments will not succeed, and cannot be modified to address Hume's challenge, because they assume empiricism.

Aquinas asserted that knowing God requires grace. This is not because of the Fall, but due to the weaknesses inherent in the human intellect:

> We have a more perfect knowledge of God by grace than by natural reason. Which appears thus. The knowledge which we have by reason requires two things: phantasms received from the sensible objects, and the natural intelligible light, by whose power we abstract from them intelligible concepts.
>
> Now in both of these human knowledge is assisted by the revelation of grace. For the intellect's natural light is strengthened by the infusion of gratuitous light. And sometimes also the phantasms in the human imagination are divinely formed, so as to express divine things better than those do which we receive from sensible things, as appears in prophetic visions; while sometimes sensible things, or even voices, are divinely formed to express some thing divine.[33]

However, if there are inherent weaknesses in my person then I cannot be blamed for them. I have an excuse.

Aquinas does afford some ability to "natural reason."

> It is written (Romans 1:19), *That which is known of God*, namely, what can be known of God by natural reason, *is manifest in them*.

---

33. Aquinas, *Summa Theologica*, 59. I q. 12, a. 13.

I answer that, Our knowledge takes its beginning from sense. Hence our natural knowledge can go as far as it can be led by sensible things. But our mind cannot be led by sense so far as to see the essence of God, because the sensible effects of God do not equal the power of God as their cause. Hence from the knowledge of sensible things the whole power of God cannot be known; nor therefore can His essence be seen. But because they are His effects and depend on their cause, we can be led from them so far as to know of God whether He exists, and to know of Him what must necessarily belong to Him as the first cause of all things, exceeding all things caused by Him.[34]

His conclusion is that we can know a few things about God through natural reason, such as that there is a first cause, but not the essence of God. This is not what the Apostle says. He affirms that we can know the eternal power and divine nature of God through the things that are made. But Aquinas's empirical epistemology limits him, and Hume will pick up on this and devastate the Thomistic approach.

Aquinas's concern to limit the knowledge of God available to humans in this life might be connected with the doctrine of the incomprehensibility and aseity of God. God, as an infinite being, can never be fully understood. Indeed, humans as finite beings can never fully understand anything, including other finite beings. Furthermore, God is wholly other and is not dependent on any other being. God as the creator possesses the incommunicable attributes of eternality, infinity, and unchangeableness—no other being can or does have these. God is therefore unique and different from the creature, and does not depend on any creature—any attempt to equate God and the creation violates this and is idolatry. However, neither of these doctrines necessitates the claim that humans cannot know God in this life. Humans will never *fully* comprehend God, nor will humans ever be like God *in eternality or infinity*, but humans can know *some things* about God. Indeed, even the claim that God is incomprehensible and other is some knowledge of God. The question is: What are humans responsible for knowing about God in this life?

A further problem for Aquinas is that reason cannot show that matter is created and not eternal.[35] "By faith alone do we hold, and by no

34. Aquinas, *Summa Theologica*, 58. I q. 12, a. 12.

35. Could matter be created and eternal, as in "eternally created"? Throughout this book the term "created" has been used to mean "with a beginning" and therefore it would be a contradiction to affirm something as eternally created. However, Aquinas is using

demonstration can it be proved, that the world did not always exist, as was said above of the mystery of the Trinity. The reason of this is that the newness of the world cannot be demonstrated from the world itself. For the principle of demonstration is the essence of a thing. . . . Hence it cannot be demonstrated that man, or heaven, or a stone did not always exist."[36] That the world is created and temporal is a necessary part of Christian theism: God only is eternal, the material world was created by God and is temporal. If this cannot be known, then unbelief (such as Aristotelianism, Platonism, Zoroastrianism, Hinduism, etc) is excusable. The "proofs" that Aquinas gives fall far short of the God of Christian theism, and this is precisely the point that Hume picks up on and criticizes.

Finally, Aquinas holds a view of faith that is incompatible with inexcusability. For Aquinas, faith is a trust in authority, and is all that most humans are capable of. This is fideism as discussed earlier. The greatest good can only be achieved through the grace of God; this is different than asserting that humans need to be forgiven:

> Since the human intellect in the present state of life cannot understand even created immaterial substances, much less can it understand the essence of the uncreated substance. Hence it must be said absolutely that God is not the first object of our knowledge. Rather do we know God through creatures, according to the Apostle (Romans 1:20), *the invisible things of God are clearly seen, being understood by the things that are made*, while the first object of our knowledge in this life is the quiddity of a material thing, which is the proper object of our intellect, as appears above in many passages.[37]

This view of faith provides most humans with an excuse. Most humans were not located in a place where they could find out about the proper tradition in which to place their trust. And for those who were, their intelligence is viewed as so low by Aquinas that it is not clear how they could even be held accountable for proper trust. Knowing what to

---

the Aristotelian framework where "created" means "dependent" and so asserts that the creation could be eternally dependent. This view is Aristotelian dualism, and not theism. The challenge for theism is to show that Aristotle's brand of dualism, as unbelief, is false, and that it can be known by reason that the creation is not co-eternal with God. Aquinas asserts that this cannot be known apart from special revelation and therefore provides an excuse for Aristotle and all other dualists.

36. Aquinas, *Summa Theologica*, 243. I q. 46, a. 2.

37. Ibid., 451. I q. 88, a. 3.

place one's trust in requires a degree of intelligence that the masses (according to Aquinas) do not seem to possess. If this was the view of humanity common in the medieval period, it is not surprising that the masses were viewed with disdain by the "intellectuals" and "nobles." Further, if this is the view held by a given thinker, it will not be surprising to also find that thinker holding to either some variety of inclusivism or eventually some kind of pluralism.

It is also worth noting that where the clarity of general revelation is denied, consistency will require an abandonment of Historic Christian claims about the inexcusability of unbelief. Sometimes this is expressed in the affirmation of the mysteries of the faith. "Mysteries" can be taken to mean things that were not originally revealed but are revealed later (the doctrine of the Trinity is not found explicitly in the O.T., and so is a "mystery" revealed in the N.T.). But often they are taken to be doctrines that are unknowable, or even paradoxes that are contradictions and therefore contrary to reason. In "Fides et Ratio" Pope John Paul II says: "To assist reason in its effort to understand the mystery there are the signs which Revelation itself presents" and "The word of God is addressed to all people, in every age and in every part of the world; and the human being is by nature a philosopher." It could be true that the word of God (as the scriptures) is addressed to all people, yet all people have not had access to the scriptures. Therefore, if humans are held accountable by God for a failure to know something that is only knowable by having read the scriptures, then they seem to have an excuse. Rather, those beliefs that humans must hold and are guilty if they do not hold, must be available through general revelation. That humans (universal) are by nature philosophers should mean that they can, by nature, think critically and examine their beliefs for meaning. They should come to know what is clear about God, and the failure to do so is a failure to live according to their nature.

Aquinas represents the best in the medieval tradition and in many ways is still among the best today. However, his empirical assumptions affect how he argues for God's existence and how he views the human condition. The conclusions of his arguments do not resemble the God of theism. As such, they are not able to support clarity. The only options are to abandon this kind of empiricism and search for an epistemology that can avoid the skepticism of Hume and serve as a ground for clarity, or abandon the claim that unbelief is inexcusable.

4.5. JOHN LOCKE

The second thinker who will be considered in relation to proofs is John Locke. Where Aquinas systematized what came before him, and is a chief representative of the Medieval view of humanity and epistemology, Locke is an important representative of the Enlightenment. Of course there are many Enlightenment thinkers, and different persons may emphasize them in different ways. But Locke stands out in his theistic view of God (as opposed to Spinoza or Leibniz), his affirmation that all humans can use reason to know God, that God is certainly known, and in his combination of the *a priori* and *a posteriori* arguments. He is also the direct object of Hume's attack.

Locke affirms that God's existence can be certainly known:

> *We are capable of knowing certainly that there is a God.* Though God has given us no innate ideas of himself; though he has stamped no original characters on our minds, wherein we may read his being; yet having furnished us with those faculties our minds are endowed with, he hath not left himself without witness: since we have sense, perception, and reason, and cannot want a clear proof of him, as long as we carry *ourselves* about us. Nor can we justly complain of our ignorance in this great point; since he has so plentifully provided us with the means to discover and know him; so far as is necessary to the end of our being, and the great concernment of our happiness. But, though this be the most obvious truth that reason discovers, and though its evidence be (if I mistake not) equal to mathematical certainty: yet it requires thought and attention; and the mind must apply itself to a regular deduction of it from some part of our intuitive knowledge, or else we shall be as uncertain and ignorant of this as of other propositions, which are in themselves capable of clear demonstration. To show, therefore, that we are capable of *knowing*, i.e. *being certain* that there is a God, and *how we may come by* this certainty, I think we need go no further than *ourselves*, and that undoubted knowledge we have of our own existence.[38]

This quote by Locke is reminiscent of Anselm. If God can be certainly known by everyone, then unbelief is foolish. Locke is affirming that there is a clear general revelation of God to all humans. He does mitigate this sometimes by implying that most people do not have time to think about such matters because they are so busy with work. However, the implica-

---

38. Locke, *An Essay*, 619. iv x 1.

tion is that if they stopped working so much they could think about such things, in contrast to the view that the masses are not intelligent enough, even when at leisure, to understand.

Unfortunately, the emphasis on the ability of all to know God leads Locke to downplay the importance of special revelation. He does not emphasize the reality that unbelief is a sin that needs redemption. Therefore, he tends to see little need for special revelation other than to reaffirm truths knowable by reason. Because of this, it is common to debate whether Locke was a theist or deist, and many of his teachings were utilized by deists. It will always be true that where given thinkers do not see unbelief as an inexcusable sin that requires redemption, they will see little need for special revelation. This is a problem to note in Locke that is criticized by later generations and has led some to rationalism (denial of all special revelation) and others to fideism (in an attempt to preserve special revelation). The principle of clarity provides a clue as to how these extremes can be avoided.

In terms of Locke's specific proofs, there is both much that is helpful and much that is left wanting. First, we will examine what is helpful. Locke uses arguments that have both *a priori* and *a posteriori* aspects. He affirms that God can be known through general revelation by arguing that it is clear that there must be something eternal. "For I judge it as certain and clear a truth as can anywhere be delivered, that 'the invisible things of God are clearly seen from the creation of the world, being understood by the things that are made, even his eternal power and Godhead.'"[39] Locke's understanding of Paul seems more consistent than Aquinas. The most helpful thing in Locke is his methodology. He affirms the clarity of God's existence and then argues for the impossibility of the opposite. He does this in steps. First, something must have existed from eternity (as opposed to the claim that nothing is eternal):

> There is no truth more evident than that *something* must be *from eternity*. I never yet heard of any one so unreasonable, or that could suppose so manifest a contradiction, as a time wherein there was perfectly nothing. This being of all absurdities the greatest, to imagine that pure nothing, the perfect negation and absence of all beings, should ever produce any real existence.

---

39. Locke, *An Essay,* 621. iv x 7.

It being, then, unavoidable for all rational creatures to conclude, that *something* has existed from eternity; let us next see *what kind of thing* that must be.[40]

Secondly, what has existed from eternity cannot be the material world.[41] Rather, what has existed from eternity must be a personal being, or spirit.[42] The material world cannot account for the reality of thought. The reality of thought in us indicates that the creator of thought is personal and not simply a material force. This spirit is infinite in power and knowledge, there is none higher.[43] If Locke can show these things, then he has gone a long way to establishing the clarity of God's existence. It is worth noting that he leaves out discussion of the goodness of God, and that his empiricism will ultimately undermine his approach. But his method is the only possible method consistent with the principle of clarity: God's existence is knowable by all because the contradictory claims are impossible (contrary to reason). If this could be established, then unbelief would be inexcusable. Locke did not establish it.

In spite of his methodology, Locke does not see the need for redemption. This causes significant trouble in his intellectual tradition. He hints at excuses for unbelief, such as the workload of the common human. He does not see the redemptive nature of special revelation and instead thinks of it as a supplement to general revelation. Even if he was not personally a deist, he opens the door to deism and the rejection of scripture, and it is not surprising to see that many in the Enlightenment tradition deny the need for scripture altogether. This reality emphasizes the necessity of the principle of clarity for Historic Christianity.

In order to make sense of the need for special revelation as redemptive revelation, unbelief must be inexcusable. In spite of the improvement of method in Locke, he does not see the inexcusability of unbelief before God or what it would cost for God to redeem unbelievers. On the other hand, if it is true that unbelief is inexcusable, and justice demands payment for wrong, then the suffering and death of Christ, as the Son of God, can be understood. This is the highest possible payment, which empha-

---

40. Locke, *An Essay,* 622. iv x 8. Here Locke only proves that something must be eternal, not that any one thing is eternal. It could be that there is an eternal process consisting of temporal beings (the flux of Heraclitus or the dependent co-arising of Buddhism).

41. Locke, *An Essay,* 626. iv x 14.

42. Ibid., 628. iv x 18.

43. Ibid., 628. iv x 18–19.

sizes the horror of unbelief as sin. If sin requires such a payment, then it is taken very seriously by God. For those who tend to downplay the serious nature of unbelief, it will not be surprising to find them also downplaying the payment. This is a consistent outcome. Christ will be seen as an example of love, motivational speaker, or wise prophet, but not as the eternal Son of God who had to suffer and die to pay for the sins of the world.

4.6. CONCLUSION: THE INEXCUSABILITY PRINCIPLE AND HISTORIC CHRISTIAN CLAIMS

If the Historic Christian view of Christ is to be maintained, then the inexcusability of unbelief must be proven. Locke came close, but he did not succeed. He was undermined by his empirical epistemology. Consequently, he did not see the need for Christ as expressed in the Historic Christian tradition, and he was a valuable source for deists who denied the historic view of Christ altogether. Understanding the failure of Locke is an important key to understanding the turn from the Historic Christian view of Christ to views found in the nineteenth and twentieth centuries.

In the next chapter we will see how empirical assumptions allowed Hume and Kant to limit the ability of reason to know God (or anything beyond experience). Their criticisms of the theistic arguments are largely correct, showing that these arguments overextend themselves.

5

Enlightenment Challenges to Theistic Belief

Having considered the traditional arguments, which continue to be relied upon today, we now turn to the challenges given in response to these. The process of challenges helps reveal ways in which the tradition has come short, and so can be healthy. This chapter considers challenges from David Hume and Immanuel Kant. In what way do these challenges call into question inexcusability, and therefore the Christian message of redemption itself? Can Christianity be content with blind faith, or even informed faith falling short of knowledge? What is the standard for inexcusability?

THE CONCLUSION AFTER HAVING viewed the best arguments thus far offered in theism is that they are more than insufficient. This point will be made all the more stark by a consideration of Hume and Kant. The failure to prove that God exists sets the stage for a general turning away from the exclusivist claims of Historic Christianity. It is important to recognize that such notable Christian thinkers as Aquinas did not even assert the principle of clarity, and that where others did, like Locke, they came short of proving that unbelief is inexcusable and requires redemption. We will now look at the devastating attack given by Hume and Kant that leads many contemporary philosophers to assert that proofs for God's existence are no longer viable.

5.1. DAVID HUME

David Hume concludes his *Enquiry Concerning Human Understanding* by undermining both *a priori* and *a posteriori* arguments for God's existence:

Whatever *is* may *not be*. No negation of a fact can involve a contradiction. The non-existence of any being, without exception, is as
clear and distinct an idea as its existence ... The existence, therefore,
of any being can only be proved by arguments from its cause or its
effect; and these arguments are founded entirely on experience. If
we reason *a priori*, anything may appear able to produce anything.
The falling of a pebble may, for aught we know, extinguish the sun;
or the wish of a man control the planets in their orbits. It is only
experience which teaches us the nature and bounds of cause and
effect, and enables us to infer the existence of one object from that
of another.[1]

To understand the challenge to theistic belief posed by David Hume
it is necessary to understand his epistemology. Hume divides knowledge
into two kinds:

All the objects of human reason or enquiry may naturally be
divided into two kinds, to wit, *Relations of Ideas*, and *Matters of
Fact*. Of the first kind are the science of Geometry, Algebra, and
Arithmetic . . . Propositions of this kind are discoverable by the
mere operation of thought, without dependence on what is anywhere existent in the universe.[2]

The relations of ideas do not tell us anything about existence. If we are to
have knowledge of what exists, it must be through a knowledge of matters
of fact. In this assertion Hume has already undermined the ontological
argument, which is an argument from the relation of ideas to what exists.
It is an *a priori* argument. Hume explains how, in his view, we can come
to know of existence:

It may, therefore, be a subject worthy of curiosity, to enquire what
is the nature of that evidence which assures us of any real existence
and matter of fact, beyond the present testimony of our senses, or
the records of our memory ... All reasonings concerning matter
of fact seem to be founded on the relation of *Cause and Effect*. By
means of that relation alone we can go beyond the evidence of our
memory and senses . . . If we would satisfy ourselves, therefore,
concerning the nature of that evidence, which assures us of matters of fact, we must enquire how we arrive at the knowledge of
cause and effect.

1. Hume, *Enquiries*, 164. Sect XII, Part III, 132.
2. Ibid., 25. Sect IV, Part I, 20.

> I shall venture to affirm, as a general proposition, which admits of no exception, that the knowledge of this relation is not, in any instance, attained by reasonings *a priori*; but arises entirely from experience, when we find that any particular objects are constantly conjoined together.[3]

Having undermined the ontological argument, he has now also dismissed any cosmological argument. All cosmological arguments proceed by using cause and effect to conclude that God exists. But Hume denies that any such conclusion can be arrived at:

> Hence we may discover the reason why no philosopher, who is rational and modest, has ever pretended to assign the ultimate cause of any natural operation, or to show distinctly the action of that power, which produces any single effect in the universe. It is confessed, that the utmost effort of human reason is to reduce the principles, productive of natural phenomena, to a greater simplicity, and to resolve the many particular effects into a few general uses, by means of reasonings from analogy, experience, and observation. But as to the cause of these general causes, we should in vain attempt their discovery; nor shall we ever be able to satisfy ourselves, by any particular explication of them. *These ultimate springs and principles are totally shut up from human curiosity and enquiry.*[4]

It is not possible to know about ultimate causes (for the theist this is God) because all knowledge is from experience, and we cannot argue from experience to an ultimate cause. "When it is asked, *What is the nature of all our reasonings concerning matters of fact?* The proper answer seems to be, that they are founded on the relation of cause and effect. When again it is asked, *What is the foundation of all our reasonings and conclusions concerning that relation?* It may be replied in one word, Experience."[5]

In his *Dialogues Concerning Natural Religion* Hume challenges both *a priori* and *a posteriori* arguments. He was aware of all the kinds of arguments for God's existence that had been given up to his day:

> Emphasis is sometimes laid on the fact that Hume devoted his attention principally to theistic arguments as found in English writers such as Clarke and Butler. This is true enough; but if the implication is intended that Hume would have changed his mind,

3. Hume, *Enquiries*, 26. Sect IV, Part 1, 21.

4. Ibid., 30. Sect IV, Part 1, 26. Emphasis mine.

5. Ibid., 32. Sect IV, Part 2, 28.

had he been acquainted with more satisfactory formulations of the arguments for the existence of God, it must be remembered that, given Hume's philosophical principles, especially his analysis of causality, he could not admit any cogent proofs of theism in a recognizable sense.[6]

The *a priori* argument is unsound because there is no such thing as a necessary being. For any being that can be thought of, both its existence and non-existence can be imagined. This is a direct challenge to Anselm's proof, and to Locke's analysis of eternal existence. It is a denial that reason applies to being. This limitation on reason anticipates Kant, and will be the major challenge that must be addressed if God's existence is to be proven.

The *a posteriori* arguments do not prove theism, according to Hume. These arguments are based on our daily experience and on analogy. However, our daily experience cannot take us beyond our daily experience. If we have a daily experience of succession in time, this does not tell us anything about the cause of the universe. If we have a daily experience of houses being designed, this does not tell us anything about the universe as being designed. The character Philo, from Hume's *Dialogues*, says:

> Mark the consequences. *First*, by this method of reasoning you renounce all claim to infinity in any of the attributes of the Deity. For, as the cause ought only to be proportioned to the effect, and the effect, so far as it falls under our cognizance, is not infinite, what pretensions have we, upon your suppositions, to ascribe that attribute to the Divine Being? You will still insist that, by removing Him so much from all similarity to human creatures, we give in to the most arbitrary hypothesis, and at the same time weaken all proofs of His existence.
>
> *Secondly*, you have no reason, on your theory, for ascribing perfection to the Deity, even in His finite capacity, or for supposing Him free from every error, mistake, or incoherence, in His undertakings.[7]

This is a challenge to the empiricism assumed behind *a posteriori* arguments. We cannot argue to universal conclusions from our limited experience. We cannot conclude "God" from "house." Our experience is extremely limited, and any argument from experience to a universal is a gross over-extension of reason.

---

6. Copleston, *A History of Philosophy: Hobbes to Hume, Vol. 5*, 311.

7. Hume, *Dialogues*, 38. V.

However, even granting that we can use an empirical argument, such an argument will not arrive at the God of theism. Why not a material cause of the universe? Philo asserts that there is no basis for maintaining that the universe must have a spiritual or ideal cause rather than a material cause. Is it possible that the first cause could be material, or that the material world needs no first cause? Remember that Locke did offer an argument as to why a material cause is insufficient and this might be worth exploring further. But Hume is correct that most theists hardly even think about this point. Many assume "the great chain of being" where spirit is "better" than matter, but why this is so must be *proven* rather than *assumed*.

Why cannot the world explain itself? Hume argues that mathematics has precision and design, and yet this does not require any other explanation than that it is the nature of numbers to be so. Is it possible to give a similar explanation of the design in the material world and simply say that it is in the nature of matter to be so? Perhaps the explanation of the universe can be found in the universe itself rather than in looking beyond it. The arguments of Aquinas have already been undermined because we cannot assume that causation applies to the whole universe, or that the universe as a whole is governed. But Hume offers another challenge in asking why not look for the explanation in the universe itself.

Hume also sees that the "theistic" proofs do not actually prove that "God," as understood in theism, exists. Why not some non-theistic cosmogony? Philo wonders if there could be an eternity of motion, or if what appears to be order and design might not be the result of ages of chaos. Are these possible explanations for what we observe? If unbelief is inexcusable, then non-theism must have no rational foundation. However, theists have generally had a very truncated view of non-theism, often equating it with naturalism. Hume shows both that the arguments themselves are unsound and that they do not show that non-theism is false. Interestingly, Hume appears to see the need for clarity if God's existence is to be relevant. He somewhat sarcastically concludes that God must be a matter of faith and not reason.

In addition to his attack on the ontological and cosmological arguments, Hume offers a devastating attack on one of the most popular theistic arguments: The argument from design. The argument from design only proves a designer and not the God of theism. It may not even prove a designer. Philo states:

But can you think, Cleanthes, that your usual phlegm and phi-losophy have been preserved in so wide a step as you have taken when you compared to the universe houses, ships, furniture, ma-chines, and, from their similarity in some circumstances, inferred a similarity in their causes? Thought, design, intelligence, such as we discover in men and other animals, is no more than one of the springs and principles of the universe, as well as heat or cold, attraction or repulsion, and a hundred others which fall under daily observation. It is an active cause by which some particular parts of nature, we find produce alterations on other parts. But can a conclusion, with any propriety, be transferred from parts to the whole? Does not the great disproportion bar all comparison and inference? From observing the growth of a hair, can we learn anything concerning the generation of a man? Would the manner of a leaf's blowing, even though perfectly known, afford us any instruction concerning the vegetation of a tree?[8]

This is an attack on the empiricism behind Aquinas and Locke. We cannot argue from our experience to a universal conclusion. There is no "causation," only succession in time. Furthermore, the opposite of any matter of fact is possible. This is devastating to Aquinas's arguments from motion and causation.

This critique is based on Hume's epistemology of empiricism: All knowledge is through sense data. Aquinas said this same thing. Locke says something very similar although he makes allowance for some knowl-edge of ideas (nevertheless, these ideas come from experience). Hume draws out the implications overlooked by Aquinas and Locke:

All the philosophy, therefore, in the world, and all the religion, which is never but a species of philosophy, will never be able to carry us beyond the usual course of experience, or give us mea-sures of conduct and behavior different from those which are furnished by reflections on common life. No new fact can ever be inferred from the religious hypotheses; no event foreseen or fore-told; no reward or punishment expected or dreaded, beyond what is already known by practice and observation.[9]

Hume is an empiricist but he takes it to its logical conclusion: Skepticism. It is this skepticism that awakens Kant from his dogmatic slumbers to search for a way to attain knowledge.

8. Hume, *Dialogues*, 21. II.
9. Hume, *Enquiries*, 146. Sect XI 113.

5.2. IMMANUEL KANT

Kant sought to avoid the mistakes that arise when people overextend the use of reason, especially in the area of metaphysics. He denied the ability of reason to reach knowledge about anything transcending our experience:

> The outcome of all dialectical attempts of pure reason does not merely confirm what we have already proved in the Transcendental Analytic, namely, that all those conclusions of ours which profess to lead us beyond the field of possible experience are deceptive and without foundation; it likewise teaches us this further lesson, that human reason has a natural tendency to transgress these limits, and that transcendental ideas are just as natural to it as the categories are to understanding—though with this difference, that while the categories lead to truth, that is, to the conformity of our concepts with the object, the ideas produce what, through mere illusion, is none the less irresistible, and the harmful influence of which we can barely succeed in neutralizing even by means of the severest criticism.[10]

Certainly mistakes are prevalent; this is one of the realities that the skeptic points out in order to deny that there is clarity. The question is: Can reason be both guarded from overextension and used to establish the existence of God, and was Kant successful in this?

While Kant sought to provide a basis for knowledge (including knowledge of God) in responding to Hume's skepticism, he is believed by many to have shown that theistic proofs are unsuccessful and impossible. "It is obvious that on Kant's premises no proof of God's existence is possible. But he wishes to make this impossibility clear by showing that every line of proof is fallacious. The task is not so great as one might suppose. For according to Kant there are only three ways of proving God's existence in speculative metaphysics."[11] Kant divides theistic arguments into three kinds (ontological, cosmological, and teleological) and shows each to be unsound.

Kant's response to Hume, and his attempt to explain how knowledge is possible, is to critique reason. Kant argues that pure reason cannot be used to make progress in cosmology because it "soon falls into such contradictions that it is constrained, in this cosmological field, to desist from any such

---

10. Kant, *The Critique*, B 671.
11. Copleston, "*A History of Philosophy: Wolff to Kant*," 295.

pretensions."[12] The first of these contradictions, what Kant calls antinomies, is that the world had a beginning in time and that the world did not have a beginning in time. Kant believed that either position could be successfully defended by reason.[13] Contemporary philosopher of religion Alvin Plantinga does not think that Kant was correct in this conclusion:

> In no case is there anything like a conclusive argument (given the assumption that we are thinking about the *Dinge*) for either the thesis or the antithesis. In some cases, we may not *know* or *be able to tell* which (thesis or antithesis) is true: but that doesn't constitute much of an argument for the conclusion that we can't think about the noumenal. What would be needed for the argument to work would be a really powerful argument for the thesis and an equally powerful argument for the antithesis. In none of these cases do we have something like that.[14]

Kant's judgment that reason cannot know being in itself comes as a conclusion to his consideration of how synthetic *a priori* truths are possible:

> Now the proper problem of pure reason is contained in the question: How are *a priori* synthetic judgments possible? . . . Among philosophers, David Hume came nearest to envisaging this problem, but still was very far from conceiving it with sufficient definiteness and universality. He occupied himself exclusively with the synthetic proposition regarding the connection of an effect with its cause (*principium causalitatis*), and he believed himself to have shown that such an *a priori* proposition is entirely impossible. If we accept his conclusions, then all that we call metaphysics is a mere delusion whereby we fancy ourselves to have rational insight into what, in actual fact, is borrowed solely from experience, and under the influence of custom has taken the illusory semblance of necessity. If he had envisaged our problem in all its universality, he would never have been guilty of this statement, so destructive of all pure philosophy. For he would then have recognized that, according to his own argument, pure mathematics as certainly containing *a priori* synthetic propositions, would also not be possible; and from such an assertion his good sense would have saved him.[15]

---

12. Kant, *The Critique*, B 433.
13. Ibid., B 453.
14. Plantinga, *Warranted*, 27.
15. Kant, *The Critique*, 55. B 19.

Kant is concerned about Hume's challenge because he understands that it would make knowledge about the world impossible—for instance, pure mathematics could not tell us anything about the world. How is this problem solved? By distinguishing between the thing in itself (the noumenal) and the thing as experienced (the phenomena):

> We commonly distinguish in appearances that which is essentially inherent in their intuition and holds for sense in all human beings, from that which belongs to their intuition accidentally only, and is valid not in relation to sensibility in general but only in relation to a particular standpoint or to a peculiarity of structure in this or that sense . . . The rainbow in a sunny shower may be called a mere appearance, and the rain the thing in itself . . . But if we take this empirical object in its general character, and ask, without considering whether or not it is the same for all human sense, whether it represents an object in itself (and by that we cannot mean the drop of rain, for these are already, as appearances, empirical objects), the question as to the relation of the representation to the object at once becomes transcendental. We then realize that not only are the drops of rain mere appearances, but that even their round shape, nay even the space in which they fall, are nothing in themselves, but merely modifications or fundamental forms of our sensible intuition, and that the transcendental object remains unknown to us.[16]

And so how are synthetic *a priori* judgments possible?

> Since the propositions of geometry are synthetic *a priori*, and are known with apodeictic certainty, I raise the question, whence do you obtain such propositions, and upon what does the understanding rely in its endeavour to achieve such absolutely necessary and universally valid truths? There is no other way than through concepts or through intuitions; and these are given either *a priori* or *a posteriori*. In their latter form, namely, as *empirical* concepts, and also as that upon which these are grounded, the *empirical* intuition, neither the concepts nor the intuitions can yield any synthetic proposition except such as is itself also merely empirical (that is, a proposition of experience), and which for that very reason can never possess the necessity and absolute universality which are characteristic of all geometrical propositions . . . You must therefore give yourself an object *a priori* in intuition, and ground upon this your synthetic proposition . . . It is, therefore,

16. Kant, *The Critique*, 84. B 62.

not merely possible or probable, but indubitably certain, that space and time, as the necessary conditions of all outer and inner experience, are merely subjective conditions of all our intuition, and that in relation to these conditions all objects are therefore mere appearances, and not given us as things in themselves which exist in this manner. *For this reason also, while much can be said a priori as regards the form of appearances, nothing whatsoever can be asserted of the thing in itself, which may underlie these appearances.*[17]

The italicized portion above highlights how Kant's critique of reason undermines any possible proof for God's existence. God transcends human experience, and so cannot be known:

I do not at all share the opinion which certain excellent and thoughtful men (such as Sulzer), in face of the weakness of the arguments hitherto employed, have so often been led to express, that we may hope sometime to discover conclusive demonstrations of the two cardinal propositions of our reason—that there is a God, and that there is a future life. On the contrary, I am certain that this will never happen. For whence will reason obtain ground for such synthetic assertions, which do not relate to objects of experience and their inner possibility? But it is also apodeictically certain that there will never be anyone who will be able to assert the *opposite* with the least show [of proof], much less, dogmatically. For since he could prove this only through pure reason, he must undertake to prove that a supreme being, and the thinking subject in us [viewed] as pure intelligence, are *impossible*. But whence will he obtain the modes of knowledge which could justify him in thus judging synthetically in regard to things that lie beyond all possible experience?[18]

Kant is certain that reason is ineffectual as far as knowing God is concerned. Post-Kantian theologians will therefore stress God as experienced, rather than God Himself. But this line of thought leads ultimately to Nietzsche's assertion of the death of God, and Freud's psychoanalytic cure for theistic illusion. If Kant is correct in his critique of reason, then not only is unbelief not inexcusable, belief becomes at best a matter of personal choice, perhaps an infantile illusion, or perhaps rationally inexcusable. This critique of reason's ability to reveal God is the challenge of the modern world for Historic Christianity.

17. Ibid. Emphasis mine.
18. Ibid., 595. B 769.

Kant asserts that there are only three ways of proving the existence of God by speculative reason. The first is the teleological proof, the second is the cosmological proof, and the third is the ontological proof. He believes all other arguments can be reduced to one of these three. He also argues that the first two can be reduced to the last, the ontological, so that if it is unsuccessful then all three are unsuccessful. Kant's attack on the ontological argument is an attack on the power of reason. Just as with Hume, Kant's epistemology will be the driving force of his challenge.

Kant believed that theoretical reason cannot be used to prove that God exists. He says: "I propose to show that reason is as little able to make progress on the one path, the empirical, as on the other path, the transcendental, and that it stretches its wings in vain in thus attempting to soar above the world of sense by the mere power of speculation."[19] Kant, like Hume, accepts that all knowledge is through experience. Unlike Hume, Kant asserts that the mind imposes categories on the world that are not part of the noumenal world. One example is causation. Therefore, the human mind cannot reason its way beyond the categories it imposes to know being in itself. This is the most fundamental aspect of Kant's critique, and his challenge to theistic proofs must be understood in light of his challenge to reason.

Kant believed that the ontological argument is unsuccessful. He thought that it assumes the concept of existence, and is in fact only an analytic assertion:

> There is already a contradiction in introducing the concept of existence—no matter under what title it may be disguised—into the concept of a thing which we profess to be thinking solely in reference to its possibility. If that be allowed as legitimate, a seeming victory has been won; but in actual fact nothing at all is said: the assertion is a mere tautology. We must ask: is the proposition that this or that thing (which, whatever it may be, is allowed as possible) exists, an analytic or a synthetic proposition? If it is analytic, the assertion of the existence of the thing adds nothing to the thought of the thing; but in that case either the thought, which in us, is the thing itself, or we have presupposed an existence as belonging to the realm of the possible, and have then, on that pretext, inferred its existence from its internal possibility—which is nothing but a miserable tautology. . . . but if, on the other hand, we admit as every reasonable person must, that all existential propositions

19. Kant, *The Critique*, 500. B 619.

are synthetic, how can we profess to maintain that the predicate of existence cannot be rejected without contradiction? This is a feature which is found only in analytic propositions and is indeed precisely what constitutes their analytic character.[20]

Kant believed that analytic truths do not tell us anything about being in itself. The ontological argument is, at best, an analytic truth. This is an important feature of Kant's epistemology. Analytic truths only tell us about how the human mind shapes the experiences given to it. They do not tell us anything about the world in itself. If this is the case then the entire project of the ontological argument is unfounded. Kant did believe that there are some synthetic *a priori* truths, such as $7 + 5 = 12$. But the concept of existence is not one of these. The ontological argument is based on arguing from an idea to existence *a priori*, and if this is not possible, and the other two forms of theistic proofs are based on the ontological argument, then theistic proofs are not possible. However, if theistic proofs are not possible, then the claim that unbelief is inexcusable and needs forgiveness is groundless. It should not be surprising that liberal theologians after Kant, accepting a Kantian framework, abandoned exclusivist approaches and became inclusivists or pluralists.

Kant argued that the teleological proof is based on the cosmological proof. This is because the teleological argument attempts to move from our perception of design to the cause of that design. He then argues that the cosmological argument is based on the ontological argument. This is because in the cosmological argument we argue from the idea of cause or motion to the existence of that which causes. But remember that causation does not apply to the noumenal realm, to being in itself. Therefore, this argument does not tell us anything about being; it only describes the categories we impose on being. If these arguments ultimately rest on the ontological argument, which makes the claim that we can know about existence *a priori*, then they are unsound. Since these are the only forms of theistic arguments, it is not possible to prove that God exists.

Kant's solution to the problem of the synthetic *a priori* is to distinguish between the noumenal world (being itself) and the phenomenal world (being as experienced by humans). Knowledge is only of the phenomenal world. Categories such as causation apply to the phenomenal world, but not to the noumenal world. "From all this it undeniably follows

20. Kant, *The Critique*, 503. B 625.

that the pure concepts of understanding can *never* admit of *transcendental* but *always* only of *empirical* employment, and that the principles of pure understanding can apply only to objects of senses under the universal conditions of a possible experience, never to things in general with regard to the mode in which we are able to intuit them."[21] There is a kind of causation that applies in the noumenal realm, and Kant discusses this when he speaks about the relationship between natural necessity and freedom.[22] The problem with Kant's discussion of causation in the noumenal realm is that it violates his claim that *nothing* can be said about the noumenal realm![23] Kant's solution about belief in God as a function of practical rationality does not overcome the problem of skepticism, as many post-Kantians see. If causation does not apply to the noumenal world, then the noumenal world cannot be said to be the cause of the phenomenal world. Further, Kant believed that free will is incompatible with causation. Freedom and necessity must be located in separate realms which do not interfere with each other because freedom and necessity are conflicting ideas (Kant rejected compatibilism).[24] He locates free will in the noumenal world which is not affected by causation:

> Reason is present in all the actions of men at all times and under all circumstances, and is always the same; but it is not itself in time, and does not fall into any new state in which it was not before. In respect to new states, it is *determining*, not *determinable*. We may not, therefore, ask why reason has not determined *itself* differently, but only why it has not through its causality determined the *appearances* differently. But to this question no answer is possible. For a different intelligible character would have given a different empirical character. When we say that in spite of his whole previous course of life the agent could have refrained from lying, this only means that the act is under the immediate power of reason, and that reason in its causality is not subject to any conditions of appearance or time.[25]

However, if free will is not affected by causation, then in what sense do my decisions cause my actions? In what sense can I cause a change

---

21. Kant, *The Critique*, 264. B 603.
22. Ibid., 478. B 584.
23. Ibid., 85. B 64.
24. Ibid., 478. B 585.
25. Ibid., 478. B 584.

in my behavior? Kant asserts that "In respect of the intelligible character, of which the empirical character is the sensible schema, there can be
no *before* and *after*; every action, irrespective of its relation in time to
other appearances, is the immediate effect of the intelligible character
of pure reason."[26] Freedom is the power to originate a series of events.[27]
However, why one series of events is originated and not another cannot
be answered.[28] These were problems that had to be addressed and often
resulted in skepticism. Perhaps the problem is not in the theistic arguments but in Kant's epistemology and the division between the noumenal
and phenomenal realms.

Kant did think that belief in God was important and necessary. Kant
postulated God's existence as necessary for morality. "By reason we cannot
either prove or disprove God's existence. The criticism of natural theology
thus leaves the way open for practical or moral faith."[29] Kant thinks that
God is necessary for practical morality. However, this approach to God
will be severely challenged when the morality that Kant wishes to justify
is called into question and rejected by post-Kantians (Nietzsche). The God
of theism may be necessary for theistic moral systems, but what if those
systems are rejected in favor of another moral or religious system, or ni-
hilism? If Kant's theistic morality is rejected then God is unnecessary.

Kant also spoke highly of the design argument:

> This proof always deserves to be mentioned with respect. It is the
> oldest, the clearest, and the most accordant with the common reason
> of mankind. It enlivens the study of nature, just as it itself derives its
> existence and gains ever new vigour from that source . . . It would
> therefore not only be uncomforting but utterly vain to attempt to
> diminish in any way the authority of this argument. Reason, con-
> stantly upheld by this ever-increasing evidence, which, though
> empirical, is yet so powerful, cannot be so depressed through
> doubts suggested by subtle and abstruse speculation, that it is not
> at once aroused from the indecision of all melancholy reflection,
> as from a dream, by one glance at the wonders of nature and the
> majesty of the universe—ascending from height to height up to

26. Kant, *The Critique*, 476. B 581.

27. Ibid., 476. B 581.

28. Ibid., 478. B 584.

29. Copleston, *A History of Philosophy: Wolff to Kant*, 301.

the all-highest, from the conditioned to its conditions, up to the supreme and unconditioned Author.[30]

For Kant this proof is persuasive. He says that more should not be expected, and that this proof should cause skeptics to be more humble in their objections:

> But although we have nothing to bring against the rationality and utility of this procedure, but have rather to commend and to further it, we still cannot approve the claims, which this mode of argument would fain advance, to apodeictic certainty and to an assent founded on no special favour or support from other quarters. It cannot hurt the good cause, if the dogmatic language of the overweening sophist be toned down to the more moderate and humble requirements of a belief adequate to quieten our doubts, though not to command unconditional submission. I therefore maintain that the physico-theological proof can never by itself establish the existence of a supreme being, but must always fall back upon the ontological argument to make good its deficiency. It only serves as an introduction to the ontological argument; and the latter therefore contains (in so far as a speculative proof is possible at all) *the one possible ground for proof* with which human reason can never dispense.[31]

Clearly Kant admires the design argument and believes it can silence, or at least humble, skeptics (he notes that proof for God's existence relies on the ontological proof, a proof that moves from thought to being). However, there are four problems with his use of the design argument with respect to our current discussion. Kant himself notes the first one, which is that this argument rests on the cosmological argument, which in turn rests on the ontological argument, which he has said cannot prove that God exists.[32] He praises the design argument, but also severely criticizes it. "Physico-theology is therefore unable to give any determinate concept of the supreme cause of the world, and cannot therefore serve as the foundation of a theology which is itself in turn to form the basis of religion."[33] In fact, he concludes: "To advance to absolute totality by the empirical

30. Kant, *The Critique*, 520. B 651.

31. Ibid., 520. B 652.

32. Ibid., 524. B 658.

33. Ibid., 523. B 656.

road is utterly impossible. None the less this is what is attempted in the physico-theological proof."[34]

While the teleological argument may not provide certainty that God exists, Kant thinks it can give personal conviction, which leads to the second problem in his use of this argument. Kant does not distinguish between being personally certain of something, and there being objective clarity on which to base inexcusability. That Kant finds the design argument so compelling tells us more about Kant than about reality. Others, when looking at the world, see disorder, pain, and misery, and conclude that there can be no God. Or they see indicators of the truth of various other religions or worldviews, such as Buddhism, Hinduism, or Platonism. The skeptic will not disagree that Kant finds the argument compelling, but will ask why he (the skeptic) should find the argument compelling.

Since Kant's time (and especially in the last decade) much interesting work has been done on "irreducible complexity" which is said to indicate design and therefore support the design argument. However, at best the design argument gives proof of a designer, as found in Platonism, and not a Creator (*ex nihilo*) as found in theism. Consequently, even if it can be shown that there is design in the world, this does not necessarily help in establishing theism.

This consideration leads to the third problem with Kant's use of the design argument, which is that it does not address the objections to this argument raised by Hume. This has already been covered so we need only mention that Hume argued against the analogical reasoning used in the design argument, pointed out the problems in its anthropomorphism, and suggested that the world exhibits such poor design that if it is the work of a designer, that one must be like an incompetent child or senile old man:

> This world, for aught he knows, is very faulty and imperfect, compared to a superior standard, and was only the first rude essay of some infant deity who afterwards abandoned it, ashamed of his lame performance; it is the work only of some dependent, inferior deity, and is the object of derision to his superiors; it is the production of old age and dotage in some superannuated deity, and ever since his death has run on at adventures, from the first impulse and active force which it received from him.[35]

34. Kant, *The Critique* 523. B 656..
35. Hume, *Dialogues*, 41.V.

Hume seems to foreshadow Kant in the person of Demea when this character says: "Good God!" cried Demea, interrupting him, where are we? Zealous defenders of religion allow that the proofs of a Deity fall short of perfect evidence!"[36] But can the design argument give proof for theism at all, or does it at best lead to a designer not unlike that found in many non-theistic religions? And if it can be used to support both theism and non-theism, does it provide a ground for the claim "it is clear that God exists so that unbelief is without excuse"?

The fourth problem with Kant's use of the teleological argument is that since Kant's time new defeaters have been raised against the design argument that require a response, so that a reliance on it as presented by Kant would be insufficient to answer the questions of non-theists. Perhaps the most important challenge is that raised by Darwinism. According to Darwinism, design is the product of time and chance, not the product of a designer. While Darwin himself may have kept God in the picture to provide the first form of life, contemporary Darwinists like Richard Dawkins reject the need even for an original designer and instead offer a mechanism that can produce what they call the "appearance of design."[37] Those qualities in the world that inspired Kant to believe in a designer are, according to this view, only the *appearance of design* and can be accounted for through purely material causes.

5.3. CONCLUSION: THE NECESSITY TO ESTABLISH THE ONTOLOGICAL ARGUMENT

The most important aspect of Kant's approach to the arguments for God's existence is that he sees that if God's existence is to be established it must ultimately be done through a form of the ontological argument. This means that if such an argument is impossible, then it is also impossible to prove that God exists, which means that unbelief cannot be said to be inexcusable. People may continue to believe in God for various reasons, but the claim that the failure to believe in God is without excuse, a claim made by the Apostle Paul, can no longer be maintained. And yet there is hope in that if Kant was wrong about the ontological argument, then it might still be possible to prove that God exists with certainty. Kant sought to protect against the many errors committed in metaphysics by a misuse of reason,

36. Hume, *Dialogues*, 19. II.
37. See Richard Dawkins *The Blind Watchmaker*.

but in so doing limited reason so as to exclude any possibility of an ontological argument. In Chapters 8–10 we will consider steps necessary to establish the clarity of God's existence. Part of doing this will be to argue that the problem with the ontological argument is not as Kant diagnosed. The problem is not in applying reason to being as well as to thought; the problem is in the overextension from "highest being" to "God" without explaining why alternatives (what Graham Oppy calls "parallel cases") are rejected. In Chapter 9 we will consider why Kant's appearance/reality, or phenomena/noumena distinction is not applicable to proof at the basic level, and in doing this we will be giving a response to his critique of pure reason and defending the possibility of theistic proofs.

6

Victory Over Theism?

What was the historic outcome of these challenges to knowing God? If God cannot be known, what is the alternative for believers? Does this give occasion for some persons to become unbelievers? This chapter explores the historical development of thinking about God after the challenges of Hume and Kant. How should Christians think about this development, and what should their response be to the challenges that developed?

THE NINETEENTH AND TWENTIETH century thinking about God's existence was shaped by Kant's skepticism about the noumenal realm. "The works of Kant, Schleiermacher, and Hegel alone determined the course of theology for at least the next century and a half."[1] Because many thinkers have uncritically accepted Kant's framework they have also assumed that theistic proofs are impossible. The following will trace some of that influence, and then the next section will examine theistic responses to Hume and Kant.

Natural theology was thought to be a dead end. Something had to be put in its place. "Philosophy of religion came on the scene as an alternative to the discredited metaphysics of natural theology."[2] Two options were thought to remain: One was to seek a new metaphysical ground for the knowledge of God, as we will see that Hegel attempted; the second was to see that no such foundation was possible and that religion is a merely human expression best understood by studying humans.[3] Both options are premised on

1. Livingston, *Modern,* Vol. I, 143.
2. Hodgson, *Hegel,* 13.
3. Ibid., 13.

the assumption that theism is not rationally justifiable and that another view must be sought. Consequently, those who adopt one or another of these options will also be seen to significantly modify Christianity—often into a form of pantheism, if not abandoning it altogether.

6.1. FRIEDRICH SCHLEIERMACHER

Friedrich Schleiermacher (1768–1834) adopted the Kantian epistemology and has had a significant effect on modern theology and religious studies. "He carried out a 'Copernican revolution' in theology as consequential as Kant's revolution in philosophy."[4] He addressed his most influential work to the "cultured despisers of religion," perhaps thinking of David Hume. Because knowledge of being in itself is not possible, the focus of theology must be *experience*. God cannot be known, so what is important is the phenomenological aspect of God. God as experienced. God as "other." This makes experience the focus and raises questions about whether God need even be discussed. "For Schleiermacher, feelings are the unique element of the religious life; religion is essentially *feeling*."[5] Later theologians will continue the emphasis on feelings and experience, and jettison talk about God as secondary or even unnecessary. Schleiermacher represents a move away from the claim that unbelief is inexcusable toward the claim that belief and unbelief are irrelevant because what matters are feelings. He denied that religion has to do with the kind of knowledge of God that philosophers try to achieve. "Though you pass from the laws to the Universal Lawgiver, in whom is the unity of all things; though you allege that nature cannot be comprehended without God, I would still maintain that religion has nothing to do with this knowledge."[6] Instead, religion is as follows:

> The contemplation of the pious is the immediate consciousness of the universal existence of all finite things, in and through the Infinite, and of all temporal things in and through the Eternal. Religion is to seek this and find it in all that lives and moves, in all growth and change, in all doing and suffering. It is to have life and

---

4. Livingston, *Modern*, Vol. I, 96.

5. Ibid., 99.

6. Schleiermacher, *On Religion*, 35. Speech II.

to know life *in immediate feeling*, only as such an existence in the Infinite and Eternal. Where this is found religion is satisfied.[7]

6.2. G. W. F. HEGEL

Georg Wilhelm Friedrich Hegel (1770–1831) "was the greatest of the German Idealists and one of the most fertile minds in the history of Western thought."[8] He came of age as the Enlightenment was ending and Romanticism was becoming established. What is relevant for our purposes here is his concern with giving a defense for Christianity, and the form this defense took. "Hegel was consumed by the problem of the reconciliation of religion and culture from the very earliest period of his career, and his philosophic reinterpretation of Christianity had a very wide appeal in the universities and seminaries in the latter half of the nineteenth century, not only in Germany but in England and the United States as well."[9] While he speaks as if he wants to defend Christianity, in actuality he abandons Historic Christianity in favor of something which uses some Christian terminology but is pantheistic, idealistic, and dialectic. He divides world history into four parts:

> Thus, the first stage we shall consider in the spirit's development can be compared with the spirit of childhood ... The second phase of the spirit is that of separation, in which the spirit is reflected within itself and in which it emerges from a position of mere obedience and trust . . . The second part of this phase is that of the spirit's manhood, in which the individual has his own ends for himself, but can only attain them in the service of a universal, of the state ... Then fourthly, there follows the Germanic age, the *Christian World*. If it were possible to compare the spirit's development to that of the individual in this case too, this age would have to be called the old age of the spirit ... In the Christian age, the divine spirit has come into the world and taken up its abode in the individual, who is now completely free and endowed with substantial freedom.[10]

---

7. Ibid., 36. Speech II. Emphasis mine.

8. Livingston, *Modern*, Vol. I, 144.

9. Ibid., 143.

10. Hegel, *Lectures*, 130. C.a. Emphasis mine.

He then explains how world history is a progress toward self-consciousness of the spirit through a dialectical process:

> World history, as already pointed out, represents the development of the spirit's consciousness of its own freedom and of the consequent realisation of this freedom. This development is by nature a *gradual progression*, a series of successive determinations of freedom which proceed from the concept of the material in question, i.e. the nature of freedom in its development towards self-consciousness. The logical—and even more so the dialectical—nature of the concept in general, i.e. the fact that it determines itself, assumes successive determinations which it progressively overcomes, thereby attaining a positive, richer, and more concrete determination . . . Each historical principle, in its concrete form, expresses every aspect of the nation's consciousness and will, and indeed of its entire reality; it is the common denominator of its religion, its political constitution, its ethical life, its system of justice, its customs, its learning, art, and technical skill, and the whole direction of its industry. These special peculiarities should be interpreted in the light of the general peculiarity, the particular principle of the nation in question, just as this general peculiarity can be detected in the factual details with which history presents us.[11]

He sets an example for the next century which is followed by many. While keeping Christian terminology the actual content of the beliefs could not be further from Historic Christianity. Consequently, we will not examine many such thinkers since our purpose here is to see how those holding to Christian theism have responded to the challenges of Hume and Kant.

What Hegel set out to do was "recover the conceptual foundations of religion by creating a postcritical speculative theology of his own."[12] Hegel implicitly, if not explicitly, admits that Historic Christianity and even theism are beyond rational defense. Hegel rejected theism and with it Historic Christianity and its message of redemption. "God could not be the extraworldly, omnipotent superperson of classical theism, or the abstract supreme being of the Enlightenment."[13] Hegel is consistent. He does not try to salvage Christianity and redemption while abandoning God. He sees that the whole message is connected, and gives an entirely new account although using the old terminology. Many theologians of

11. Hegel, *Lectures*, 138. C.c. Emphasis mine.
12. Hodgson, *Hegel*, 13.
13. Ibid., 14.

the nineteenth and twentieth centuries follow him in this attempt at re-construction. Others do not even see the challenge and the problem and continue on defending theism as if Hume and Kant had never existed. A third option would be to show that it is clear that God exists so that unbelief is inexcusable. Doing so would require responding to Hume and Kant by showing that reason can be used to know God.

Hegel rejected the focus on feelings found in Schleiermacher. He is noted to have said that if religion is essentially a feeling of dependence, then the dog is the best Christian.[14] Rather, he saw Christianity as the best religion because it could be re-interpreted to fit his dialectic system:

> Historical Christianity had grasped the truth in representational form, but philosophy grasps this same truth in its rational neces-sity. Nevertheless, truth is now not something abstract and ahis-torical for Hegel. 'The universal must pass into actuality through the particular' and only then can it be seen in its rational necessity. The truth of Christianity, therefore, is not to be reduced to certain abstract principles but seen in the historical actualization of the unity of the divine and human and the coming into being of the Absolute Spirit.[15]

But note that Hegel has abandoned Historic Christianity in favor of ideal-ism. In a way this is an acceptance of the inability to know God after Kant's challenge. Rather than attempt to justify theism Hegel gives a completely new interpretation of Christian belief. But can theism be salvaged?

6.3. LUDWIG FEUERBACH

Ludwig Feuerbach (1804–1872) rejected the need for God and instead said God is a human projection.

> The object of the senses is out of man, the religious object is within him, and therefore as little forsakes him as his self-consciousness or his conscience; it is the intimate, the closest object . . . the ob-ject of religion is a selected object; the most excellent, the first, the supreme being; it essentially presupposes a critical judgment, a discrimination between the divine and the non-divine, between that which is worthy of adoration and that which is not worthy. And here may be applied, without any limitation, the proposition: the object of any subject is nothing else than the subject's own

14. Livingston, *Modern*, 145.
15. Ibid., 150.

nature taken objectively. Such as are a man's thought and dispositions, such is his God; so much worth as a man has, so much and no more has his God. Consciousness of God is self-consciousness, knowledge of God is self-knowledge. By his God thou knowest the man, and by the man his God; the two are identical. Whatever is God to a man, that is his heart and soul; and conversely, God is the manifested inward nature, the expressed self of a man—religion the solemn unveiling of a man's hidden treasures, the revelation of his intimate thoughts, the open confession of his love-secrets.[16]

Feuerbach takes God out of the noumenal realm, and places him in the phenomenal realm as an invention of the human mind. If belief in God is an invention of the human mind then unbelief is not inexcusable, but is rather enlightened. This approach anticipates both Nietzsche and Freud.

6.4. ALBRECHT RITSCHL

Albrecht Ritschl (1822–1889) accepted Kant's epistemology. Since knowledge of the noumenal world is not possible, the focus must be on the phenomenal world, the world of experience. "Ritschl agreed with Schleiermacher that religion is a matter of experience and that Christian theology is a matter of Christian experience. Where the two giants of Protestant liberal theology differed was on the nature of religious experience."[17] Ritschl argued that what is important is not God and the noumenal realm but the effects of belief in God in this life. "The Ritschlian school rejected the romanticism of Schleiermacher and the idealism of Hegel by aligning itself with the philosophical and theological precepts of neo-Kantianism. Ritschlianism could be described as antimetaphysical, antimystical, and historical-empirical in character. Following Kant, the Ritschlian theologians insisted that what can be known is not the 'thing-in-itself,' but only its effect or felt value for the individual."[18] This easily leads to inclusivism and pluralism. If unbelief (non-Christian worldviews) can have a positive effect on human life, then it is justified as not inexcusable. The important question will be "what is a positive effect?" It would be worthwhile to explore this approach further as it is found in "historic criticism" and the search for the historic Jesus. These can be understood as

16. Feuerbach, *The Essence of Christianity*, 12. I.2.

17. Livingston, *Modern*, 247.

18. Demarest, *General Revelation*, 98.

responses to the inability to know God and the lack of need for redemption from unbelief.

6.5. FRIEDRICH NIETZSCHE

Frederich Nietzsche (1844–1900) is well known for his claim that God is dead. This statement can be viewed as the claim that belief in God is no longer relevant to society. Nietzsche's position is a move beyond Ritschl because it claims that the effects of belief in God are negative. Nietzsche saw faith and belief in God as a weakness, and theology as an attempt to rationalize one's beliefs. Reason is viewed by Nietzsche as a tool to be used to gain power rather than as a means for knowing God:

> Plato, more innocent in such matters and lacking the craftiness of the plebeian, wanted to employ all his strength—the greatest strength any philosopher so far has had at his disposal—to prove to himself that reason and instinct of themselves tend toward one goal, the good, 'God.' And since Plato, all theologians and philosophers are on the same track—that is, in moral matters it has so far been instinct, or what the Christians call 'faith,' or 'the herd,' as I put it, that has triumphed. Perhaps Descartes should be excepted, as the father of rationalism (and hence grandfather of the Revolution) who conceded authority to reason alone: but reason is merely an instrument, and Descartes was superficial.[19]

Unbelief is not only not inexcusable, it is valuable and enlightened. One reason that God is no longer relevant or necessary is that Nietzsche rejects the morality that Kant needed God to support and in so doing rejects God. He calls this a slave morality. Without this morality there is no need for God. In fact, even with this kind of morality, God only serves the purpose of propping up a slave morality that harms humanity. Belief is therefore harmful. Belief, not unbelief, is inexcusable.

6.6. SIGMUND FREUD

Entering the twentieth century, Sigmund Freud (1856–1934) views belief in God as immature, and likens it to childhood illusions, thus implying its falsehood. The child relies on his father. But he soon discovers that his father is limited and weak, unable to help him through the hardships of life. He therefore abstracts a "heavenly father," not unlike the process

19. Nietzsche, *Beyond*, 104. Part V, 191.

described by Feuerbach. This heavenly father serves as a security blanket and helps the child get through life. However, a person who believes in God is believing an illusion. This illusion is used to comfort, but ultimately illusions are false. A person who must rely on illusions throughout adulthood is immature. Freud believed that humanity was emerging from an immature stage where belief in God was the norm to an age of maturity where humanity could face the hardships of life without the need to refer to God, and yet the masses of common people were still held in the grips of illusion:

> In my *Future of an Illusion* I was concerned much less with the deepest sources of religious feeling than with what the ordinary man understands by his religion—with the system of doctrines and promises which on the one hand explains to him the riddle of this world with enviable completeness, and, on the other, assures him that a careful Providence will watch over his life and will compensate him in a future existence for any frustrations he suffers here. The common man cannot imagine this Providence than in the figure of an enormously exalted father. Only such a being can understand the needs of the children of men and be softened by their prayers and placated by the signs of their remorse. The whole thing is so patently infantile, so foreign to reality, that to anyone with a friendly attitude to humanity it is painful to think that the great majority of mortals will never be able to rise above this view of life. It is still more humiliating to discover how large a number of people living to-day, who cannot but see that this religion is not tenable, nevertheless try to defend it piece by piece in a series of pitiful rearguard actions. One would like to mix among the ranks of the believers in order to meet these philosophers, who think they can rescue the God of religion by replacing him by an impersonal, shadowy and abstract principle, and to address them with the warning word: 'Thou shalt not take the name of the Lord thy God in vain!' And if some of the great men of the past acted in the same way, no appeal can be made to their example: we know why they were obliged to.[20]

Freud gives an argument to show that God does not exist: the objects of immature beliefs do not exist. God is the object of immature belief, therefore God does not exist.

---

20. Freud, *Civilization*, 22. II.

6.7. CONCLUSION: AFTER KANT

As we look at responses offered to the Kantian challenge it is important to note how pervasive the acceptance of Kantianism had become. Those wishing to hold an exclusivist position and assert the inexcusability of unbelief became a minority in the intellectual circles. "In the quarter century before World War I, a host of young American theologians went to Germany to complete their theological studies. There they sat at the feet of many of the leaders of the Ritschlian school, men such as Herrmann, Harnack, and Kaftan."[21] While the liberal theologians did not become explicitly Ritschlian, the Kantian emphasis on experience and de-emphasis on the doctrine of God was obvious. It is not possible to tell a person that their experiences are invalid or unimportant. Thus, with the emphasis on experience came the acceptance of all religious experience and the de-emphasis on inexcusability of unbelief.

This is a necessary conclusion of a process started by Kant. The noumenal realm is unknowable by reason. God is part of the noumenal realm. Therefore God is unknowable by reason. Some other way must be sought to justify belief in God. Whether it is morality, or the sense of the other, or the sense of the holy, or religious experience, or the benefits of religion, all of these share in common the underlying assumption that it is not clear that God exists. Consequently, inexcusability for unbelief is no longer justified. It is not surprising that during this time the view of redemption is changed. Redemption is no longer the necessary payment of God's only son to achieve forgiveness for sin (including the sin of unbelief), but becomes a metaphoric act of love on the part of an enlightened person. It is also not surprising that during this time religion becomes viewed as a matter of the emotions or feelings. Some, like Schleiermacher, find this beneficial. Others, like Marx, find it to be a hindrance. Once religion is relegated to the realm of emotions it is no longer a matter of true and false. As such, the need for redemption can no longer be based on the idea of inexcusability.

We therefore enter a time in history where the idea of the clarity of God's existence has been undermined in a way that it never had before. Religion is viewed as subjective and based on feelings. Belief in God is a matter of personal taste. Matters of truth, like the reality of gravity, are not personal tastes but are public matters. Belief in God, by implication,

---

21. Livingston, *Modern,* 262.

is not a matter of truth. Not surprisingly, many Christians altered their view of sin, inexcusability, and redemption to accommodate the assumptions of the age. The question still remains as to whether the redemptive claims of Historic Christianity can be justified by showing that unbelief is inexcusable. Later, a response to the Hume/Kant critique of reason will be given by arguing that at the basic level there is clarity, and skeptical problems about appearance and reality do not apply. However, many forms of Christianity in the contemporary age have abandoned the historic views and conceded to the critique of reason in an attempt to accommodate popular intellectual trends.

This section ends with a very bleak view of the possibility of theistic proofs. The next looks at Christian responses to these challenges. The focus will be on the failure of these responses to see the problem. They collectively fail to see the need for clarity as the ground for inexcusability and redemption. As such, the twentieth century concludes in a deeper state of skepticism than when it began.

7

Theistic Responses
to the Challenge of Hume and Kant

Undoubtedly, Christians have been aware of the mounting challenges to knowing God and the use of reason. How have they responded? Indeed, it is sometimes claimed that there is currently a renaissance in Christian philosophy, with centers in both Protestant and Catholic universities, as well as influence at secular schools. If there is such a renewed energy, is it based on seeing the need to respond to these challenges, and is the response addressing the basic problem? In this chapter we will consider some of the most popular Christian philosophers and movements, and how these attempt to defend belief in God. Are Christian philosophers addressing the need to show that the existence of God is clear so that there is no excuse, or do their responses provide fodder for further excuses?

CHRISTIAN BELIEF PRESUPPOSES THE existence of God. It also claims that the failure to believe in God is inexcusable. These claims have been undermined by Hume, Kant, and the post-Kantian thinkers. Many have abandoned Historic Christian belief for some other form of worldview. Most often these views have seen Christ as a wise person who, through example, showed the rest of humanity how to love. This is no longer redemption. Bertrand Russell challenged even this watered down version of Christianity by arguing that Christ is not a very good moral example: "I cannot myself feel that either in the matter of wisdom or in the matter of virtue Christ stands quite as high as some other people known to history. I think I should put Buddha and Socrates above Him in those respects."[1] Without its claims about sin and redemption, it is unclear

1. Russell, *Why I Am Not A Christian*, 19.

whether Christianity can survive as a worldview. These claims *require* clarity and inexcusability.

Consequently, it is necessary for Christians, especially those holding to the Historic form of Christianity, to respond to the challenges of Hume and Kant. It is necessary in order to support the inexcusability of unbelief, and explain the clarity of God's existence. This section will examine seven prominent and common responses. The common thread through each will be the failure to see the need for clarity and the consequent ineffectual nature of the responses. None of them establish that ignorance of God is culpable. By the end of the twentieth century fideism is still the most common response, and religion is still viewed as the realm of feelings and not of truth.

It is one thing to be challenged and shown to be falling short. Such a challenge can be a source of growth. It is another to go through the challenge and not adequately understand it. This seems to be the nature of the responses offered to date. However, this need not lead to the conclusion that Historic Christianity is beyond hope. Historic Christianity has always developed in light of challenges. In the past the development often resulted in a creed addressing the challenges of the day with successful responses. What is important is identifying the exact challenge so that the response can be as helpful as possible. If the last round of responses is to be found in the Reformation, in confessions like the Westminster Confession of Faith, then it is not surprising that Historic Christianity is due for another set of responses. This section will conclude by considering what is necessary for such responses to be effectual.

7.1. FINE-TUNING THEISTIC ARGUMENTS

In order to consider some standard arguments it will be helpful to look at two contemporary thinkers who have attempted to reformulate the traditional arguments in light of challenges from philosophers like Hume and Kant. Alvin Plantinga and William Lane Craig have done such work (as have many others). There is a great amount of work done on specific arguments, but the contention here will be that these arguments *in kind* do not get around the challenge given by Hume and Kant. What a successful argument must do is show that reason can be used to know the existence *and* nature of God. To argue for a highest being, first cause, or designer is significantly less than the view of God in theism and Historic Christianity.

Furthermore, the Hume/Kant challenge is aimed at the ability of reason to arrive at even these conclusions, conclusions which go beyond the limits of reason. A successful response *must* address this challenge to reason.

An example of how Plantinga fine-tunes the ontological argument is as follows. After giving his restatement of the ontological argument (too long to reproduce here), Plantinga concludes about the reformulated versions of Anselm's argument that: "They cannot, perhaps, be said to *prove* or *establish* their conclusion. But since it is rational to accept their central premises, they do show that it is rational to *accept* that conclusion. And perhaps that is all that can be expected of any such argument."[2] What is important for our purposes here is not the argument itself, but Plantinga's view of what it can be used to do. It is rational to hold to the conclusion in the sense that the alternative view does not have a conclusive argument to prove that God does not exist. Both positions are based on their adherents' intuitions about one of the premises (#36) concerning whether or not maximal greatness is possible.[3] For those who think it is, then the argument is sound. For those who think it is not, then the argument is not sound. Surely there is much interesting work to be done in thinking about this.

However, Plantinga's concession that the argument does not *prove* or *establish* the conclusion, and that a person can be rational while holding that premise 36 is false, means that the argument cannot support the claim that unbelief is inexcusable. Why should I believe? Because I find the premise intuitively plausible. But what if my intuitions are wrong? They have been at other times. If the best that the ontological argument can do is to lead to the conclusion that one is rational to believe in God based on this argument, but one can also be rational to reject this argument, then we are still left in the arena of skepticism or uncertainty. And if Kant is correct that all theistic arguments are based on the ontological argument, and Plantinga is correct that this argument cannot *prove* that God exists, then unbelief is not inexcusable. What those who hold to Historic Christianity must do is show that Kant is incorrect in his assessment of reason's capability to know about God, and Plantinga is incorrect in concluding that the ontological argument cannot *prove* that God exists (in the sense of demonstrating the impossibility of the opposite). In order

---

2. Plantinga, *The Nature*, 221.

3. "(36) Maximal greatness is possibly exemplified." Ibid., 214.

to do the latter it will be necessary to critically examine Plantinga's reliance on intuition.

Most theists have simply tried to rework the theistic arguments that have been critiqued by Hume and Kant. An example of how William Lane Craig fine-tunes the teleological and cosmological arguments is as follows: In his published debate with Walter Sinnott-Armstrong, Craig gives five reasons to believe that God exists. He says: "I'm going to present five reasons why I think theism (the view that God exists) is more plausibly true than atheism (the view that He does not)."[4] To say that it is plausible that God exists does not provide a basis for inexcusability. Either such claims about plausibility simply mean "I prefer it," and are therefore matters of taste which cannot be settled, or they are terms that refer to probability and make no sense. Probable in respect to what? The believer's preferences? Then the probability is 1. The non-believer's preferences? Then the probability is 0. What is commonly held in our society today? Common agreement is no guarantee of truth and cannot establish probability with respect to truth. Without having considered his actual arguments we can already conclude that Craig is not providing grounds for inexcusability, and as an Evangelical Christian who holds to Historic Christianity this will be a problem for him. What will be done below is to consider each of the five reasons that Craig gives in support of theism. It will become evident that Craig does not respond to the central challenge (that reason is inadequate to settle such matters) and therefore it can be concluded that even after fine-tuning the cosmological and teleological arguments, the inexcusability of God's existence has not been established.

The first reason Craig offers is that God makes sense of the origin of the universe.[5] He states this argument as follows: "1. Whatever begins to exist has a cause. 2. The universe began to exist. 3. Therefore, the universe has a cause."[6] He gives as support of this that there cannot be an actually infinite regress of events in time, and that recent work on the Big Bang shows that the universe had a beginning. Notice that both of these miss the objection. Hume called into question the very idea of causation and the ability of reason to make the analogy of causation as we experience it to a cause of the universe itself.

---

4. Craig and Sinnott-Armstrong, *God?* 3.
5. Ibid.
6. Ibid., 5.

The second reason he gives is that God makes sense of the fine-tuning of the universe for intelligent life. Much of this rests on discoveries made in the last 30 years and so Hume did not have access to this information. Craig states it in the following manner: "1. The fine-tuning of the universe is due to either law, chance, or design. 2. It is not due to law or chance. 3. Therefore, it is due to design."[7] However, this is a kind of design argument. How can we know that the fine-tuning thus far observed applies to all of the universe? Or why not conclude that this fine-tuning is part of the nature of the universe itself rather than positing that it is the result of another being? Most importantly, why believe that reason can settle such questions at all? If reason cannot go beyond our experience of the world, which is very limited, then it cannot arrive at universal conclusions about God.

The third reason that Craig gives is that God makes sense of the objective moral values in the world. He states it in the following manner: "1. If God does not exist, objective moral values do not exist. 2. Objective moral values do exist. 3. Therefore, God exists."[8] The problem here is that both (1) and (2) are contentious. Must the theistic view of God exist for there to be objective moral values? Have not other worldviews provided moral systems based on their view of what is eternal? Essentially, Craig's claim becomes "theistic morality cannot be justified without theism," which is true but uncontroversial (what is controversial is whether any morality can be justified without theism). And why believe there are objective moral values? Why not, with Nietzsche, reject objective morality?

The fourth reason that Craig gives is that God makes sense of the life, death, and resurrection of Jesus. He bases this on four facts: Jesus was buried in the tomb of Joseph of Arimathea; on the Sunday after his crucifixion the tomb was found empty; Jesus was seen alive after this by multiple individuals and groups; the original disciples had the sincere belief that he had risen from the dead.[9] Even granting that Jesus did rise from the dead, which the materialist will most likely not grant, there are still two problems with this line of argument: knowledge of Jesus is not available to most people throughout history, and other worldviews can grant that Jesus did rise from the dead and give this event their own in-

7. Craig, *God?* 15.
8. Ibid., 19.
9. Ibid., 22.

terpretation. The pragmatist may agree that Jesus rose from the dead and ask what that has to do with the practicalities of life 2000 years later; the Hindu may agree that Jesus rose from the dead and is an incarnation of Krishna; or Jesus may be said to be an enlightened one (a Buddha), etc. That Jesus rose from the dead does not form a basis for the inexcusability of unbelief, but is instead part of redemptive revelation, which *assumes* that there is a clear general revelation of God's existence.

The final reason that Craig gives is that God can be immediately known and experienced. He says that belief in God is a properly basic belief, such as belief in the material world or other minds.[10] Here is an appeal to inner experience which has already been considered. Craig believes his religious experience to be genuine and all others which lead to different religious convictions to be erroneous. This is asserting what must be proven, and does not provide a basis for inexcusability.

What is helpful about this consideration of Craig is both that he does not adequately address the challenges given by Hume and Kant, and he does not aim at establishing clarity. Instead, he seems to want to persuade his audience by giving what might appear as plausible to them. He does not prove that reason can be used to know about God, nor does he establish the inexcusability of unbelief. This is what is important for our purposes here. There are many other thinkers who have attempted to update the theistic arguments or give a defense of Christian belief, such as C. S. Lewis or Josh McDowell. But rather than consider each one, what will be done is to consider some general schools of thought that have attempted to defend theistic belief. The question will be: Do any of them respond to the challenge aimed at reason, and do they establish that it is clear that God exists so that unbelief is inexcusable? If not, then what they offer are arguments that they find personally convincing, which is more a statement about them than it is about reality and what exists.

7.2. FIDEISM

The first response to Hume/Kant has already been seen earlier in this work. It is fideism. "From Kant onward the dominant motif in Protestant theology has been fideistic. This is evident in Schleiermacher's emphasis on the experience of a feeling of dependence, in Kierkegaard's view of truth as subjectivity, and in Albrecht Ritschl's desire to exclude metaphys-

10. Craig, *God?* 26.

ics from theology, focusing instead on nominalistic-phenomenalistic ethical values."[11] Fideism has already been shown to be contrary to clarity and undermines the inexcusability of unbelief. And yet it is still popular. "Today, not only are Christians in general (and neo-orthodox ones especially) fideistic, but even Evangelical, Orthodox Christians tend to be so. At least many, indeed, most Evangelical scholars reject the theistic proofs, and it is very difficult, if not logically impossible, to avoid fideism without them."[12] As a response this is a non-response. It does not take seriously the challenge. It does not see that if Christianity cannot respond to the challenge, then its redemptive claims are unintelligible.

Some contemporary fideists have gone beyond the claim that blind belief is necessary. In response to the nineteenth century, some fideists argue not only that reason cannot know God but also that reason is harmful.

> In explicating his claim about the inertness of reason the fideist usually tells a story. The story consists essentially of divorcing reason from feeling, from the motives of the will, and from the practical side of life. By restricting reason to a formal function, the fideist contends that any theoretical exercise terminates in mere concepts and that these cannot move to a religious belief. The fideist strategy seems to be one of positing a bifurcation between logic, reason, and concepts on the one side, and affectivity, will, and praxis on the other.[13]

This is accepted without question by many persons. It is found in the distinction drawn between the head and the heart. Religion is said to be a matter of the heart. This is a version of the claim that knowledge is unimportant and does not affect how one lives.

These claims must be responded to by Historic Christianity. If religion is a matter of the feelings, then unbelief cannot be said to be inexcusable. If knowledge does not affect how we live, then unbelief is irrelevant and unimportant. The assumption behind the claim that unbelief is inexcusable is that beliefs matter, they affect how we live, and false beliefs result in wrong actions. The assumption is that we are responsible not only for the wrong actions, but for the beliefs that lead to them. The assumption is that belief in God matters, that it makes a difference in

---

11. Sproul, "Classical Apologetics," 33.

12. Ibid., 35.

13. King, "Fideism and Rationality," 435.

how one lives. Contemporary fideism, accepted by such a large part of Christianity, undermines these claims. It should be no surprise that contemporary Christianity is unable to defend the historic views of redemption and instead tends toward syncretism as the expression of inclusivism and pluralism.

The neo-orthodox believers, such as Karl Barth (1886–1968), encouraged the view that reason cannot lead to God. "Man cannot capture the Truth about the eternal God in his own finite formulas. Man can only witness to the paradoxicality of God's own self-revelation."[14] However, this undermines both Christianity and rationality. "When Barth and Bultmann protest that God does not need to justify himself before man, the proper response is to re-echo Jasper's answer to Bultmann, 'I do not say that God has to justify himself, but that everything that appears in the world and claims to be God's word, God's act, God's revelation, has to justify itself."[15] The claim that God does not need to justify himself before the bar of human reason undermines inexcusability. Jasper saw that the claims of any given worldview must be tested by reason. If God does not need to justify himself, does Brahman? This path leads to the same skepticism that all fideism tends toward.

Consider Barth's explanation of "faith":

> Christian faith has to do with the object, with God the Father, the Son, and the Holy Spirit, of which the Creed speaks. Of course it is of the nature and being of this object, of God the Father, the Son, and the Holy Spirit, that he cannot be known by the powers of human knowledge, but is apprehensible and apprehended solely because of His own freedom, decision and action. What man can know by his own power according to the measure of his natural powers, his understanding, his feeling, will be at most something like a supreme being, an absolute nature, the idea of an utterly free power, of a being towering over everything. This absolute and supreme being, the ultimate and most profound, this "thing in itself", has nothing to do with God. It is part of the intuitions and marginal possibilities of man's thinking, man's contrivance. Man is able to think this being; but he has not thereby thought God. God is thought and known when in His own freedom God makes Himself apprehensible.[16]

14. Livingston, *Modern*, 328.

15. Pojman, "Rationality and Religious Belief," 172.

16. Barth, "Dogmatics in Outline," 23.

This same theme is found in his commentary on Romans where Barth gives his interpretation of 1:20. Barth takes this passage to mean that, at best, a vague notion of a higher power is available to humanity.

> *That which may be known of God is manifest unto them.* The truth concerning the limiting and dissolving of men by the unknown God, which breaks forth in the resurrection, is a known truth ... We know that God is He who we do not know, and that our ignorance is precisely the problem and the source of our knowledge. We know that God is the Personality which we are not, and that this lack of Personality is precisely what dissolves and establishes our personality. The recognition of the absolute heteronomy under which we stand is itself an autonomous recognition; and this is precisely *that which may be known of God* ... But—*in spite of knowing God.* The knowledge of God attainable through a simple observation of the incomprehensibility, the imperfection, the triviality of human life, was not taken advantage of.[17]

There may be a confusion here between the doctrine of God and soteriology. It could be true that the change from rejecting God to knowing God requires the work of God's grace in a person's life. In that sense Barth might hold to the traditional Augustinian/Calvinist view expressed in total depravity and the effectual calling. However, this is consistent with inexcusability in that if it is clear that God exists, then there is no rational justification for rejecting God. Thus, an unbeliever like Russell does in fact reject theistic belief, and he gives arguments to support his rejection and subsequent acceptance of a different view. But if it is clear that God exists, then it must be shown that his arguments are unsound and his rejection of theism irrational. If this can be done then it can be held that unbelief is inexcusable. Note that Augustine did something similar in his own personal journey from unbelief to belief, arguing that his non-theistic beliefs had no justifiable foundation because God is Truth. But he also maintained that God's grace is required to know God. The problem with Barth is that he extends the soteriological principle to the knowledge of God and thereby cannot provide a basis for the clarity of God's existence or inexcusability. Barth simply begins with Christian theism, and cannot answer the question posed by the ethics of belief (why should I believe this?).

Søren Kierkegaard (1813–1855) perpetuated the divided view of the human. He gave a response to Hegel, in whose system there was no

---

17. Barth, "The Epistle to the Romans," 45. Emphasis mine.

room for the individual. He emphasized paradox and subjectivity. "As we have seen, the theme of the Paradox is central to Kierkegaard's thought. The necessary counterpart to that theme is Kierkegaard's doctrine that *Truth is subjectivity.*"[18] Kierkegaard emphasized the individual against the system of Hegel. He emphasized feeling against thought. There is much that is attractive in Kierkegaard. However, Kierkegaard's approach cannot support inexcusability. "The fact is that Kierkegaard belongs more to the twentieth century than to his own in terms of the influence of his life and writings."[19]

Kierkegaard denies the ability for the human mind to reason from the creation to God:

> The works from which I would deduce his existence are not directly given. The wisdom in nature, the goodness, the wisdom in the governance of the world—are all these manifest, perhaps, upon the very face of things? Are we not here confronted with the most terrible temptations to doubt, and is it not impossible finally to dispose of all these doubts? But from such an order of things I will surely not attempt to prove God's existence; and even if I began I would never finish, and would in addition have to live constantly in suspense, lest something so terrible should suddenly happen that my bit of proof would be demolished.[20]

He thinks there will always be doubts, which provide an excuse. He does not define "faith" in the same way that it is defined in Hebrews, where it is spoken of as the evidence of things not seen. Instead, he replaces objective certainty with a blind acceptance based on uncertainty:

> Without risk there is no faith. Faith is precisely the contradiction between the infinite passion of the individual's inwardness and the objective uncertainty. If I am capable of grasping God objectively, I do not believe, but precisely because I cannot do this I must believe. If I wish to preserve myself in faith I must constantly be intent upon holding fast the objective uncertainty, so that in the objective uncertainty I am out 'upon the seventy thousand fathoms of water,' and yet believe.[21]

---

18. Livingston, *Modern*, 320.
19. Ibid., 311.
20. Kierkegaard, *Philosophical Fragments*, 51. Chap III.
21. Kierkegaard, *Concluding*, 183. Part II, Chap II.

But of course the problem is that one does not know which worldview to accept with uncertain passion. Why the Christian worldview? Why not Hinduism? Why not Materialism? It becomes a matter of taste and personal choice. And if Kierkegaard happened to be right in his personal choice, it cannot be maintained that unbelief is inexcusable. It cannot be maintained that all persons should believe in God. And yet this is precisely what Kierkegaard's worldview (Historic Christianity) has maintained.

Kierkegaard's approach cannot explain which religion or worldview we should blindly leap into. Further, if the mark of the correct religion is its distance from reason, then the more irrational the religion the better:

> There is another problem with the contention of the fideists in claiming that religious belief cannot have and ought not to have rational justification. This problem is that it tends to lend itself to an infinite regress of irrationalism. If a religious belief is religious to the extent that it lacks justification, then it would seem that the less justification I have for believing something, the more religious is my believing.[22]

There is no room in Kierkegaard for the idea of the inexcusability of unbelief. The need for redemption becomes unintelligible. Kierkegaard might view this as a positive development, reveling in the absurd. However, he cannot tell us which absurdity to revel in, or why the Christian absurdity is better than the non-Christian absurdity.

The bifurcation between thought and feeling ignores the cognitive reality of religious claims. Christianity makes claims about the nature of reality. It makes claims about God, good and evil, and the need for redemption. If reality is not the way that Christianity claims it is, then Christianity is false. If God does not exist, then the entire claim about redemption and unbelief is false. This is the crux of Historic Christianity. Any attempt to adapt these claims changes Christianity beyond recognition from a redemptive religion into a moral system based on an enlightened teacher. The contemporary response to Hume and Kant which weakens reason is unsuccessful as an attempt to justify Christian belief.

> My primary thesis is that a religion such as Christianity is (among other things) an explanatory theory or hypothesis about the world, which as such is as much in need of rational justification as any

---

22. Pojman, "Rationality and Religious Belief," 168.

other explanatory theory or hypothesis. That is, while a religion is also a form of life, a set of practices, it contains a cognitive aspect which claims to make sense out of one's experience. It answers questions as to why we are here, why we suffer, why the world is the way it is. These answers form a coherent network which call for reasons why they (or the network as a whole) are to be preferred to other answers (or no answer at all).[23]

7.3. NON-COGNITIVISM

Another response being what I will call non-cognitivism. This is the position of thinkers like Schleiermacher and other romantics. "Reacting against the rationalistic tradition, Schleiermacher established religious belief on the foundation of pious subjectivity. Man, he argued, is first and foremost a feeling rather than a thinking being."[24] Besides abandoning Historic Christianity, many abandoned Christianity as well due to the influence of non-cognitivism. If the basis of religion is non-cognitive, then unbelief is irrelevant, not inexcusable. The category of "inexcusability" does not apply to feelings. One either has certain feelings or does not. *De gustubus non disputandum est.* The idea that the Son of God had to die in order to redeem his people from sin does not make sense to this approach. Christ is romanticized along with everything else. Christ becomes a romantic figure who teaches us how to love through his sacrifice. Christ becomes a revolutionary figure who fights the conservatives of his day in favor of a more loving moral system.

While this is contrary to Historic Christianity, it is also rejected by many non-believers. Russell notes many aspects of Christ's moral teachings that he finds distasteful. It is possible that one could be blamed for not having certain emotions under certain conditions (such as empathy). But this could only be the case if one could know that one should have such emotions, or could know that one should develop one's character in a given way so as to have those emotions. Again, the prerequisite for responsibility is that one can know. But if religion is non-cognitive, then Russell's feelings about Christ are as justified as anyone else's feelings. Without determining if religion is in fact non-cognitive, it can be con-

23. Pojman, "Rationality and Religious Belief," 159.
24. Demarest, *General Revelation*, 94.

cluded with certainty that as a response, the non-cognitive approach is insufficient to support the claim that unbelief is inexcusable.

Karl Rahner (1904–1984) takes this approach. He accepts Heidegger's version of Kant and instead of seeking to respond he seeks to modify:

> In opposition to the neoscholastic Thomism of Jacques Maritain and Etienne Gilson, Rahner attempts a modern reinterpretation of Aquinas guided by insights from Kant, Heidegger, and Joseph Marechal, the Belgian Jesuit proponent of transcendental Thomism.... Rahner imparts a new twist to the Thomistic epistemology by maintaining that human knowledge, structured to the objects of immediate sense experience, transcends the space-time world to gain a partial knowledge of absolute Being-itself ... man knows ultimate Being, not extrinsically as a subject in relation to an object, but intrinsically as an instance of spirit in the world. Rahner, in other words, attempts to work a Heideggerian exposition of Thomas Aquinas.[25]

Belief in God is not what is important; it is a disposition to have certain experiences that is important. These experiences can be had in non-Christian religions. Consequently, Rahner speaks of implicit Christianity. A given person, while claiming to be a Hindu, might actually be an implicit Christian. The beliefs of these two worldviews are utterly contrary. However, beliefs are not important. Why not say the Christian is an implicit Hindu?

Hans Kung (1928–) takes a similar approach:

> Clearly what Kung, like Rahner, has done is to construct a natural theology founded on experience—but an experience that involves no necessary assent to cognitive truths. ... Since all religions accept the underlying reality of the world and attempt to answer the basic questions of existence, their adherents enjoy a valid spiritual experience of God.[26]

Once religion has been reduced to experience, has been based on the non-cognitive, then it is impossible to evaluate religion or judge one as true or false. What one person "feels" to be positive another may "feel" to be negative. The Historic Christian claims about the inexcusability of unbelief and the need for redemption become unintelligible. A new system is offered in their place. This new system does not respond to Hume and Kant, but has instead accepted their criticism and abandoned the theism and the redemp-

25. Demarest, *General Revelation*, 188.
26. Ibid., 197.

tive claims of Christianity. As such it is not a response but an acceptance of the Kantian epistemological and metaphysical framework.

The problem with this response is that it fails to respond to challenges of the nineteenth century and instead abandons theism and the cognitive aspects of Christianity. "What kind of statements does Schleiermacher make about the object of one's feeling of absolute dependence? That of which man is immediately aware is God, the Universe, the Whole. Schleiermacher's God, however, is not a personal, transcendent Being distinct from the world."[27] It should not be surprising that the non-cognitivists end in inclusivism or pluralism, thus rejecting the inexcusability of unbelief and the need for redemption through Christ. This is a perfectly consistent move, granting non-cognitivist assumptions. But why should these assumptions be granted? Questioning them requires backing up and questioning the epistemology of Hume and Kant. This is worth doing because their epistemology ends in skepticism about religious knowledge. If Historic Christianity is to respond successfully to the challenges considered thus far, it must take a different approach from the non-cognitivists.

7.4. CLASSICAL APOLOGETICS

A much more promising response to the Hume/Kant challenge is Classical Apologetics. Unlike the first two responses considered here, this one takes seriously the challenges and seeks for an intellectual solution. Proponent William Lane Craig says: "The methodology of classical apologetics was first to present arguments for theism, which aimed to show that God's existence is at least more probable than not, and then to present Christian evidences, probabilistically construed, for God's revelation in Christ. This is the method I have adopted in my own work."[28] Its methodology is to build up the theistic proofs against the attacks of Hume and Kant. It argues that their challenges went wrong at some point. As such, it is a return to the traditional theistic arguments, often explicitly looking to Aquinas, as do the Neo-Thomists. There are two problems with this response. First, it does not overcome the central challenge to reason made by Hume and Kant. Reason itself was called into question by Hume and Kant. Classical

---

27. Demarest, *General Revelation*, 95.
28. Craig, "The Classical Method," 48.

Apologetics assumes that reason can successfully offer a proof and seeks to find that proof.

Second, it does not see the need for the clarity of God's existence. It is one thing to offer a sound proof that is extremely difficult to understand and is knowable by only a few. It is another to assert that unbelief is inexcusable; Classical Apologetics is not based on the idea that unbelief is inexcusable, instead it aims at plausibility and probability. In returning to Aquinas there must also be a return to his views about the knowledge of God and reason. These, as was seen earlier, are incompatible with the claim that unbelief is inexcusable.

A related aspect of this approach that appears in some thinkers is an appeal to the Holy Spirit. This can be done by any of the approaches to apologetics considered here and is not unique to Classical Apologetics. One thinker who makes such an appeal is William Lane Craig, who falls somewhere between Classical Apologetics and Evidentialism. He asserts that "in answering the question 'How do I know Christianity is true?' we must make a distinction between *knowing* it is true and *showing* it is true. We *know* Christianity is true primarily by the self-authenticating witness of God's Spirit. We *show* Christianity is true by demonstrating that it is systematically consistent."[29] The appeal to the Holy Spirit to avoid clarity was considered earlier. It is a non-response that can be made by any religion. Craig's appeal demonstrates the influence of post-Kantian theology and the shift toward feelings in his thinking. A strong feeling about the truth of Christianity is said to be the Holy Spirit working in his life. But the Holy Spirit restores a person to seeking and understanding, thus the Christian should be able to show that it is clear that God exists. It should be noted that this view (Craig's view) is not the Historic Christian view of how the Holy Spirit works,[30] and that it confuses how one feels about the nature of reality (or about some belief system) with the nature of reality (or the truth of a belief system).

It is also worth noting that Craig relies heavily on the Kalam argument for the existence of God. "On the basis of philosophical arguments against the existence of an infinite, temporal regress of past events, al-Ghazali sought to demonstrate that the universe began to exist. Contemporary interest in the argument arises largely out of the startling empirical evi-

---

29. Craig, "Reasonable Faith," 350.

30. See the Westminster Confession, chapter 10.

dence of astrophysical cosmology for a beginning of space and time."[31] This argument has both *a priori* and *a posteriori* aspects. It argues *a priori* that there cannot be an actual infinite regress. It argues *a posteriori* that there was a beginning to the universe. Both kinds of arguments were challenged by Hume and Kant. Why should we believe that reason can tell us about the transcendent? Why should we believe that the evidence indicates creation *ex nihilo* instead of an oscillating universe? It is my assertion that because thinkers like Craig ultimately rest on an appeal to plausibility and inward feelings, they approach the need for arguments as a secondary matter. Such arguments are for some Christians who are interested, and for convincing those few unbelievers who will accept the arguments. What is not seen is that sin is not seeking and not understanding, and that seeking and understanding requires inferences and arguments. The Classical Approach has traditionally provided arguments, but their aim has not been the clarity of God's existence. Furthermore, this move toward plausibility is much less than clarity and provides an excuse. If unbelief is inexcusable then arguments are not just for some—they are necessary for all humans as rational beings who wish to make sense of the world. Consequently, while some might view Craig's efforts as admirable although unnecessary for the genuine believer, it is the contention here that they are harmful because they do not affirm the principle of clarity.

Classical Apologetics is a large group and includes many thinkers with varying degrees of awareness of the Hume/Kant challenge. William Lane Craig hardly replies at all to this challenge, and when he does it is to peripheral issues such as miracles or "great making properties." R.C. Sproul sees the challenge much more clearly and attempts to explain how the use of reason can lead to knowing God.

> We know that different philosophers adopt different theoretical starting points and that the epistemologies present in the debate extend far beyond those employed merely by Kant and the apostle Paul. The starting point of Descartes was different from that of Locke, at least in theory. Were there, however, common assumptions operating in both Locke and Descartes, in Hume and Aquinas, in Russell and Kierkegaard? We are searching for assumptions which are neither arbitrary nor subjective, but which

---

31. Copan and Craig, *Creation Out of Nothing*, 198.

function by practical necessity, are objective, and are or should be non-negotiables in any discussion of truth.[32]

There is much to be said for this approach when it correctly identifies the challenges, and it could be very helpful if it focused on the need to show that it is clear that God exists. In a later chapter we will discuss these non-negotiables that are necessary for truth and intelligibility.

7.5. EVIDENTIALISM

One of the most popular responses within Evangelical Christianity has been Evidentialism. This is unfortunate because it is hardly a response at all. It proceeds as if Hume's challenge had not been made.

> The evidential method of apologetics has much in common with the classical method, with the chief difference being the way in which historical evidences are used. Evidentialism may be characterized as the 'one-step' approach to this question, in that historical evidences can serve as a species of argument for God. Instead of having to prove God's existence *before* moving to specific evidences (the 'two-step' method), the evidentialist treats one or more historical arguments as being able both to indicate God's existence and activity and to indicate which variety of theism is true. Like the other methods, evidentialism can be rather eclectic in its use of various 'positive' evidences and 'negative' critiques and answers to detractors. Yet it tends to focus chiefly on the legitimacy of accumulating various historical evidences for the truth of Christianity.[33]

It continues the approach taken by thinkers like Samuel Clarke. It argues for God's existence from events like the resurrection, miracles, or the Bible. This approach is circular, and does not take into account the challenge of Hume. Some Evidentialists do attempt to respond to Hume's critique of miracles, but miss the greater point that such events must be interpreted, and the interpretation given by the Evidentialists is only one among many.

This is perhaps the most significant failure of this response. The Evidentialist proceeds as if experience and events are interpreted in the same way by all persons. For example, according to the Evidentialists, if

---

32. Sproul, *Classical Apologetics*, 71.
33. Habermas, "The Evidential Method," 92.

the resurrection of Christ could be proven to have occurred through historical evidence, then God must exist and Christianity is true. However, many different worldviews can acknowledge the resurrection of Christ without thereby granting theism or the redemptive claims of Christianity. Evidentialism fails to see that experiences must be interpreted.

Because of this, it does not establish the inexcusability of unbelief. It often uses the probability model, arguing that the evidence at hand makes Christianity probably true. This is often done with an extreme naïveté about the other world religions. Why doesn't the evidence at hand make it probably true that Christ is an avatar of Vishnu? This question does not appear to concern the Evidentialist. Consequently, this approach gives the entire project of offering a response in support of Historic Christianity a bad name in the minds of most non-Christian intellectuals.

While the Evidentialist approach claims to establish the probability of Christianity it falls far short of this. The problems in a probabilistic approach have already been mentioned. However, proponents of this view often think narrowly in terms of Christianity vs. naturalism instead of recognizing the diverse religions of the world. Not only is this approach unhelpful at this stage in world history, it falls far short of the Christian claim that unbelief is inexcusable.

7.6. CUMULATIVE CASE THEORY

A related theory is the Cumulative Case Theory. This is so similar that in many respects it can be lumped in with the Evidentialist response. The same criticisms made about that response are relevant here. However, one aspect stands out as important for consideration on its own. Where Evidentialism naïvely assumes a pre-Humean empiricism, this approach seems to recognize the need for a modified epistemology. It accepts skepticism and instead uses a "court" model. It asks: "Is there enough evidence to convince a jury?" The evidence needed to convince a jury is significantly less than is needed to convince Hume or Kant, but it is more realistic and applicable to the "real world." Proponent Paul Feinberg says:

> There is a rational approach that has been called a variety of names, the *cumulative case approach* or the *inference to the best explanation approach* being the most common. Such an argument is rational but does not take the form of a proof or argument for probability in the strict sense of these words. This approach un-

derstands Christian theism, other theistic religions; and atheism as systems of belief. Such systems are rationally supported by a variety of considerations or data. The model for defending Christianity is not to be found in the domain of philosophy or logic, but law, history, and literature.[34]

What convinces a jury could be spurious reasoning (as is found in some of the high profile cases of recent history, or the trial of Socrates). That a jury is convinced tells us more about the jury than it does about reality. It tells us more about the society out of which the jury was chosen than it does about reality. It does not tell us about the way the evidence should be interpreted. This is central if unbelief is inexcusable.

Further, this approach hardly considers the reality of non-Christian religions, instead it focuses on a one-dimensional opponent called "atheism." What about the cumulative case for non-Christian religions? Could not a similar approach be used to prove the truth of Hinduism, Buddhism, or Zoroastrianism? Cannot these religions incorporate the Resurrection and miracles of Christ? This response cannot establish the clarity of God's existence, nor does it see the need to do so. As such it is unsuccessful as an attempt to justify Historic Christianity in the face of challenges (as was true of Evidentialism, this is a popular response among Evangelicals who wish to hold to an exclusivist view).

7.7. PRESUPPOSITIONALISM

One of the more thoughtful responses of the twentieth century is Presuppositionalism. This view takes into account the reality of non-Christian worldviews and considers the presuppositions behind them. It specifically focuses on the manner that presuppositions affect how a person thinks. "Christian faith governs reasoning just as it governs all other human activities. Reasoning is not in some realm that is neutral between faith and unbelief. There is no such realm, since God's standards apply to all of life. We may not lay our faith aside when we study God's world."[35]

Presuppositionalism draws attention to the presuppositions behind the critiques of Christianity.

> Van Til is concerned, therefore, to deal with the foundations of a philosophy of life or a worldview, on the conviction that the mean-

---

34. Feinberg, "The Cumulative Case Method," 151.
35. Frame, "The Presuppositional Method," 209.

ing of particular terms and aspects of life is determined by those foundations. However, he does not seem to argue for a more or less arbitrary postulation of the Christian foundation as merely one of several alternatives, each of which is viable. Rather, he is arguing that though there are a number of ostensible alternatives, only one is in fact viable.[36]

When Marx or Freud criticize Christian theism they do so from within a worldview. They were materialists. Of course a materialist will find problems with Christian theism. However, the Presuppositionalists point out that there are significant problems in the materialist's presuppositions that affect all aspects of their worldview. Their claim is that the naturalists cannot account for knowledge, cannot explain the nature of being, and cannot provide a foundation for values.

Unfortunately, there are some limitations in how this method has been pursued. It often relies on a negative critique of non-Christian worldviews. It seems to assert that since naturalism is based on inadequate presuppositions, then Christianity must be true. It also often falls into the antinomy that other responses have fallen into: Naturalism or Christianity. Most philosophers throughout history have noted the weaknesses and simplemindedness of the materialist worldview. Plato and Aristotle responded to Greek naturalism. This means that Christianity must address not only naturalism, but all forms of unbelief. This is not an inherent weakness in Presuppositionalism because in theory this method could be extended to consider all non-Christian views.

A more serious problem is that it does not adequately respond to Kant and his critique of reason. Presuppositionalism asserts that what counts as "reason" is relative to a person's worldview. It confuses "how a person reasons" with reason in itself as the laws of thought (such as the law of non-contradiction). The law of non-contradiction transcends worldviews and applies to all thinking. How given persons reason is often shaped by their specific worldview. Presuppositionalism does not provide an answer to Kant's critique of reason as being inapplicable to being in itself. If reason does not apply to being in itself, then "presuppositional reasoning" about which presuppositions are best is not about being in itself, but only about human experience. The assertion that Christian "reasoning" is better than materialist "reasoning" becomes a statement about

36. Spencer, "Fideism and Presuppositionalism," 89.

the preferences of the Presuppositionalist, or about the human mind, and not about the nature of reality. This produces a second problem.

Presuppositionalism becomes fideistic and based on question-begging appeals to scripture. "Both [Gordon] Clark and [Cornelius] Van Til seem to say that general revelation is not sufficient in itself to give sinless man a definite knowledge of God; it must be interpreted by the aid of special revelation."[37] It argues that "autonomous human reason" is fallen and is insufficient to lead humans to knowledge. This really means that general revelation is not general: General revelation cannot be understood apart from special revelation, and so it can only be understood by those who have access to special revelation—it is not universally (generally) understandable. It relies on standard skeptical arguments to show that human knowledge is not possible. It claims that what is needed is a divine source of knowledge. This is the Bible.

This position undermines the claim that unbelief is inexcusable. The problem in starting with the Bible is that this fails to make sense of the Biblical claim that the failure to know God is inexcusable. If human reason is insufficient to provide knowledge of God, then humans have an excuse. We have already considered the problems in claiming that the Fall is the cause of unbelief. This aspect of Presuppositionalism is devastating; while proponents desire to defend Historic Christianity they render unintelligible the claim that all humans are inexcusable in their unbelief and need redemption. If human reason cannot understand general revelation, why think it will fare any better with special revelation? It is not possible to justify Christianity as a whole without first making sense of the central claims it makes about redemption and its assumptions about God. If these claims are unjustifiable, then Christianity as a whole cannot be justified.

Additionally, Presuppositionalism provides no basis for determining which set of scriptures should be the foundation. Why not the Vedas or the Koran? As soon as the Presuppositionalist offers an answer he has violated his Bible-based epistemology. In offering an answer, he is suggesting a non-Biblical basis for knowledge and critiques of other alleged scriptures. Or, if the Presuppositionalists merely reasserts the superiority of the Bible, he begs the question. It is a non-response; it is dogmatic table-pounding.

37. Diehl, "Evangelicalism and General Revelation," 9.

One important aspect of the Presuppositionalists approach is the Transcendental Argument for God's existence (TAG).

> This is the heart of Van Til's transcendental argument for God's existence. All argumentation involves presuppositions, but only the presupposition of the Christian God renders any kind of argument meaningful. In that case, the unbeliever's 'argument' against God or the gospel, if it can make any sense whatsoever, already 'stands upon the emplacement' of belief in God's existence. Rational argumentation already assumes the Christian position to be true, even when unbelievers argue against this truth.[38]

It is true that all argumentation has presuppositions. These presuppositions can be arranged into levels of more basic and less basic. It may be true that if God exists then at one point this is a necessary presupposition to other discussions. However, it is not the most basic presupposition. Van Til's own method reveals that he holds the law of non-contradiction to be most basic. He uses this law to justify TAG. He says that Christianity is true because the opposite is impossible. But this presupposes that the law of non-contradiction is valid. The problem is that Van Til and other Presuppositionalists reject placing the law of non-contradiction as the most basic and instead insist that the Triune God of the Bible be placed at the foundation. They assert that all worldviews have first principles, and this (the Triune God of the Bible) is their first principle. Needless to say, this has not been a first principle that has been universally available. Supposing that it is ontologically true that the Trinity is the ground of knowledge, it does not follow that the Trinity is epistemologically prior to the knowledge of other facts. When asked why the Trinity should be accepted rather than some other worldview, they assert that other first principles are contradictory. "The alternatives of biblical theism sooner or later break down through their forfeiture of internal consistency."[39] But again, this places the law of non-contradiction in the ultimate position of determining which view to hold. This seems to be a potentially helpful method to pursue, but it is not the method they wish to pursue.

Ultimately, the Presuppositionalists have ended by reasserting a form of fideism. They have merely asserted that theistic presuppositions should be our starting point, but they have not shown that the failure to know God

38. Bahnsen, "Van Til's Apologetic," 139.
39. Henry, "God," 408.

is inexcusable as culpable ignorance. They correctly recognize that all beliefs are parts of systems and should be understood in light of the whole. They correctly point out that there is an order between beliefs within a system beginning with what is most basic to what is less basic. They correctly point out significant problems in the basic beliefs of the materialist worldview. Yet, they fail to explain why all the basic beliefs of systems of unbelief are inexcusable. They fail to show why the basic beliefs of Christian theism are to be universally accepted, since they have not been universally accessible. Consequently, they render the Christian claims about redemption unintelligible.

7.8. REFORMED EPISTEMOLOGY

A final response to the Hume/Kant challenge to be considered is Reformed Epistemology. We considered this position earlier as an attempt to avoid the need to give an argument. It is also a major response to the challenges from Hume, Kant, and others. As we will see it shifts the focus from justification to warrant and in so doing undermines the requirement of inexcusability by focusing on immediate, intuitive, knowledge of God. This leads to circular reasoning with respect to a central concept (what it means to be "properly functioning"). Where the Enlightenment sought for evidence to support beliefs, Reformed Epistemology asserts that some beliefs do not need evidence or other kinds of rational support, but are instead *prima facie* "warranted." Just what counts as warrant, and whether or not a person really is *prima facie* warranted, or can be in the modern world, needs attention. Warrant is a weaker requirement than justification, and depends on factors such as the proper function of the cognitive faculties of the person rather than argumentation and the laws of thought.

Reformed Epistemology uses a parity, or analogy, argument to defend its assertion that belief in God is warranted:

> Penelhum is accurate, I think, in suggesting that Plantinga incorporates a 'permissive parity' argument in his defense of the rationality of religious belief. The 'permissive' version of the parity argument, given by Plantinga, argues that many of our common sense beliefs are taken as 'properly basic' (not groundless), such as the belief that 'I see a computer in front of me,' or 'I had lunch this afternoon,' or 'There are other minds.' According to Plantinga, theistic belief is on an epistemic *par*; thus a condition of parity exists between certain religious and non-religious beliefs. Belief in God,

for example, may be just as much of a basic belief as belief in other minds. Thus, if our epistemic situation is such that some common sense beliefs are properly basic, it is *permissible* to include belief in God as 'properly basic.'[40]

This argument equates theistic belief with such beliefs as the existence of other minds and the existence of the material world. These are widely accepted without much proof. Most people would not demand that their neighbor give justification for his or her belief in a material world. In the same way, the theist should not be held to a higher standard but should be seen as warranted in his or her belief that God exists. "If the parity thesis captures a central claim of Reformed epistemology, then Reformed epistemology puts forth an intriguing claim. That theistic beliefs may have the same epistemic status as other more commonly accepted nontheistic beliefs is a suggestion many theists would surely welcome."[41]

The important term to define is "warrant." "Put in a nutshell, then, a belief has warrant for a person S only if that belief is produced in S by cognitive faculties functioning properly (subject to no dysfunction) in a cognitive environment that is appropriate for S's kind of cognitive faculties, according to a design plan that is successfully aimed at truth."[42] Belief in God is warranted because it is part of the design plan for humans. Just as the eye was designed to provide information about the world, so too the human mind was designed to believe in God. Unbelief is a result of improper function, not of rational inexcusability, and as such there is an excuse for unbelief. "This capacity for knowledge of God is part of our original cognitive equipment, part of the fundamental epistemic establishment with which we have been created by God."[43]

Reformed Epistemology also focuses on epistemic "rights." Is a theist within his or her epistemic rights to remain a theist in the modern world? After the challenges from Hume and Kant, is the theist within his or her rights? What about "average," or "non-intellectual" believers? Are they within their rights? Reformed Epistemology answers in the affirmative, and explains why by relying on the *sensus divinitatis* considered previously. It is a focus on the immediate, intuitive, knowledge of God.

---

40 Askew, "On Fideism," 13.

41. McLeod, *Rationality*, 9.

42. Plantinga, *Warranted*, 156.

43. Ibid., 180.

Let me suggest four or five theses on rationality which, in my opinion, have become characteristics of the Calvinist tradition . . . It has characteristically been held to be (rationally) justified in being a theist, one does not have to accept the crucial tenets of theism on the basis of some argument or some reasons. A person may be well within his rights if he accepts those tenets *immediately*. . . . Similarly, it has characteristically been held that one may well be within one's rights in believing immediately that the Christian Scriptures are the revelation of God, or the Word of God. . . . It has characteristically been held that sin has darkened our capacities for acquiring justified beliefs and for acquiring knowledge. Reason is, in this way, not insulated from the devastation which sin has wrought in our existence. It is not that sin has affected our will but not our reason. It has characteristically been held that a specimen of science (*Wissenschaft*) may well be intellectually and scientifically competent and yet not neutral with respect to the Christian faith. . . . The Calvinist has insisted that in the face of an awareness of this conflict, one should re-do the science rather than surrender the faith. . . . It has characteristically been held that when the Christian engages in science, his activity ought in appropriate ways to be directed by his faith.[44]

Belief in God is a natural response on the part of humans to their environment. This view implies that unbelief is due to improper function. A person is warranted if that person's cognitive faculties are properly functioning based on the circumstances and according to a design plan aimed at attaining truth. This definition of warrant assumes part of what the theist must prove, that there is design, and is therefore problematic. It is also difficult to define "properly functioning" without begging the question.

Reformed Epistemology undermines the inexcusability of unbelief. If unbelief is due to improper function (and the improper function cannot rationally be expected to be detected and corrected by the individual alone) then unbelief is excusable. It cannot be culpable ignorance if it is due to improper functioning. Reformed Epistemology often seeks to justify its view of warrant by arguing that the standards of justification coming out of the Enlightenment were too stringent. Rather than offer responses to the challenges of Hume and Kant, it complains that their standards are unfair:

> If evidentialism is true, then my grandmother has a noetic defect—she believes in God without sufficient propositional evi-

44. Nicholas Wolterstorff, "Introduction," v.

dence. I prefer to look at the matter in my grandmother's favor. My grandmother does not have a noetic defect—hence evidentialism is false. It is difficult for me to imagine that God has put her in a cognitive situation which makes her belief in God positively ir-rational. I am constrained by the goodness of God to believe that he has created her with the noetic faculties that produce belief in him in the appropriate circumstances.

Why consider the experience of my grandmother? I believe that evidentialism, motivated by a quest for mathematical certainty in all believings, has offered an inappropriate paradigm of rationality. The Enlightenment conception of rationality, as we have demonstrated, is foreign to our believing experience. This reduces rationality to the model of a calculating machine: a mere algorithm for calculating the deductive consequences of beliefs that are independently verified. The more closely one's mental life resembles the workings of a com-puter, the more likely one is to be rational. If the arguments of the preceding chapters are persuasive, then it should be clear that human cognition is vastly different from computer calculation. Rationality is not simply a relation that obtains between one's beliefs. Rather, it is the complex relation between one's cognitive equipment—divinely designed—one's experiences, and the world.[45]

Reformed Epistemology is vaguely correct when it suggests that the stan-dards for knowledge in the Enlightenment era might be incorrect. But this is a result not of having too high a view of reason, but of limiting reason as Hume and Kant did. However, Reformed Epistemology fails to see that some standards are universal (apply to all "eras") and transcen-dent (apply to all worldviews). Asking that a worldview not violate the law of non-contradiction is not too stringent. Reformed Epistemology could have been helpful if it had called into question the empirical epistemology assumed by both Hume and Kant. It could not do this because it is based on a form of empiricism, seeking an intuitive knowledge of God. Like Hume and Kant, it limits the powers of reason, and in this respect accepts their position and the accompanying skepticism, rather than providing a response and basis for the knowledge of God.

Warrant is too weak to support inexcusability and the need for re-demption. It seems that non-theists could be warranted in their beliefs, or that we would not know if they are unless we also know if God exists. This means we would need some way of knowing if God exists apart from the

45. Clark, *Return to Reason*, 158.

"warranted basic beliefs" in question in order to defend them as warranted in contrast to other basic beliefs. Consequently, warrant provides no foundation for the concept of inexcusability and therefore is not sufficient to defend the claim that all humans need redemption. Rather, it provides unbelief with an excuse. Unbelief is due to improper functioning. Further, "proper functioning" is defined as functioning according to a design plan, and yet that there is a design plan assumes a designer, which is what the non-theist may be calling into question.

> What is it that determines whether a given way of acting or believing, given that your circumstances are thus-and-so, is rational or reasonable, in the relevant sense? Here is my suggestion: what determines this is what a creature of our kind with *properly functioning* reasoning would do or believe, given that she was in those circumstances. Or perhaps it is what someone with ideal *ratio* would do or think in the circumstances.[46]

To say that theistic belief is the result of proper functioning and Hindu belief is not becomes a matter of table pounding, because the Hindu can make the same assertion. This does not bother Plantinga, who says:

> The Christian will of course suppose that belief in God is entirely proper and rational; if he doesn't accept this belief on the basis of other propositions, he will conclude that it is basic for him and quite properly so. Followers of Bertrand Russell and Madelyn Murray O'Hare may disagree, but how is that relevant? Must my criteria, or those of the Christian community, conform to their examples? Surely not. The Christian community is responsible to *its* set of examples, not to theirs.[47]

But this is far from showing that unbelief is inexcusable. And if it turns out that the central redemptive claim of Christianity is unjustifiable, and involves believing a contradiction, then even in Plantinga's view it would lose its warrant. This means that Plantinga must either give up the claim that unbelief is inexcusable, or provide a better account of it than his view of proper functioning and warrant (as expressed to date) is able to do.

Reformed Epistemology sees that theists must respond to challenges, or "defeaters." If a defeater is offered and there is no response, then the person is no longer warranted. Many believers have not encountered the

---

46. Plantinga, "Warranted," 134.
47. Plantinga, "On Taking," 498.

defeaters of Hume or Kant and so their warrant is safe. But this oversimplifies the reality of challenges.

> It is, of course, abundantly plain that countless thousands of Christians have managed to fight the good fight of faith without ever having heard of Wittgensteinian language games or even of Wisdom's gardener . . . The fact remains, however, that church members and others will persist in demanding a reason for their hope; they will crave an account of 'the meaning of life'; and if office and factory skeptics do not challenge them on the problem of evil, the grounds of belief, immortality and the like, the circumstances of life probably will.[48]

The unexamined life is not worth living. This is even true for our grandmothers. Reformed Epistemology might be a good response to the *de jure* objection, but what about helping in critically examining basic beliefs—living the examined life? It should be noted that Plantinga does see the challenge to reason made by Kant. He states: "Our main interest here does not lie in trying to resolve the question of what Kant intended: that is perhaps necessarily beyond our powers. Instead, we are looking to see if there is good reason, either given by Kant or constructible from materials given by him, for the conclusion that our concepts do not apply to God."[49] Plantinga's typical response to such challenges is to show that they are not convincing:

> It doesn't look as if there is good reason in Kant or in the neighborhood of Kant for the conclusion that our concepts do not apply to God, so that we cannot think about him. Contemporary theologians and others sometimes complain that contemporary philosophers of religion often write as if they have never read their Kant. Perhaps the reason they write that way, however, is not that they have never read their Kant but rather that they *have* read him and remain unconvinced. They may be unconvinced that Kant actually claimed that our concepts do not apply to God. Alternatively, they may concede that Kant did claim this, but remain unconvinced that he was *right*; after all, it is not just a given of the intellectual life that Kant is right. Either way, they don't think Kant gives us reason to hold that we cannot think about God.[50]

---

48. Sell, *Philosophy*, 244.

49. Plantinga, *Warranted*, 14.

50. Ibid., 30.

Plantinga gives helpful insights into how our concepts apply to God and why Kant was wrong to restrict reason. We can hope for more in this direction.

7.9. CONCLUSION: THE ESTABLISHMENT OF CLARITY AS A PRECONDITION TO EXCLUSIVIST CLAIMS

The foundations of Christian theism have been called into question. Christian theism is not merely belief in God. It makes claims about good and evil. It asserts that unbelief is sin, that the failure to know God is inexcusable. It further claims that redemption from this sin is necessary and could only be achieved through the death of Christ. This is a high cost. It emphasizes the serious nature of unbelief as sin. The challenge from Hume and Kant has undermined the Christian claim that unbelief is sin. If unbelief is excusable, it is not sin, and does not require redemption.

Many thinkers in the Enlightenment and Post-Enlightenment eras have seen the failure of Christianity to demonstrate the clarity of God's existence and have chosen to abandon the claim that unbelief is sin. This failure required an abandonment of the exclusivist claims made about redemption by Historic Christianity. This has been done in favor of some form of inclusivism or pluralism. Abandoning inexcusability and the need for redemption through Christ involves an abandonment of Historic Christianity. It also often involved (historically) an abandonment of theism in favor of something like pantheism. Since inclusivists and pluralists abandoned Historic Christianity they have not been considered here as offering responses to Hume and Kant. The foregoing responses were made by those who wish to defend the exclusivist claims of Historic Christianity.

The responses by exclusivists were insufficient. Collectively they did not see that in order to defend the exclusivist claims of Historic Christianity the inexcusability of unbelief must be established. As responses they attempted to dogmatically reassert Christian belief, deny the need for rationality and proof, change the meaning of proof, reassert old arguments based on empirical evidence, or revive traditional theistic proofs. All of these methods have already been successfully challenged by Hume, Kant, and others. What is needed is *either* to defend the inexcusability of unbelief *or* to abandon Historic Christianity. If the former approach has any promise it must be in focusing on the crux of the challenge as a challenge to reason and the knowledge of God.

Graham Oppy's book *Arguing About Gods* reemphasizes the failure of Christians to show the clarity of God's existence. The arguments given after Hume and Kant are simply revisions of the traditional arguments without adequately dealing with the challenge to reason or the need for clarity. He asserts:

> That it may well be the case that theism and non-theism are both reasonable responses to the evidence that people have, and yet that any case that theists put forward for the existence of an orthodoxly conceived monotheistic god can be 'paralleled' by cases for the existence of other gods about which: (i) theists reasonably judge that the cases are not genuinely parallel (but often for reasons that they have not yet, and perhaps that they shall never have, successfully articulated); and (ii) non-theists reasonably judge that the cases are genuinely parallel (where this judgment is typically a natural expression of—or a companion to—their view that there is insufficient evidence for belief in the existence of an orthodoxly conceived monotheistic god).[51]

Oppy gives clear direction as to what must be done if Christianity is to maintain that unbelief is inexcusable because of the clarity of God's existence. The alternatives to belief in God, the "parallel cases," must be identified and shown to be impossible. This would leave no excuse for unbelief. Oppy correctly points out that this has not been done. The next two chapters will consider what steps must be taken in order to accomplish this.

51. Oppy, *Arguing*, 47.

8

The First Step toward the Clarity of God's Existence

If contemporary Christian philosophers has not provided the foundation for inexcusability and clarity, is such a foundation possible? Hume and Kant denied that reason can be used to know God. Is this the case, or can the use of reason be defended? And can reason be used to show that it is clear that God exists so that there is no excuse for unbelief? If so, what would such an argument look like, what would the steps be for showing this? In this chapter we will consider such steps, and consider if Hume and Kant were inexcusable in their worldview.

8.1. SHOWING THE CLARITY OF GOD'S EXISTENCE

IF THERE IS TO be a successful demonstration of the clarity of God's existence, it must begin by demonstrating that reason can be used to know that something has existed from eternity. The failure of previous arguments was in not aiming to establish clarity (the impossibility of the alternatives) and overextending from premises to conclusion ("highest being = God," "first mover = God," "designer = God"). A successful argument must avoid these mistakes. It must be able to identify alternatives to belief in God, and it must be able to show that these are contradictory. It must then show that what is eternal is a spirit, and that this eternal spirit is infinite and unchanging in properties such as knowledge, power, and goodness.

Identifying the alternatives requires defining "God." In Historic Christian theism, God is a Spirit who is infinite, eternal, and unchanging in being, wisdom, power, holiness, justice, goodness, and truth.[1] Unbelief is the denial that this God exists, and the affirmation that something else

1. Westminster Confession of Faith, chapter 2.

is eternal (has existed from eternity). If clarity is to be established, it must be proven that only God is eternal, and all other claims about what is eternal are contradictory. It requires showing that there is a clear distinction between eternal and non-eternal. The first step in doing this requires proving that something must have existed from eternity, and that reason can be used to know this. The alternative to this is that there was an uncaused event in which being came from non-being. Locke was quoted earlier as saying that nothing could be more absurd than holding that being came from non-being. But the following two chapters are going to consider this possibility in order to argue that it is clear that something has existed from eternity. To do this requires clearly defining what "being from non-being" and "uncaused event" mean, and considering important philosophers who have maintained that it is possible that being came from non-being. This analysis will help to show what is meant in saying "it is clear that something has existed from eternity," and that the alternative to clarity is a self-contradiction which ends in silence. One must be silent when one's assertions are self-contradictory and thus are not about anything. They are about nothing.

8.2. STEPS FOR SHOWING THE CLARITY OF GOD'S EXISTENCE

Beyond finding such a proof, we must also come to understand why it is inexcusable to not know God. This entails understanding what steps are needed to show that God exists. I have maintained that the traditional proofs overextend themselves in that they do not support theism. What is necessary to arrive at theism and then successfully defend it from challenges? Here I am going to suggest 10 steps that are based on work by Surrendra Gangadean in his book *Philosophical Foundation: A Critical Analysis of Basic Beliefs*, and in his chapter "The Necessity of Natural Theology" in my book *Reason and Worldviews*. They are:

1. Show that there must be something eternal.
   Show that only some is eternal by showing:
2. Show that matter exists (vs. spiritual monism, and idealism).
3. Show that matter is not eternal (vs. material monism).
4. Show that the soul exists (vs. material monism and Advaita Vedanta)

5. Show that the soul is not eternal (vs. Dvaita Vedanta and other forms of spiritual monism).

6. Respond to the problem of evil (moral and natural).

7. Respond to natural evolution (vs. uniformitarianism and materialistic reductionism).

8. Respond to theistic evolution (the original creation was very good—without evil).

9. Respond to deism (the necessity for special revelation).

10. Show that there is a moral law that is clear from general revelation.

This approach avoids the criticism of overextension because it identifies what must be proven: God is a spirit who is infinite, eternal, and unchanging in being, wisdom, power, holiness, justice, goodness, and truth. It then identifies the historic challenges to this position and argues against them: material monism, spiritual monism, and dualism. It then further identifies the major challenges to theism from cosmology and teleology: evolution, theistic evolution, and the problems of evil and suffering. For a development of each of these steps and how they are worked out the reader can follow-up with *Philosophical Foundation*. Here my concern is to ask: Can the challenge to reason from the Enlightenment be successfully answered, and can reason help us in making the first step toward a proof for the clarity of God's existence?

8.3. CLARITY AND THE INEXCUSABILITY OF HUME AND KANT

What does it mean to be without excuse? Persons can come up with excuses for just about anything in order to justify themselves, so we must distinguish between *being* without an excuse and *seeing* that oneself has no excuse. Being without excuse is objective and can be seen by others who know what to look for. Earlier it was stated that one is inexcusable if:

1. One holds to self-contradictory beliefs.

2. One does not have integrity—does not live according to the principles one teaches.

3. One does not know what is clear—since thinking is presuppositional (the less basic assumes the more basic), if anything is clear, the basic

things are clear. Thus, one is inexcusable if one does not know what is basic.

4. One does not see what is clear. Clarity requires distinguishing between *a* and *non-a*. An example of a basic belief that is clear is the distinction between *being* and *non-being*. There is no excuse for failing to distinguish these because their distinction is the foundation of all thought—to give an excuse requires this distinction.

As I move from arguing about the necessity for clarity and inexcusability within Christian theism, and the failure to provide these, to a criticism of Hume and Kant, I want to lay out the steps that would lead to a successful proof for God's existence. These steps are necessary to show that God as understood in Christian theism exists. In this book I mainly deal with the first step because the challenges from the Enlightenment are challenges to reason's ability to make even this step. Once we have laid the foundation for how reason can indeed make this step, then the important work of the following steps can be addressed.[2] I want to sharply distinguish my approach from the common method of apologists who believe that if they have shown that the material universe had a beginning, and perhaps that the cause of that beginning is personal, then they have just about exhausted the content of general revelation and somehow moved us closer to Christian theism. But this does not move us closer to Christian theism—it does not address the possibility of dualism, or spiritual monism both of which have been maintained by influential world religions. If general revelation cannot get us past simply a first mover who might be personal, then it cannot provide the inexcusability necessary for the redemptive claims of Christianity.

Consider the steps for showing the clarity of God's existence given previously. These steps avoid one of the major problems of the traditional proofs—they *clearly identify* the opposites to theism. But they are still susceptible to the challenge from Hume and Kant because those challenges aimed to undermine reason's ability to make even the first step. Therefore, the following will ask if Hume and Kant were consistent in their own position, or if their positions can be used to show that something must be eternal, and therefore that they were inexcusable in their failure to know

---

2. This has been done in Surrendra Gangadean's *Philosophical Foundation: A Critical Analysis of Basic Beliefs*, University Press of America, 2008.

God (Kant may have believed, but he provided a basis for objections and never moved from believing to knowing).

In light of those considerations, we must first consider if a response can be given to the challenges of the Enlightenment, the essence of which is that reason cannot provide a proof for God's existence. We have studied the challenges to theistic proofs from Hume and Kant. What does a response to these challenges require? Hume criticized the theistic proofs by limiting knowledge to the relation of ideas and sense data. Kant argued that reason cannot tell us about being and what exists. One move is to respond to these challenges by challenging their assumptions about the sources of knowledge. Indeed, the empiricism of Hume has many problems, as does Kant's phenomenal/noumenal distinction. But an even more potent response is one that shows how both Hume and Kant have no excuse for their unbelief, and that while they may have issued important and relevant corrections to the theistic proofs, showing the need for more work, they could have and should have gone further themselves and provided a clear proof for God's existence. Here I will argue that working within the confines of Hume's epistemology, and Kant's critique of reason, there is no excuse for their unbelief.

To say that Hume and Kant are inexcusable is to say that they did not see what is clear, they were not consistent within their own worldviews, and they did not live the implications consistently. To not see what is clear is to confuse and distort what is basic—it is to confuse *being* and *non-being* in alleging that there could be uncaused events or that all could come from nothing; it is to fail to consistently address the question "what is eternal," and allow that to be a fixed point in one's system. In this we will see the extent to which persons must go to avoid the clarity of God's existence—rather than know God they will posit that all being can come into *being* from *non-being* as a possibility (Hume), or they will undermine our ability to use reason while at the very same time using reason to do so (Kant).

8.4. HUME'S CHALLENGE TO REASON

First, consider Hume's epistemology. Allowing that the only sources of knowledge are sense data and the relationship between ideas, he gives a devastating criticism to the traditional proofs. Essentially, Hume's line of argument is: We cannot know if God exists through the use of reason (we cannot use reason to know if any particular being exists), and we cannot know if God exists through sense data, therefore we cannot know if God exists. But there is something Hume overlooked: While we cannot make the move from reason to existence directly, we can know from reason what cannot exist. Then, by eliminating the impossible, whatever is left, must exist. Hume allows for this methodology himself when he says that in the relation of ideas, what is contradictory cannot be.

But Hume also says that the opposite of any matter of fact is possible, or thinkable. Thus, no matter of fact bears logical necessity. Matters of fact are known through the senses, and Hume claims the senses give us data that we then put together due to habit. We then come to view some sequences of events as necessary, and say that one causes the other. But if the opposite of any fact is also possible, then there can be no necessity in this "causation." And if causation bears no necessity, then one cannot argue from effects to causes, and the basis for the cosmological and teleological arguments is undermined. Hume arrived at this conclusion due to his understanding of knowledge and sense data, and if a response is to be found that shows Hume to be inexcusable, it must show that he did not hold this view consistently, and he did not see what is clear at the basic level.

Hume is answering the question: "How do humans come to know?" which is different than "What ought humans know?" An insufficient way to answer the former question is by observing others and how they claim to come to know. In the Enlightenment it was common to recognize two sources of information, the senses and the rational faculty. Different schools placed differing emphasis on each, and indeed this distinction can be traced in Western Philosophy to Plato. Some argued that the rational faculty gave the foundational intuitions that were then used to understand the senses, others that the rational faculty was blank—without information—and only reflected upon what information the senses provided. Falling within the British Empiricist tradition, Hume is developing a form of the latter view.

The problem in giving an explanation of how people come to know is that one must explain how one came to know this. Experience cannot be the explanation as it cannot provide a universal, and the range of persons that philosophers have met is very limited. Fundamentally, the explanation must rest on an explanation that is not itself in need of explanation: that is, an explanation that is authoritative and self-attesting. What is self-attesting does not need to be proven because it makes proof possible. Because Hume could not provide this foundation he saw the role of philosophy as skeptical, and advocated this role in contrast to the overextension of reason beyond experience (by the rationalists) and fideism. Kant described Hume's failure as follows:

> The celebrated Locke, for want of due reflection on these points, and because he met with pure conceptions of the understanding in experience, sought also to deduce them from experience, and yet proceeded so inconsequently as to attempt, with their aid, to arrive at cognitions which lie far beyond the limits of all experience. David Hume perceived that, to render this possible, it was necessary that the conceptions should have an *a priori* origin. But as he could not explain how it was possible that conceptions which are not connected with each other in the understanding must nevertheless be thought as necessarily connected in the object—and it never occurred to him that the understanding itself might, perhaps, by means of these conceptions, be the author of the experience in which its objects were presented to it—he was forced to drive these conceptions from experience, that is, from a subjective necessity arising from repeated association of experiences erroneously considered to be objective—in one word, from *habit*. But he proceeded with perfect consequences and declared it to be impossible, with such conceptions and the principles arising from them, to overstep the limits of experience.[3]

But the descriptive element of his answer to the question "how do people know?" does not address the normative issue—what should people know? It might be true that many persons rely on sense data for what they claim to know, and that they only use reason in reflecting on sense data—they are not critical thinkers, or systematic thinkers, but instead wait for experiences in life in order to learn lessons. But should they learn this way? And if this is how they learn, do they have an excuse for not knowing God? Answering this question will offer a response to Hume's challenge from the inside out—taking Hume's epistemic assumptions, I will argue that he is still without excuse because he is inconsistent with his own skeptical philosophy, and because he did not see what is clear.

---

3. Kant, *Critique of Pure Reason*, B 127.

8.5. CRITIQUING HUME FROM WITHIN: THE IDEA OF THE ETERNAL

I want to show this in two ways: first, by showing that reflection upon sense information leads to ideas about what is eternal, and second, by expanding on Hume's claim that a contradiction between ideas is meaningless. First, granting that all ideas originate in sense data, but that from there the mind reflects on these ideas, what kind of reflection can be expected from a person? Hume says that when he introspects all he sees are changing mental images. Indeed, *change is the constant* with respect to sense data. This has been noted from the beginning of philosophy (Heraclitus), and arguing past change to universals is a problem for all empiricists.[4]

Thus, upon reflection, all humans will notice that the senses are continually offering changing information—the idea of change is thus basic to all other claims that are made using sense data. But once we have this idea of change, we can also reflect on its opposite, the idea of changelessness (these go together like *a* and *non-a*). Immediately some basic questions arise: Is everything changing, or is there anything changeless? Is there simply a series of changing moments reaching into eternity (change is eternal), or was there a beginning to the changing world (the world of change was created by something that is not changing)? Simply by working within Hume's framework these questions naturally arise—they are basic questions in that all other beliefs formed within Hume's system assume answers to these questions, and these answers have ramifications for the entire system. I am contending here that this level of reflection is basic and natural—all thinking humans can reflect in this way, and to not do so is to live the unexamined life. Therefore, while it might be the case that many/most humans live without reflecting on sense data or their assumptions, they are responsible for the consequences of this unreflecting life, and they are without excuse if they do not see what is clear due to this method.

The implication for belief in God is that Hume's epistemology leads naturally to ask the question *what is eternal?* Here "eternal" means what is without beginning and therefore changeless (either no change or changeless in the sense of recycling the same changes). This is because any being that has unique change, and has existed from eternity, would already have

---

4. Hume's position, consistently developed, leads to the doctrine of momentariness. Some Buddhist schools of thought more consistently draw out the implications of empiricism than did Hume. See *Buddhists, Brahmans, and Belief,* by Dan Arnold.

achieved such change (such as burning out, or growing to enlightenment) or reaching such change is impossible (if it has not been reached after eternity then it cannot be reached). So while the senses only give changing information, they provide the basis for asking questions about what is eternal and changeless.

Hume's position seems to be that such questions cannot be answered, since the only source of an answer is sense data which is always changing—we cannot have sense data of what is changeless and eternal. And, he contends, the mere relation of ideas cannot tell us about what exists, so that if an eternal being does exist, we cannot know of that being through the senses or the relation of ideas—the only two sources of knowledge. But he overlooks a point he made about meaninglessness and ideas: a contradiction between ideas yields meaninglessness. This means that if the claim that "none is eternal" is a contradiction, then it is meaningless, it cannot be true, and its contradiction "something is eternal" must be true. I am going to argue that "none is eternal" is a contradiction, and this means that within Hume's own system it is clear that there must be something eternal. Now, this is not yet to say that it is clear that God exists. To show that it is God that is eternal requires other steps to be taken (indicated earlier). But this is the first step. Theism claims that God is eternal, so if it is the case that none is eternal, then theism is false. The first step in the proof is to show that something must be eternal, and this can be shown within Hume's system.

And yet Hume did not see this. This is the normative aspect of the knowledge question. What should Hume have known? In Hume's case, he can be held to his own standard, so that if he constructs a system of epistemology, and in that system it can be shown to be clear that God exists, then Hume should have seen this. One might try to defend Hume and say that he only started the theory, and left it to others to develop its implications. This can and does happen in all areas of knowledge at the constructive level—drawing out implications and further implications over time. But at the basic level, the level assumed in all other knowledge claims, this defense does not work, either at the professional level or at the personal level. Professionally, Hume wanted to influence philosophical speculation, which means he is making claims that have assumptions which need a defense. This is the tradition of philosophy going back to Socrates—asking persons to explain their positions to see if they know or only claim to know. Personally, Hume faces the existential problem of meaning—what is the meaning of life, what is of lasting value? His failure to see that the claim that *nothing is eternal* is a contradiction, and therefore something must be eternal, affects his ability to come to know what is of lasting value, and he cannot blame this failure on anyone else.

8.6. SOMETHING MUST BE ETERNAL: NO UNCAUSED EVENTS, NO BEING FROM NON-BEING

In order to understand why "none is eternal" is a contradiction we must understand more about what it means, and about Hume's system. In Hume's epistemology a strict contradiction has to do with the relation between ideas, and he discusses these relations among which are *comparison* and *causation*. Both of these are important in understanding the claim "none is eternal," although ultimately it is the causal relation that is central. Comparison helps us to identify what each of the concepts mean. "Eternal" is compared with "temporal." What is eternal has no beginning, while what is temporal has a beginning. What is temporal is changing (at the very least in going from not existing to existing), while what is eternal is not changing (or the change is a matter of eternal cycle). To say that *none is eternal* is to say that *no being is eternal, nothing exists that is eternal.* "None" is contrasted with what "is," with "being," and therefore refers to "non-being." Therefore, this claim has both quantitative and substantive parts. Taking it for granted that something now exists, the claim "none is eternal" is equivalent to saying that *being* came from *non-being.* This is claiming that what now exists, or the chain of temporal being leading to the present, does not extend to eternity and was not brought into being by an eternal being—it came into being from non-being.

This is where the causal relationship becomes central and important. Hume is famous for his work on causation and his claim that causation is a matter of constant conjunction in time, that it is based on sense data and is not known by necessity. This analysis of causation leaves the possible couplings wide open—any two senses can possibly be united as cause and effect without contradiction. Hume gives numerous examples of this, and examples to show that we could not anticipate causation in experience but only think we do because of habit. But assumed in all his examples is the distinction between *being* and *non-being.* All of his examples are examples of *being.* The one possible coupling that is not possible is that of *being* and *non-being* because *non-being* is not a *thing* that can be coupled.

In the *Treatise*, Hume raises the broader question as to our right to postulate that events must always be causally determined. In other words, he there questions the validity of the *universal* causal principle, that whatever begins to exist must have a cause of existence; and he does so on the explicit ground that it demands as necessary the connecting of two concepts, that of an event and that of an antecedent cause, between which *no connection of any kind* can be detected by the mind.[5]

The principle, that is to say, is not self-evident; it is synthetic:

> The concept of an event and the concept of a cause are quite separate and distinct ideas. Events can be conceived without our requiring to think antecedent events upon which they are dependent. Nor is the principle capable of demonstration. For if it be objected that in questioning its validity we are committing ourselves to the impossible assertion that events arise out of nothing, such argument is only applicable if the principle be previously granted. If events do not require a cause, it is as little necessary to seek their source in a generation out of nothing as in anything positive.[6]

This analysis of causation leaves the possible couplings wide open—any two sense experiences can be united as cause and effect without contradiction.

Stated again, all of Hume's examples are examples of beings. The one impossibility of a causal connection within Hume's system is being from non-being. Indeed, all cause *presupposes* being, and all intelligibility *presupposes* cause. Perhaps Hume did not see this because, as was noted earlier, he was arguing from how he observed people to come to understanding, rather than considering what people ought to understand. This kept him from a kind of critical analysis of his own system, and from a critical examination of basic beliefs in a search for meaning. He is not seeing what is clear at the basic level: The distinction between *being* and *non-being*, and the impossibility of *being from non-being*.

8.7. THE IMPOSSIBILITY OF UNCAUSED EVENTS

But why can't being come from non-being, why is it impossible? A more common way of phrasing this question is to ask if there can be uncaused

5. Smith, *A Commentary*, xxvi.
6. Ibid., xxvi.

events. These propositions are equivalent in that if no being is the cause, then *non-being* is bringing about a state of affairs, something that is. Here, *non-being* is both a substantive and a quantifier in that it refers to *no* (quantifier) *being* (substantive). So this is not committing the error of attributing action to non-being, as if non-being were a being. But rather it is affirming that uncaused events are equivalent to the claim that *no being caused this to happen*. Hume explicitly states that uncaused events are possible,[7] and I think this is a failure on his part to see what is clear (this is a criticism from the inside out to emphasize Hume's inexcusability). This failure kept Hume from knowing God, and was the basis of his criticism. If he had seen what is clear, he might have criticized the traditional proofs as insufficient (we can agree they are), and then gone on to provide a foundation on which to show the clarity of God's existence.

Hume maintains that uncaused events are possible because there is no basis from experience to say that they are not, and he does not think they involve a contradiction of ideas. And yet, if causation is a habit of the human mind developed due to constant conjunction in experience (of beings), then being from non-being would always be ruled out—we can never experience non-being. *Non-being* is known as a concept through the act of reason in reflecting on the opposite of being. Everything that is experienced is a being, or quality of a being, or state, relation, etc., of a being. So in arguing that there cannot be being from non-being, and that the implication is that something must be eternal, we are not violating Hume's rule against arguing from relation of ideas to existents. *Non-being* is not an existent that we are ruling out, it is non-existence. Rather, we are saying that if there is now being then there has always been being (something is eternal, without specifying what).

Hume maintains, nevertheless, that uncaused events cannot be ruled out because, although not yet experienced, perhaps they will one day be experienced, or perhaps they occur all the time in a part of the universe not currently experienced. Perhaps they can never be experienced by humans, but they are still the case. There are three problems with this. If uncaused events are possible, how can they be distinguished, in experience, from caused events? We might think that *a* caused *b*, but really it was uncaused. Indeed, it is possible that all events are like this. How can this be consistently ruled out? But this leads to the second problem: If all

7. Hume, *Treatise,* 79.

events are uncaused then what happens to intelligibility and the possibility of knowledge? All knowledge claims presuppose causation to hold, and when I tell you something I presuppose that my claim will cause some understanding in you (at least enough for you to disagree with). If there is no causation then there can be no intelligibility, and no consistent purpose in attempting to communicate. The only consistent option is silence. And yet Hume is not silent, but wants to maintain an entire philosophical system. He must presuppose causation, he does presuppose causation—he wants his words to cause us to think.

But why not have most events be caused, and just one or two be uncaused? Notice that this is not what is maintained by the Copenhagen interpretation of quantum physics, which claims that billions and billions (more than that) of uncaused events occur each moment, which has troubling implications for knowledge that we will consider later. But what if there was just one uncaused event, the uncaused event of all being coming into being, and after that all events have been caused? Perhaps the universe came into being from non-being, but once it exists there are laws established that rule out uncaused events. Or perhaps there can be no uncaused events (after the first one that brings everything into being) because new beings would have to occupy space, and that would be causing some other being to go out of existence to "free up some space." The problem should be obvious: If the entire universe can come into being from non-being, then once the universe exists new laws can come into being from non-being, or new space can come into being from non-being.

A further problem with claiming that uncaused events are possible is that it results in a contradiction and blurs the distinction between being and non-being, once again landing us in unintelligibility and silence. But where is this contradiction? Many have argued that there is no strict contradiction since the claim is not that being is non-being. Furthermore, there are many cases of *a* from *non-a,* such as a chicken from an egg (or an egg from a chicken). So what is the problem with being from non-being as a logical possibility? It can be shown to be a strict contradiction by considering that all "from" claims presuppose being. Obviously, "from" in "being from non-being" is not a spatial term, such as "I came from Phoenix." Nor can it be a term denoting origination such as "that noise came from me" since non-being cannot *do* anything. Upon analysis, all uses of "from" involve being, and it can never be used with non-being. It has been commonplace to say that from nothing *nothing* comes, or nothing begets nothing, and indeed, this is basic to all areas of study. It is presupposed in the laws of motion: If nothing acts on an object, then nothing changes (it either continues in motion, or continues in rest). If being can come from non-being then the laws of motion can no longer be maintained. Similarly in banking: If nothing is added or subtracted from one's account, then it remains the same. Consider receiving your bank statement, and although nothing has been added or subtracted, the balance is less than the last statement's. Upon inquiry, the banker tells you that this is due to an uncaused event where a withdrawal came into being from non-being. We can continue to consider "real life" scenarios, and examples from the sciences, to make the point that people do not accept even the remote possibility of uncaused events, and the more important something is to them (e.g., their bank account), the less patience they will have with such answers. It is inconsistent to maintain that uncaused events are possible but then not accept them or live as if there are any in the most important areas of life. This is inexcusable.

Perhaps it will be maintained that the use of "from" is misleading, and instead it should simply be stated that there exists a finite series of changing events, the first of which was not caused; it is incorrect to say "caused by nothing" since this makes nothing a substantive. Nor was there an infinite amount of time in which nothing happened, since time is an aspect of change, and nothing was changing before the first event. But this first event is the event of coming into existence. Such an event is unavoidably a dependent event, and so in this description there is still the element of an event which is dependent and depends on nothing (a contradiction). Taking the objection earlier that there are many instances of *a* from *non-a,* this situation becomes: *a* from neither *a* nor *non-a* (*a* from nothing) since all descriptions of non-being or nothing become substantive where nothing is doing something. More consistent would be the statement: "on the issue of where *a* came from I remain silent," or "on the issue of on what *a*'s existence depends I remain silent."

But is there a strict contradiction to meet Hume's criterion for meaninglessness? There is, and it can be seen in what happens to the distinction between *being* and *non-being* if being from non-being is possible. Remember that in Hume's system making distinctions is one of the relations of ideas, and *a* and *non-a* is an absolute distinction. While *being* from *non-being* follows this formally, it is different from all other distinctions between *a* and *non-a*. All other such cases are cases of beings. "Table" falls into the category of "non-egg," and yet both are beings. So too with all the examples Hume considers. Behind all of these is the distinction of being and non-being, and the reality that in causal relations being is only related to being. If being could come from either *being* or *non-being*, then on this point the two are not different—they are not *a* and *non-a* on this point, just as *table* and *egg* are not *a* and *non-a* with respect to the category *material objects*. Here then is the contradiction: if being can come from either being or non-being, then on this point they are not different, which is to say that being is non-being. *Tables* are equivalent to *eggs* with respect to being material objects. But *being* and *non-being* are different on all points and in every respect, which means if being comes from being, then it can *never* come from non-being. This holds true for whatever sense of *from* that one wants to hold, and for the example where a series of changing and dependent events is preceded by nothing. If Hume wants to be able to refer to either *being* or *non-being* as the source of other being, then what is the difference between these?

8.8. KANT'S RESPONSE TO HUME

On this basis I believe we can say that Hume was inexcusable in his failure to know God. His objections to belief were based on his epistemology, which he did not apply consistently, and if applied consistently could provide the first step to knowing God—showing that something must be eternal. But Kant's objection would seek to undermine even this gain—in attempting to solve the problem of necessity and causation Kant argues for a system that denies reason's ability to arrive at conclusions about being in itself. Our next step will be to offer a response to Kant in the same way we did to Hume, from the inside. Given Kant's system, can it be shown that there is no excuse for unbelief? Kant builds on the work of Hume by taking the central insight of Hume to be the analysis that causation is not necessary, and then seeks to find a solution to the problem this raises for knowledge. Norman Kempt Smith, one of the most famous commentators on Kant, says:

> Now it was these considerations that, as it would seem, awakened Kant to the problem of *a priori synthesis*. He was, and to the very last remained, in entire agreement with Hume's contention that the principle of causality is neither self-evident nor capable of logical demonstration, and he at once realized that what is true of this

principle must also hold of all the other principles fundamental to science and philosophy. Kant further agreed that inductive inference from the data of experience is only possible upon the prior acceptance of rational principles independently established; and that we may not, therefore, look to experience for proof of their validity. Thus with the rejection of self-evidence as a feature of the *a priori*, and with the consequent admission of its synthetic character, Kant is compelled to acquiesce in the inevitableness of the dilemma which Hume propounds. Either Hume's sceptical conclusions must be accepted, or we must be able to point to some criterion which is not subject to the defects of the rationalist and empirical methods of proof, and which is adequate to determine the validity or invalidity of general principles. Is there any such alternative?[8]

The basic problem that Kant struggled with is:

> As the principles which lie at the basis of our knowledge are synthetic, they have no intrinsic necessity, and cannot possess the absolute authority ascribed to them by the rationalists ... They are conditions of *sense*-experience, and that means of our knowledge of appearances, never legitimately applicable in the deciphering of ultimate reality. They are valid within the realm of experience, useless for the construction of a metaphysical theory of things in themselves.[9]

The difficulty is not in explaining analytic judgments, because these must be the case due to the law of non-contradiction. Nor is there, for Kant, a problem in explaining synthetic judgments that are empirical in that the predicate is related to the subject as part of an empirical whole.[10] But what about non-empirical judgments that are not analytic. Indeed, until Kant the terms *a priori* and analytic were not much distinguished. In order to respond to Hume's analysis of causation, Kant attempts to show that there are *a priori* but synthetic (not analytic) judgments that are necessary to explain experience at all. Causation is one of these, and therefore is given a kind of *necessity* in relation to human experience or understanding of experience, but not a necessity with respect to being in itself. Kant's solution relativises causation to the human mind and disconnects it from reality—this is the Kantian revolution. This is the transcendental method.

---

8. Smith, *A Commentary*, xxvii.

9. Ibid., xxxv.

10. Ibid., 30.

8.9. THE TRANSCENDENTAL METHOD

Kant's method of proof is the transcendental—he seeks for that which makes apprehension possible.[11] His proof of the objective validity of categories is that they are the only possible way for perception to be empirically objective.[12] There is an important sense in which Kant's transcendental method is not different from the hypothetical method of the natural sciences. "It proceeds by enquiring what conditions must be postulated in order that the admittedly given may be explained and accounted for. Starting from the given, it also submits its conclusions to confirmation by the given."[13] The "given" is the reality of perception as different from the self, and the self that is aware.

The perceptions do not give knowledge because they must be interpreted. Kant distinguishes between the information of the senses and the meaning that this is given by the mind. Kant teaches that there is no consciousness or awareness without apprehension of meaning.[14]

> Meaning . . . always involves the interpretation of what is given in the light of wider considerations that lend it significance. In the awareness of meaning the given, the actually presented, is in some way transcended, and this transcendence is what has chiefly to be reckoned with in any attempt to explain the conscious process. Kant is giving expression to this thesis when he contends that all awareness, no matter how rudimentary or apparently simple, is an act of judgment, and therefore involves the relational categories . . . this, of course, commits Kant to the assertion that there is no mode of cognition that can be described as immediate or unreflective. There is an immediate *element* in all knowledge, but our consciousness of it is always conditioned and accompanied by interpretive processes, and in their absence there can be no awareness of any kind.[15]

We have already considered Kant's objections to the theistic proofs, and their central challenge to reason. Now we want to see if Kant is without excuse. Does his epistemology provide an alternative to knowing God, or a viable challenge to theistic proofs? Kant begins his *Critique of Pure*

11. Smith, *A Commentary*, 250.
12. Ibid., 250.
13. Ibid., xxxviii.
14. Ibid., xli.
15. Smith, *A Commentary*, xlii.

of Reason by affirming that all knowledge is through the senses, although it is given recognizable form by the human mind. The senses provide the information that is then used by the mind to make judgments. "It is therefore correct to say that the senses do not err—not because they always judge rightly but because they do not judge at all" (297). Nor is error due to the understanding when it is used properly—according to the laws of understanding. So what is the source of error?

Kant says:

> In any knowledge which completely accords with the laws of understanding there is no error . . . Thus neither the understanding by itself (uninfluenced by another cause), nor the senses by themselves, would fall into error. The former would not, since, if it acts only according to its own laws, the effect (the judgment) must necessarily be in conformity with these laws; conformity with laws of the understanding is the formal element in all truth. In the sense there is no judgment whatsoever, neither a true nor a false judgment. Now since we have no source of knowledge besides these two, it follows that error is brought about solely by the unobserved influence of sensibility on the understanding, through which it happens that the subjective grounds of the judgment enter into union with the objective grounds and make these deviate from their true function.[16]

Thus if we are in error about God, or about the proofs for God's existence, it is due to subjective elements entering into our formation of judgments. The influence of this claim on later thinkers like Marx, Feuerbach, and Freud, is abundantly clear, as are the implications for appeals to religious experience. Kant himself does not maintain that God is such an error, but he provides the groundwork that is used by others to make this claim.

8.10. THE TRANSCENDENTAL ILLUSION

Kant speaks about the *transcendental illusion* by which we make claims about being in itself that go beyond our empirical abilities.

> We are concerned only with *transcendental illusion*, which exerts its influence on principles that are in no wise intended for use in experience, in which case we should at least have had a criterion of their correctness. In defiance of all the warnings of criticism, it carries us altogether beyond the empirical employment of cat-

16. Kant, *Critique*, A294.

egories and puts us off with a merely deceptive extension of *pure understanding.* We shall entitle the principles whose application is confined entirely within the limits of possible experience, *immanent*; and those, on the other hand, which profess to pass beyond these limits, *transcendent.*[17]

Obviously, all proofs for God's existence fall into this error and are thus illusions. Not all concepts can be experienced, such as *eternal* and *changeless*, Kant is committing himself to claiming that these are imposed by the mind rather than knowable about being in itself. These are not the same as the *unconditioned* about which Kant sometimes speaks—we have clear concepts (not images) of *eternal* and *changeless*; we can distinguish them from temporal and changing. Kant believes that God must be postulated for practical judgments, but this is not the same as knowing God, and provides an excuse for those who have not heard of God (and therefore cannot postulate him) or those who find an alternative postulate for practical judgments.

This illusion is not due to a mistake in thinking, as in the case of an informal fallacy, and therefore cannot be corrected the way that fallacies can be corrected. Kant does not think that this kind of illusion can be altogether overcome or avoided. The best we can do is recognize it and realize when it is occurring so that we are not fooled. He says:

> Logical illusion, which consists in the mere imitation of the form of reason (the illusion of formal fallacies), arises entirely from lack of attention to the logical rule. As soon as attention is brought to bear on the case that is before us, the illusion completely disappears. Transcendental illusion, on the other hand, does not cease even after it has been detected and its invalidity clearly revealed by transcendental criticism (*e.g.* the illusion in the proposition: the world must have a beginning in time). The cause of this is that there are fundamental rules and maxims for the employment of our reason (subjectively regarded as a faculty of human knowledge), and that these have all the appearance of being objective principles. We therefore take the subjective necessity of a connection of our concepts, which is to the advantage of the understanding, for an objective necessity in the determination of things in themselves. This is an *illusion* which can no more be prevented

17. Kant, *Critique*, B352.

than we can present the sea appearing higher at the horizon than at the shore.[18]

A theist might take this and claim that belief in God, and the transcendental illusion, is unavoidable. Or, that belief in God is part of our framework, our make-up, and is therefore natural for all humans. Of course, the adherents of other religions can claim that their beliefs are part of the mind's framework, are natural for all religions, and theism is due to improper functioning. So this line of thinking does not help in establishing the status of belief in God, and this has been borne out in our philosophy of religion since Kant.

In order to help illustrate how this illusion works, Kant gives examples called the antinomies of pure reason. These are cases where both sides of a claim can be equally defended or argued for by reason. For instance, the first antinomy considers the claim that the world had a beginning and that it did not. According to Kant, Both can be defended by reason so that we do not know which to accept from pure reason alone. The mistake is that we are imposing intuitions, which are immediate, onto being in itself which is given mediately through the senses. The mind has the intuitions of sequence, duration, and causation, and imposes these onto perception. This first antinomy arises because of the application of these intuitions to matter and time. There cannot have been an infinite regress of sequence, nor can there have been a beginning that was uncaused (such as God creating, but God is uncaused in his action—nothing outside God caused him, and nothing in him could have changed to make him create at one point rather than another). The 2nd antinomy undermines the principle of sufficient reason, and the fourth antinomy addresses the issue of necessary being.

Aquinas struggled with this same problem with respect to the creation of the world. He concluded that humans cannot know if the world was created or extends to eternity from reason alone, but must have special revelation to inform us on this point. Of course, trusting the content of special revelation raises the same problems—it makes claims that go beyond what is possibly experienced and therefore is the transcendental illusion. So we see that this has been a longstanding problem in philosophy—both of these thinkers claim to believe in God and yet both cannot see a way for reason to know God. But I think we can see that within Kant's

---

18. Kant, *Critique*, A297.

framework there is a key to finding inexcusability and even going a step further to defending reason as not only transcendental but also ontological.

8.11. RESPONDING TO KANT

The key is provided in the ideas that Kant says are part of our intuition and imposed on experience. The ideas of sequence, duration, and causation, are for Kant at the heart of the transcendental illusion. And yet they cannot simply be jettisoned because they are necessary to understand anything in experience, and Kant maintains that all knowledge is from experience.[19] These intuitions particularly apply to the idea of change; what changes has sequence, duration over time (through the sequence), and causation to explain the change. This means that we also have the intuition of changelessness to which these do not apply (if we have the intuition of *a*, we also have the intuition of *non-a*). Sequence does not apply to what is changeless—there is not one step after another as this would be change—what is changeless simply *is*. It might be thought that duration applies to what is changeless, and it does in that it simply *is*, but not duration in the sense meant above by Kant because that imports the idea of change over time—what endures as time passes. The changeless is not going through steps in time and therefore there is not this question of duration through time. Similarly, causation does not apply to the changeless as it does not have change, growth, or decline that would require causal explanation. Furthermore, what is changeless is also without beginning—it does not change from non-existent to existent—and therefore does not require a cause to explain its existence.

Thus, with the intuitions of sequence, duration, and causation (under the heading of "changeable") comes the intuition of what is changeless and eternal (without beginning). Perhaps these were not discussed by Kant in the above quotes because they cannot be applied to experience. Kant noted what is clear about experience—it is always changing, and it is experience of a world that is always changing. But here is where Kant's own framework provides a basis for his inexcusability.

In his fourth antinomy Kant considers the claim that the world is a necessary being, and the claim that the world was started by a necessary being, and believes that both have sound arguments in their favor, and sound arguments against the other, showing that reason cannot help

19. Kant, *Critique*, A1.

us in this matter. However, I believe that he gets into this difficulty due to an analysis of causation that is similar to that done by Sextus Empiricus (which we will consider in the next chapter). We need not think that causation applies to eternal being in the way that it applies to temporal being (one event after another), without giving up the idea of an eternal being causing a temporal sequence. This requires distinguishing between cause applying to the eternal being, and a temporal sequence caused by an eternal being. But Kant dismisses this discussion as beyond the powers of reason.

In a previous quote Kant spoke about the self and perceptions (and the distinction between the two) as a given. Because these are changing, the implication is that change is also a given. Here he is importing assumptions from his Western Philosophical Tradition about what is real and then dealing with the problems that those assumptions raise. But within World Philosophy, and even with the Western Tradition, it is not a given that change is a feature of the real. For instance, Parmenides and his disciple Zeno used paradoxes to argue that the idea of change always leads to contradictions and that what is real is without change. Since the world of experience is always changing, they concluded that it is an illusion. Philosophers in the Hindu and Buddhist traditions have made similar insights and developed this philosophy further. So why begin with changing experience and a changing self as givens? Here he is committing the transcendental illusion—he is claiming that among the things that exist, being in itself, there are changing selves and perceptions.

He commits this error because of a failure to apply his own method. He is offering a critique of pure reason, but what is he using to offer this critique? If his critique of pure reason is based on field research then he is notorious for his lack of such exposure. Furthermore, even someone with much wider experience than Kant could not come close to a universal conclusion about the nature of pure reason since experience can never give universals. Instead, his critique of pure reason is issued through the use of reason. Kant seeks to explain what are the necessary presuppositions to make sense of the self and empirical perception as objective. Norman Kempt Smith says:

> The ultimate ground of the possibility of consciousness and therefore also of empirical self-consciousness is the transcendental unity of apperception. Such apperception, to use Kant's ambiguous phraseology, precedes experience as its *a priori* condition. The interpretation of given appearances through *a priori* categories

is a necessity of consciousness because it is a condition of self-consciousness; and it is a condition of self-consciousness because it alone will account for the transcendental apperception upon which all empirical self-consciousness ultimately depends.[20]

8.12. THE ONTOLOGICAL ROLE OF REASON

Kant is self-consciously giving what he calls the *transcendental* use of reason—reason is authoritative and self-attesting; it cannot be questioned because it makes questioning possible. But what Kant fails to see, and what I want to argue for here, is that he falls into maintaining that reason is authoritative for human thinking, but not about being in itself because he fails to see that reason is ontological. Reason as transcendental alone is insufficient and cannot even support the conclusions Kant claims to make. Unless reason can also speak about being in itself, all claims about the self, perceptions, and whatever else, are examples of the *transcendental error*.

These are examples of the transcendental error because they move beyond making claims about experience to what that experience signifies, and this can never be experienced. Kant's fixed point is the desire to make knowledge possible—he is searching for the necessary presuppositions for knowledge. He maintains that the self and the objectivity of experience are two such presuppositions—they are givens. But other traditions have denied that there is a self as conceived of by Kant (consider the concept of *atman* in Hinduism), or have been willing to give up the possibility of knowledge (consider the striving for detachment in Zen). Kant is importing the idea of a self as a finite, temporal, changeable conscious being, noting that there is a difference between knowing and thinking one knows, and then within these confines asking what is necessary for knowledge. Kant insists that hypotheticals cannot get to existence, but here he is making such a move: If there is knowledge, what is necessary for this knowledge? But perhaps there is no knowledge, and perhaps there are not any of these prerequisites. These are examples of the transcendental error—they are presuppositions of Kant's that cannot be proven through experience but on which the rest of his system depends. Kant is inexcusable in identifying this error and then committing it at the very foundation of his system.

20. Smith, *A Commentary*, 250.

Kant's insistence that hypotheticals do not lead to existence, and his assumptions about the self and perception as given, and his search for the necessary foundation for knowledge, illustrate the need for presuppositional thinking. His position is: we must take as given that there is a world and a self with the faculty to understand because all knowledge presupposes this. This is unhelpful in many respects because just which view of the world and self are necessary for knowledge is not established by Kant, and indeed he imports views of each that are not clearly necessary for knowledge. What he should say is: if knowledge is to be had, then there must be a world to know and a self who can know. But then his own insight can be applied: this hypothetical does not tell us that there *is* knowledge, and therefore we cannot take as a given the *world* and the *self*. Consider this hypothetical: if either *none is eternal* or *some is eternal*, and it is not the case that *none is eternal*, then it must be the case that *some is eternal*. Here we have the hypothetical linking thoughts to what exists, but also the use of non-contradiction to rule out one of only two possibilities at the most basic level (the level of being).

Kant recognizes the authority of the law of non-contradiction, and that "the internally impossible is impossible in every respect."[21] Kant, like Hume, saw the problems in the claims of rationalism. And, like Hume, the impossibility of empiricism. But he did not want to end with the skepticism of Hume, where the purpose of philosophy becomes a negative work in checking claims to knowledge that go beyond what is possible for humans. Kant wants to provide a basis for positive claims about the world, and his solution is to look for the necessary presuppositions for knowledge claims. Taking this as his central insight and contribution, can this be applied further? Kant distinguished between being in itself and human understanding, and in many ways he was right about this. But at the most basic level, does this distinction hold up? It is often the case that a perception is mistaken, say about color or size. But can a perception be mistaken about the distinction between being and non-being?

And so what Kant's framework should give us is a pre-antinomy that he did not consider. That is, reason can be used to show that there is a world of change, and it can be used to show that there is no such world—it is an illusion. This is not to say that the material world exists in the mind, but that there is no world of change at all—material or ideal; change is an

---

21. Smith, *A Commentary*, 451.

illusion and what is real is changeless. Like Hume, Kant did not apply his own system far enough. But also like Hume, I think that there is a further step to be taken with Kant's system that will end up defending the claim that reason is transcendental. Using the insight from Hume, that what is contradictory is not possible, and applying this to Kant's framework, that what is contradictory cannot be imposed on experience and therefore cannot even rise to the level of the *transcendental illusion*, what is the outcome?

Kant refers to the laws of understanding. These laws distinguish between *a* and *non-a*, which is a formal distinction. Thus we have in the understanding the idea ("intuition" in that these ideas are immediate, not mediated through experience) of change and non-change (changelessness). But more basic than this idea is the idea of being and non-being. If there is any being that changes, and if there is any being that is changeless, either one is a being. Non-being is changeless in that there is nothing that changes, but there is not some being, called "nothing," that does not change. Therefore, our most basic idea, intuition, is that of being and non-being.

8.13. PRESUPPOSITIONAL THINKING

The process we have used here is "presuppositional thinking" to discover what is most basic. Enlightenment philosophers, including Kant, have tended to use the concept of "basic" or "basic belief" to refer to immediate beliefs. But the process I am using here indicates that immediate beliefs have presuppositions which are logically more basic. The most basic of which is the idea of being and non-being. Here is another step in showing Kant's inexcusability—he makes assumptions about being that his own framework does not allow, and this is because he did not think presuppositionally. In taking our experiences of change as real instances of the noumenal world imposed on our senses, rather than as illusions, he is making an assumption about being that he does not prove. But what can be known about being within Kant's system? We saw earlier that in Hume's system there can be no being from non-being. I think that in Kant's system we can arrive at that same conclusion for the same reasons, and go a step further to show that reason is ontological.

The basic ideas of being and non-being are presupposed by all other intuitions, judgments, and perceptions. The possibility for error comes in at the level of judgments and perceptions—Kant noted formal error due to fallacious thinking, and error due to importing subjective concerns. We have noted one of each in Kant thus far: it is a formal error to not notice the influence of logically basic beliefs on one's system and to draw conclusions that rest on unproven assumptions about what is logically basic; Kant's subjective influence about the reality of perception is such that he never considers the possibility that it is an illusion—not the possibility of idealism, but that perception itself is an illusion. But now we get to his most serious error: not applying his system far enough to see what is clear about God.

If we want to avoid the errors that Kant identifies, then we must be careful to identify the logically most basic ideas, and not make logical mistakes in how we form judgments and infer conclusions about these. And then we must not apply to experience what is impossible in experience. Avoiding the first kind of error requires us, in light of the previous discussion about Hume, to conclude that there cannot be being from non-being, and that if anything exists something has always existed. Avoiding the second kind of error requires taking this insight and carefully distinguishing between what is eternal and changeless, and what is temporal and changing—any blurring of these two, or mistaken identification, is inexcusable because it is clear that what is changeless is not changing (a is not non-a).

Could our ideas of the eternal and changeless be only perceptions that do not apply to reality? I maintain that at the most basic level, the level of being, this distinction cannot apply—both appearances and reality presuppose *being*. Clearly, perceptions are changing, and so to make such a claim is to go beyond what can be experienced. But what this indicates is that while there is the perception of change, there is also the idea of the eternal, and the problem is to understand how to relate these. The underlying challenge was to both avoid the overextension of reason committed by the rationalists, and yet to explain how to avoid the skepticism that follows empiricism. Kant's solution involved coming to understand that reason is transcendental: reason can be used to identify the necessary prerequisites for knowledge, and as such it is authoritative and self-attesting. Authoritative in that it is what makes thought possible, all other "authorities" presuppose thought and therefore presuppose reason. Self-attesting in that it cannot be questioned because it makes questioning possible. Kant seeks to give a critique of pure reason, and the tool he uses to do so is reason. There could be second, and third, and fourth critiques, all of which would be examples of using reason.[22]

8.14. THE ERROR OF KANT'S SOLUTION AND THE RESPONSE

But this insight from Kant did not solve the problem. Indeed, it made things worse. Now humans were cut off from being in itself, and could only speak of phenomena and the structuring of the human mind on perceptions. The solution comes in noticing that reason is *ontological*—reason applies to being as well as thought. This was identified above in noting that *being* is presupposed by all of Kant's categories, as well as everything else he speaks of. Thinking is about being. Thinking is the activity of a being, as well as about being. This is not to say that one can think something into being. Rather, it is to say that what is contrary to the laws of thought is contrary to both *thinking* and *being*. There are no square-circles or uncaused events. Attempts to show there are amount to attempts to show that these are not contrary to reason, which is to concede the point that reason is ontological. If it did not matter that they are contrary to reason, then there would be no incentive to show that they are free of contradiction.

Thus, in thinking about being we are thinking about the most basic concept. And through our discussion above we came to see that we have the concept of temporal, changing being, and the concept of eternal, changeless being. The first use of reason as ontological is to see that there must be something eternal. The alternative leads to a contradiction that undermines reason and makes being unintelligible. This does not commit the ontological mistakes that Kant identifies—it does not argue that existence is a great making property, nor does it argue from thinking to existing directly (the two reasons Kant rejects the ontological argument). Instead, it is an argument to the existence of eternal being by *identifying* the logically most basic beliefs, then *demonstrating* the impossibility of the contradiction, and the necessity of the conclusion for being as well as thought. This level of critical use of reason is unlike any other—all other levels of thinking, and all other objects of thought, presuppose *being* and so this is truly the most basic and unique. Furthermore, it is consistent with the claim that for all matters of fact the opposite is possible in that

---

22. For a more in-depth discussion of *reason* see Surrendra Gangadean's *Philosophical Foundation: A Critical Analysis of Basic Beliefs.*

all matters of fact *presuppose being*. Basic claims about being are, in a sense, matters of fact, but they are also the necessary presuppositions for all other matters of fact. This is precisely what Kant wanted to identify, and yet he missed it, and in so doing missed the opportunity to solve the problem that awoke him from his dogmatic (rationalist) slumbers.

Kant could have, and should have, seen this, and his critical philosophy is the very method that can lead to it—and yet he did not do so. Hume and Kant offered important challenges that should encourage theists to go further in their thinking about the clarity of God's existence and the goal of knowing God. And yet Hume and Kant themselves did not do this, and held positions for which there is no excuse. Their own views are inconsistent, were not lived consistently, and neither Hume nor Kant came to see what is clear to reason.

8.15. CONCLUSION: THINKING ABOUT BEING OR SILENCE

In order to better understand the claim that reason is ontological, I want to consider many other attempts to justify uncaused events. This will help demonstrate how reason is ontological in showing how each attempt ends in the abandonment of reason and the possibility of knowing. Kant said that we must begin with the givens of a world and the faculty of understanding the world.[23] The alternative is that there is no world (no being), and therefore nothing to think about (nothing to understand). Or that there is a world, but we do not have the faculty to understand it. Either way ends in silence.

---

23. Smith, *A Commentary*, 453.

9

Historical Overview of Being from Non-Being

The ontological function of reason says that reason applies to being as well as thought. This means that if uncaused events are contrary to reason, then they are also contrary to being and cannot "be." What has been said about uncaused events, and how have philosophers and scientists who maintain that there are uncaused events defended this position? Does skepticism require believing that uncaused events are possible? In this chapter we will consider the influential thinkers who have held to the possibility of uncaused events, and argue that in each case reason can be used to show that uncaused events are impossible. If reason is ontological, and uncaused events are impossible, then it follows that there must have existed something from eternity, which is the first step in showing that God exists.

I F IT IS CLEAR that there are no uncaused events because there is no being from non-being, then humans as rational beings are responsible to know this. If the implication of this is that there has existed something from eternity (something is eternal), then humans are also responsible for knowing this. Noted philosophers have played with the idea of uncaused events. These range from thinkers such as Sextus Empiricus to Quentin Smith and Allan Guth. Ancient skepticism is based on the distinction between appearance and reality. Modern skepticism also uses this distinction. How can we know that what appears to be is truly the case? How can we know if there really is causation, or there only appears to be causation? At the basic level claims about being and non-being, and something being eternal, transcend the difference between appearance and reality.

Skepticism comes in various forms and with numerous nuances. However, what is relevant for our purposes is when its claim that we cannot know is extended to include causation. If we cannot know whether or not there are uncaused events, then this implies that uncaused events are possible. An important source of skepticism is empiricism. Because empiricism limits knowledge to what can be experienced, universal claims such as "there are no uncaused events" are outside the possibility of knowledge. Skepticism which results from empiricism is often a response to overextended rationalism. This form of rationalism, sometimes called dogmatism, attempts to deduce all knowledge from reason alone. This is rejected by empiricists and skeptics and it is insisted that reason only leads to contradictions and so appearance should be trusted. Empiricism leaves open the door of possibility for uncaused events, and therefore it leaves open the possibility that nothing is clear.

9.1. SEXTUS EMPIRICUS

Sextus Empiricus raised questions about our ability to know causes by pointing out difficulties in causal theory. These are not unlike the paradoxes raised by Zeno about motion. They serve the same purpose: The use of reason to understand the world only ends in contradictions. Three problems with causation are: The "contiguity objection," the "regress objection," and the "demand for a causal mechanism."[1] The first two are like Zeno's paradoxes in that they analyze change in terms of infinite numbers of points. In the continuity objection, it is stated that for A to be the direct cause of B, there must be no time between A and B. However, time is dense, and so between any two points there are an infinite number of other points. Or, in the regress objection, for A to cause B the end of A affects the beginning of B. But for the end of A to be caused it must be affected by the middle of A. And for the middle of A to be caused it must be affected by a prior point in A, etc. Because this is infinitely analyzable, we never get to a point where we can say A caused B. A must go through an infinite number of causes before it can get to B. The conclusion from these is that the idea of causation is paradoxical, unknowable.

These problems are skeptical issues concerning the nature and description of change. Zeno gave paradoxes to show that motion and change are impossible. Sextus Empiricus discusses physical change and shows its impossibility.[2] He extends these sorts of problems into change

1. Chakravartty, "Causal," 10.
2. Sextus, *Scepticism*, 116.

and becoming, place and the void, and time.[3] Clearly, the issue here is with knowledge itself, and the supposed objects of knowledge. By showing that descriptions of reality, change, becoming, and time are incoherent he is showing that knowledge is not possible. All attempts to describe the world end in these kinds of problems, the "self-conceit and rashness of the dogmatists."[4] *Causality* is a necessary part of the *intelligibility of anything*; once this is given up, global skepticism is the consistent alternative.

The third problem deals with the causal mechanism. What is the mechanism that brings about change? Any suggested mechanism can be further analyzed until one gets to a simple cause. But what can be said about a simple cause? If we can say nothing about simple causes then we may as well postulate that nothing is the cause. Yet this is a mistake because it confuses epistemological and metaphysical categories ("unknown" and "nothing"). We tend to explain complex causes by breaking them into their smaller causal units. If this can be done indefinitely, then we are not actually explaining causation. This is true for simple causes between material objects, but also between material and non-material objects, such as the mind and brain. The present concern is not to identify the mechanism of causation itself but to argue that there are no uncaused events and no being from non-being. That there is causation can be known even if the mechanism is unknown.

Sextus Empiricus also rejects the idea that all things are caused and permits the possibility that no things are caused.[5] He recognizes the self-referential absurdity of denying causation:

> Whoever declares that there is no cause is even refuting himself. For if he asserts that his declaration is made absolutely and without any cause, he will be disbelieved. But if he says there is some cause for his assertion, he is positing cause in his wish to abolish it, since he is giving us a cause why cause does not exist.[6]

But his approach is to also affirm the opposite, in order to move his audience to suspend belief. "It is also plausible to say that nothing is a cause of anything."[7] He does this by showing the entire notion of cause

3. Sextus, *Scepticism*, 118–128.
4. Ibid., 128.
5. Ibid., 113.
6. Ibid.
7. Ibid.

is incoherent and therefore we are "unable to declare that anything is the cause of anything."[8]

The implication of this skepticism about causation is that causation is paradoxical, cannot be known, and therefore uncaused events are possible. But, working the other way, we can argue that if uncaused events are impossible, then causation can be understood and is not paradoxical. Both approaches use the same principle: what is self-contradictory is unknowable. And both consistently affirm that if there are uncaused events, if causation is paradoxical, then there can be no knowledge about reality. Where there is no knowledge nothing can or should be said. Skeptics like Sextus Empiricus are consistent on this point in their move to silence, and contemporary persons who wish to posit uncaused events should also be consistent by moving to silence.

If causation is paradoxical then knowledge claims about reality should be abandoned. However, the paradoxes given by Sextus Empiricus and Zeno are based on the assumption that space can be divided into an infinity of points. This requires that these points have no size. However, if they have no size, then they cannot be added together to form objects and distances that do have size. The implication is that these paradoxes rest on a false assumption and causation (and motion in Zeno's case) is not paradoxical. This does not address the mechanism of causation, but it does offer a principle for doing so. If all causes are complex causes and can be broken into other causes, then the implication is an infinite regress similar to the first two paradoxes. On the other hand, if this infinite regress is to be avoided, then it must not be the case that all causes are complex; instead there must be simple causes which cannot be further divided for explanation. In a simple cause, A simply causes B. There is no further explanation, and the search for a causal mechanism must be understood in light of this. Even so, a causal mechanism need not be known to affirm the reality of causation. To say that this is the same as affirming no cause is to confuse the epistemological and metaphysical categories.

9.2. LEIBNIZ AND OCCASIONALISM

Occasionalism shifts causation from the creation to God.[9] This need not be an absolute denial of causation, but can come in degrees, such as deny-

8. Sextus, *Scepticism*, 114.
9. Clatterbaugh, *The Causation*, 97.

ing causation to bodies while granting it to minds.[10] "For the occasional-ist, God's will acts directly on the world to produce change and motion."[11] This view affirms the necessity of causation and is an attempt to explain the mechanism of causation in relation to certain presuppositions. However, it is relevant for our discussion because it raises questions about appearance and reality: What appears to be the cause is not the cause. This could be altered slightly to say "while there appears to be a cause there is no cause." This is ineffective for reasons to be discussed in a moment.

One attempt to avoid the need for a causal mechanism is Leibniz's "pre-established harmony":

> The Cartesians themselves admit that the soul cannot give any new force to matter, but they claim that it can give a new determina-tion—i.e. direction—to the force which the matter has already. I on the other hand maintain that souls can make no change in the force or in the direction of bodies, that one of these would be as inconceivable and irrational as the other, and that to explain the union of soul and body we must avail ourselves of the pre-estab-lished harmony.[12]

This view of pre-established harmony can lead to the claim that there are uncaused events, and to avoid this God is appealed to as the source of causation, a view called "Occasionalism." To avoid the problems faced by Descartes between the mind and brain, Leibniz posited that what we think is causation is really only the appearance of causation:

> Both Spinoza and Leibniz deny that there is any causal interaction between mind and body or between bodies and minds. Spinoza explains the correlation between mind and body by means of a dual aspect theory, wherein a mental state and a physical state are simply two aspects of one and the same reality. For Leibniz, mind and body are related by the pre-established harmony.[13]

Both Spinoza and Leibniz are responding to the failure to give a mecha-nism for cause, as in the case of the mind and brain. In Spinoza, the prob-lem is avoided by positing monism—the mind and the brain are the same substance. For Leibniz, God established what appears to be causation.

10. Clatterbaugh, *The Causation,* 97.

11. Ibid., 97.

12. Leibniz, *New Essays,* 224.

13. Clatterbaugh, *The Causation,*132.

Neither is a denial of causality nor an affirmation of uncaused events. Both are more a debate about causal mechanism which is a different debate than being from non-being.

That there is only appearance and not causation can be the result of relying on empiricism, since no thinker claims that cause itself can be seen. As we saw in our discussion of Hume above, experience gives distinct sense impressions that we put together and call this "causation." Empiricism gives only appearance, not reality. This leads to skepticism about causation. The distinction between appearance and reality does not apply to being and non-being. Both *appearance* and *reality* are being, and so it can neither appear that there is being from non-being nor be so in reality. *Does being only come from being in appearance alone or also in reality?* is a pseudo-problem. Occasionalism does not work when applied to being from non-being: There is no appearance of causation or harmony between these. To say: "non-being did not cause being; there is simply the appearance of causation between them" is to say "there is no cause for being." This is exactly the problem. There is no being that is the cause, and to have no cause for being is to say being came from non-being.

It is also worth noting that Leibniz formulated the "principle of sufficient reason." He says that God "does nothing without harmony and reason."[14] Kant's second antinomy addresses the principle of sufficient reason to show that it is not necessary. Indeed, it begs the question—what *must* be proven is that there are no uncaused events in order to support the claim that there must be a sufficient reason. Skeptics will not accept the conclusion that there are no uncaused events simply because the principle of sufficient reason has been invoked—they will require that it be proven that a sufficient reason (a cause) is necessary. Numerous modifications have been given to this principle to try and make it acceptable to all, but skeptics continue to argue that these modifications beg the question.[15] More basic, and required by the principle of sufficient reason, is the claim that there is no being from non-being—if there is being from non-being then this principle cannot stand. It is also worth noting that Leibniz affirms that: "if there had ever been nothing, there would always have been nothing, since a being cannot be produced by nothing."[16] This is what is at

---

14. Leibniz, *New Essays*, 56.
15. Gale and Alexander, "A Response," 89.
16. Leibniz, *New Essays*, 436.

stake in the discussion about uncaused events: Is it clear that there must have existed something from eternity?

9.3. DAVID HUME

In the modern world, the person most identified with undermining the idea of causation is David Hume. He is said to have reduced causation and causal laws to phenomenal regularities.[17] As a skeptic, Hume rejected prior rationalist and empiricist attempts to explain causation. Instead he focuses on causation as constant conjunction in experience. This definition still involves a kind of empiricism, but it focuses on human explanation and understanding. Hume's approach could be extended to apply to being from non-being. It might be argued that in our experience being always comes from being, but our experience is not infinite, and so there might be, in some part of the universe, being from non-being. That is, being from non-being is possible.

Hume considers the claim "whatever begins to exist, must have a cause" and rejects that it is a necessary truth:

> Tis suppos'd to be founded on intuition, and to be one of those maxims, which tho' they may be deny'd with the lips, 'tis impossible for men in their hearts really to doubt of. But if we examine this maxim by the idea of knowledge above-explain'd, we shall discover in it no mark of any such intuitive certainty; but on the contrary shall find, that 'tis of a nature quite foreign to that species of conviction.[18]

This is because all certainty about any subject is a result of comparing ideas, and "from the discovery of such relations as are unalterable, so long as the ideas continue to remain the same."[19] But in the comparison of ideas, only resemblance, proportions in quantity and number, degrees of a quality, and contrariety are found, and not anything to do with the claim that what begins to exist must have a cause.[20] This claim is therefore not intuitively certain, which means it is possibly false. It is possible that being can come from non-being.

---

17. Sankey, *Causation*, xi.
18. Hume, *Treatise*, 79.
19. Ibid., 79.
20. Ibid., 79.

Hume's argument is straightforward and devastating: The necessity for a cause requires that it is true that everything which comes to exist must have a cause; that the latter claim is not certain can be proven by our ability to conceive of an object not existing one moment, and then existing the next, without conjoining to it the distinct idea of cause or productive principle.[21] "The separation, therefore, of the idea of cause from that of a beginning of existence, is plainly possible for the imagination."[22] The necessity of connection between cause and effect is a requirement of the mind rather than an aspect of reality. "Hume himself believed that we do have an immediate experience of necessity as the propensity of the mind to pass naturally from idea of a cause to idea of an effect. This would be an example of psychological regularity."[23]

Hume rejects Locke's argument, quoted earlier, that if there is no cause then nothing is the cause, and nothing cannot be a cause. This, Hume says, makes the mistake of supposing that in denying any cause Hume is still positing a cause, and therefore nothing must be the cause.[24] "Tis sufficient only to observe, that when we exclude all causes we really do exclude them, and neither suppose nothing nor the object itself to be the causes of the existence; and consequently can draw no argument from the absurdity of these suppositions to prove the absurdity of that exclusion."[25] What Hume is rejecting is that there is a cause. He is arguing that the claims "no cause" and "nothing is the cause" are different.

Is it true that cause and effect can be isolated in the mind? Sextus Empiricus argued that they cannot, and used this to undermine our ability to know about causation. He argued that they are so interconnected that they cannot be defined separately, and therefore to know the cause one must know the effect, but to know the effect one must know the cause, and therefore one knows neither.[26] Here we have skeptic against skeptic. Both can be wrong. Sextus Empiricus has already been considered. If a response to Hume is to be found, it must be in questioning his assump-

21. Hume, *Treatise*, 79.
22. Ibid., 80.
23. Smart, in Sankey, 163.
24. Hume, *Treatise*, 80.
25. Ibid., 81.
26. Sextus, *Scepticism*, 114.

tions about *a priori* knowledge and the ability to imagine cause and effect separately from the idea of change.

Hume's analysis is based on the appearance/reality distinction: It appears that there is causation, but this appearance can be explained as a mental product rather than a feature of reality. But can being from non-being be a mental product? To be a mental product requires that it is meaningful. "Being from non-being" is equivalent to "being from neither *a* nor *non-a*," which is meaningless. It is true that we can isolate any given events from prior or posterior events as long as we do not think of the event as an instance of change. But if it is a change from one being, state, relation, etc., to another, then event coupled with the change requires the idea of causation. To deny this is to claim that there can be being from non-being and to lose all intelligibility. In chapter 8 we saw why this is, and the necessity of affirming both the transcendental and the ontological functions of reason. Hume's analysis is insufficient, but it lays the groundwork for subsequent centuries of thinking about causation. It perpetuates skepticism which has at its core the appearance/reality distinction.

9.4. IMMANUEL KANT

This approach to causation (arguing from our experience) is reflected in most subsequent thought on the subject. "Kant, we must bear in mind, accepts much of Hume's criticism of the category of causality. The general principle that every event must have an antecedent cause is, Kant recognizes, neither intuitively certain nor demonstrable by general reasoning from more ultimate truths."[27] Kant's response to Hume is an attempt to justify causation as more than an inference from experience. Causation is part of the framework of the mind by which sense experience of the noumenal world is organized into the recognizable phenomena. It is *a priori*, not inferred from experience. But it is also synthetic, as opposed to analytic, because it is not just about the meaning of words but gives information. It is part of the structure of the human mind.

"For the *Critique of Pure Reason*, the first controversy in the history of philosophy concerns appearance and reality: Are ideas or experience the final court of appeal?"[28] In this *Critique*, Kant's purpose is to explain the limits of pure reason. One way he does this is by distinguishing be-

27. Smith, *Commentary*, 364.
28. Neiman, *Evil*, 11.

tween the phenomenal and the noumenal realms. "We have seen that everything which the understanding derives from itself is, though not borrowed from experience, at the disposal of the understanding solely for use in experience."[29] This means that "the sensibility (and its field, that of appearances) is itself limited by the understanding in such fashion that it does not have to do with things in themselves but only with the mode in which, owing to our subjective constitution, they appear."[30] But if causation is only known empirically then it cannot be a universal rule, nor can the effect be said to follow necessarily from the cause.[31] "It must either be grounded completely *a priori* in the understanding, or must be entirely given up as a mere phantom of the brain."[32] For Kant, causation is a necessary requirement for any experience:

> If, then, we experience that something happens, we in so doing always presuppose that something precedes it, on which it follows according to a rule. Otherwise I should not say of the object that it follows. For mere succession in my apprehension, if there be no rule determining the succession in relation to something that precedes, does not justify me in assuming any succession in the object . . . The experience of an event [*i.e.* of anything as *happening*] is itself only possible on this assumption.[33]

This rules out being from non-being (a being preceded by nothing), but Kant's solution leaves open the possibility of uncaused events and being from non-being in the noumenal realm. He makes absolute the distinction between appearance and reality in a way that rules out being from non-being in appearance, and uncaused events in appearance, but allows their possibility in reality (the noumenal realm). That this reality is beyond our reach and therefore cannot be spoken of does not stop Kant from speaking about it.

Kant's explanation leaves open the possibility of uncaused events and therefore skepticism. First, there is the noumenal realm (being in itself). In this realm causation does not apply, because causation is part of the framework of the human mind and not part of mind-indepen-

29. Kant, *Critique*, B296.
30. Ibid., A251.
31. Ibid., B124.
32. Ibid., A91.
33. Ibid., A195.

dent reality. Second, while in some sense the noumenal is responsible for the phenomenal, the noumenal cannot be said to *cause* the phenomenal without *violating* the claim that causation is part of the human mind and not part of being in itself. A critic of Kant could use these two points as reasons for rejecting his system. The majority of philosophers after Kant have adopted his approach (it is deeply embedded in both continental and analytic philosophy, although in different ways). For this reason both have had strong skeptical attitudes about the possibility of knowledge in metaphysics and about being in itself. Causation is universal because every time the human mind experiences something it does so through its categories, one of which is causation. But this leaves us in skepticism about reality.

For Kant an important area in which to keep out causation is the freedom of the will. He attempts to preserve both causality and freedom in his distinction of the phenomena and noumena:

> The principle of causality therefore applies only to things taken in the former sense, namely, in so far as they are objects of experience—these same objects, taken in the other sense, not being subject to the principle—then there is no contradiction in supposing that one and the same will is, in the appearance, that is, in its visible acts, necessarily subject to the law of nature, and so far *not free*, while yet, as belong to a thing in itself, it is not subject to that law, and is therefore *free*.[34]

Besides his empirical assumptions, Kant is also a libertarian; he believes that freedom and determination are incompatible. "Freedom in the practical sense is the will's independence of coercion through sensuous impulses"[35] and the power to begin a series of events.[36] He preserves freedom by locating it in the noumenal realm where causation does not apply: "The effect may be regarded as free in respect to its intelligible cause, and at the same time in respect of appearances as resulting from them according to the necessity of nature."[37] Morality assumes that there is a difference between *is* and *ought*:

---

34. Kant, *Critique*, Bxxvii.
35. Ibid., A534.
36. Ibid., A533.
37. Ibid., A537.

That its cause, [as found] in the [field of] appearance, is not, therefore, so determining that it excludes a causality of our will—a causality which, independently of those natural causes, and even contrary to their force and influence, can produce something that is determined in the time-order in accordance with empirical laws, and which can therefore begin a series of events *entirely of itself.*"[38]

Freedom cannot be determined by any experience.[39] And yet in this very description and attempted solution there is the claim that the noumenal *causes* a series of events in the phenomenal world. This causal relationship between the noumenal and phenomenal realms is contrary to Kant's claim that the noumenal cannot be known and the *a priori* categories do not apply to it:

The possibility of freedom transcends our powers of comprehension. The proof that it can at least be conceived without contradiction is, however, all-important. For otherwise no arguments from the nature of the moral consciousness could be of the least avail … By means of the Critical distinction between the empirical and the supersensible worlds, *these conceptions are now for the first time rendered possible of belief.*[40]

Kant's view of freedom is based on the claims that one is free if one is not coerced and if one could have done otherwise. This has come to be called the principle of alternative possibilities (PAP). An alternative to PAP is to affirm that freedom is compatible with causation: I am free when I act according to my will, or I am free when my actions are caused by my wants. If PAP requires uncaused events, then which one should be abandoned: PAP or causation?

9.5. WILLIAM JAMES

Where a person has libertarian presuppositions they may be psychologically inclined toward uncaused events. This will be impossible to overcome apart from addressing the presupposition of libertarianism. For instance, William James said:

The principle of causality, for example: what is it but a postulate, an empty name covering simply a demand that the sequence of

38. Kant, *Critique,* A534.
39. Ibid., A533.
40. Smith, *Commentary,* 21.

events shall some day manifest a deeper kind of belonging of one thing with another than the mere arbitrary juxtaposition which now phenomenally appears? It is as much an altar to an unknown god as the one that Saint Paul found at Athens. All our scientific and philosophic ideals are altars to unknown gods. Uniformity is as much so as is free will. If this be admitted, we can debate on even terms. But if anyone pretends that while freedom and variety are, in the first instance, subjective demands, necessity and uniformity are something altogether different, I do not see how we can debate at all.[41]

Can causality be given up and freedom preserved? Are these incompatible? James defines "freedom" as having alternative possibilities (PAP).[42] "The indeterminists say another volition might have occurred in its place."[43] James holds that there are alternative possibilities because there is no guarantee of what will happen; events may fall out one way or another, and once they have happened they still might have happened otherwise.[44] All this is to say that there could be uncaused events (or must be for freedom), and that it is possible that being can come from non-being.

The kinds of alternative possibilities James focuses on are not basic possibilities. They include the path one takes on the way home, and heinous actions like murder. Basic possibilities involve basic actions, such as believing (basic in the sense of being presupposed by other actions like choosing a path to walk). Choice assumes thought. Freedom at less basic levels presupposes freedom at the basic level. Are we free to believe what we want? When I believe something to be true (say, "there are no uncaused events"), is it possible that I could have believed the alternative ("there are uncaused events")? The response is "yes, if I had failed to use reason." Freedom at the basic level therefore becomes: Am I free to use reason in thinking critically about basic beliefs?

James rejects the idea that you are free if, from eternity, it has been impossible for you to walk home by a path other than the one you actually walk home on.[45] Or, at the basic level, if from eternity it was predetermined that I would not use reason in selecting what to believe. But this

---

41. James, *The Dilemma of Determinism*, 2.
42. Ibid., 3.
43. Ibid., 4.
44. Ibid., 6.
45. Ibid., 7.

view of freedom need not be contrary to causation, and if uncaused events are postulated then it seems freedom is undone. Granting that there are alternative possibilities, freedom can only be preserved if it is related to what a person wants. I could have chosen a different path home, if I had wanted to. For me to have wanted to I would have had to go through a different thought process for the choice. And I could have done this, if I had wanted to. To posit that at some point there must be a volition that is not caused by my wants is to deny that volition is mine. To posit that my wants must be uncaused is to detach them from my deliberation process. To posit that this must be uncaused is to disconnect it from my willingness to be thoughtful and use reason. This willingness is fundamental and essential to who I am; to posit that it must be uncaused is to assert that I myself must be uncaused—I must be a *being* from *non-being*. I want my action to be caused by my wants, I don't want there to be uncaused events because this will interfere with getting what I want—I may decide to act to choose but be interrupted by an uncaused event. Agent causation seeks to solve this by allowing causation between wants and actions, but positing an uncaused agent. This only moves the problem back one step—if as an agent I am uncaused, what is to guarantee continuity of my being and the relevant causal relationship?

James recognizes that the issue, while having significant psychological facets, is at its root metaphysical.[46] To arrive at this point he considers the idea of regret.

> Hardly any one can remain *entirely* optimistic after reading the confession of the murderer at Brockton the other day: how, to get rid of the wife whose continued existence bored him, he inveigled her into a desert spot, shot her four times, and then, as she lay on the ground and said to him, 'You didn't do it on purpose, did you, dear?' replied, 'No, I didn't do it on purpose,' as he raised a rock and smashed her skull. Such an occurrence, with the mild sentence and self-satisfaction of the prisoner, is a field for a crop of regrets.[47]

His dilemma is: "Are we stubbornly to stick to our judgment of regret, and say, though it *couldn't* be, yet it *would* have been a better universe with something different from this Brockton murder in it?"[48] We either give

---

46. James, *The Dilemma of Determinism*, 8.
47. Ibid., 10.
48. Ibid.

up determinism or give up regrets and give approval to everything that comes to pass:

> What interest, zest, or excitement can there be in achieving the right way, unless we are enabled to feel that the wrong way is also a possible and natural way—nay, more, a menacing and an imminent way? And what sense can there be in condemning ourselves for taking the wrong way, unless we need have done nothing of the sort, unless the right way was open to us as well?[49]

James dismisses metaphysical views that he calls "monism" because they require a subjectivism about good and evil. Such views say there is not actually good or evil but only what we call good and evil. He also considers the claim that his view of free will is incompatible with Divine Providence.

> The belief in free will is not in the least incompatible with the belief in Providence, provided you do not restrict the Providence to fulminating nothing but *fatal* de[c]rees. If you allow him to provide possibilities as well as actualities to the universe, and to carry on his own thinking in those two categories just as we do ours, chances may be there, uncontrolled even by him, and the course of the universe be really ambiguous; and yet the end of all things may be just what he intended it to be from all eternity.[50]

To illustrate this he uses the example of an expert and a novice playing chess.[51] It is known from the beginning who will win, but not the exact path the game will take. "Let now the novice stand for us finite free agents, and the expert for the infinite mind in which the universe lies."[52] The problem with this analogy is that in it the expert, or the infinite mind, is not the originator of the being of the novice, or finite mind. If God brought into being the finite agent, then this includes having brought into being that person as either being *willing* or *not willing* to use reason. And it includes the continued work of God in that person's life to either change him from one state to the other, or to continue him in existence in his state of willingness or unwillingness. The entire debate then comes down to this: Does freedom require that my self/being be uncaused (from non-being)?

49. James, *The Dilemma of Determinism*, 18.
50. Ibid., 21.
51. Ibid., 22.
52. Ibid.

Obviously there are metaphysical issues that must be resolved in order to proceed: Does God exist as creator *ex nihilo* or is "all one"? Is there a self or is the mind the brain? But another psychological block can be removed here in a way relevant to considering clarity about being from non-being. The hesitancy to allow causation in free will is rooted in the *ought/can principle*. If one ought to do something then one must be able to do it, but determinacy seems to deny this. This principle can be affirmed and causation upheld by introducing the concept of "wants." This could be named the *ought/can/want principle*. If one ought to do something then one must be able to do it, and to be able to do it one must want to do it. My want is the cause of what I do, and I am responsible for my want. The source of the want becomes irrelevant as long as it is my want; scenarios where I am given a want by an evil demon or mad scientist presuppose that I can distinguish those instances from times when it really is my want, and that when I find out about the source of my wants (an evil demon) I would no longer have that want. But it is not clear that I would abandon my want just because I find out about its origin in this way, perhaps I will continue to have the want in question.

There is significant literature about free will and causation, and much of this is theological. However, it can be reduced to the question about the origin of the self and being from non-being. The use of uncaused events (and all other nuances such as "insufficiently caused," "indeterministically caused," etc.) does not help in matters of the will. If my action was un-caused, then it was not caused by me and I cannot be held responsible. If my action was caused by me but I am uncaused, then what is the source of change in me? If change occurs without cause, then it is *being* from *non-being*. The concern about ultimate causes of my want assumes I would change my want if I were not so caused.

9.6. JOHN STUART MILL

John Stuart Mill affirms the universality of causation, and yet his empiricism allows for the possibility of uncaused events. "The truth that every fact which has a beginning has a cause, is co-extensive with human experience."[53] Mill notes that the idea of cause is essential for any theory of induction.[54] In doing this he is affirming that no experience is intelligible

53. Mill, *A System*, 212.
54. Ibid., 213.

apart from causation; if the skeptic wishes to hold that there is no causation, then consistency requires a move to silence.

Mill's empiricism requires him to focus on defining causation in terms of what can be experienced.

> The Law of Causation, the recognition of which is the main pillar of inductive science, is but the familiar truth that invariability of succession is found by observation to obtain between every fact in nature and some other fact which has preceded it, independently of all considerations respecting the ultimate mode of production of phenomena, and of every other question regarding the nature of 'Things in themselves.'[55]

Here again is the theme of appearance and reality. Mill argues correctly that without causation what appears to us in experience is unintelligible. For every consequent there must be an antecedent, or antecedents, that precede it,[56] and for it to be the cause this antecedent must invariably and unconditionally precede it.[57] From the necessity of causation Mill argues to the claim that for every fact that has a beginning something preceded it.[58] But by leaving aside questions regarding the nature of things in themselves, or reality, there is the possibility that causation does not really apply and there are uncaused events.

Mill's theory of the law of causation is based on his empiricism. The problem arises in trying to distinguish between the experience of something that was caused and something that was uncaused. Later empiricists, like Russell, will allow that the law may not be universal. From experience it cannot be determined if a consequent follows invariably and unconditionally from the antecedent which preceded it. The empirical approach shaped the twentieth century and much thinking about uncaused events.

9.7. BERTRAND RUSSELL AND ANALYTIC PHILOSOPHY

Mill's influence on Russell is pronounced, and allowed the latter to question the law of causation. Russell is relevant because he stands at the head of the analytic tradition, which has been unable to rule out the possibility of uncaused events or being from non-being. Russell's limits to human

55. Mill, *A System*, 213.
56. Ibid., 213.
57. Ibid., 222.
58. Ibid., 213.

knowledge are empirical. This leads him to reduce causation to induction, and therefore deny the universality of the law of causation:

> 'If, in a great number of instances, a thing of a certain kind is associated in a certain way with a thing of a certain other kind, it is probable that a thing of the one kind is always similarly associated with a thing of the other kind; and as the number of instances increase, the probability approaches indefinitely near certainty.' It may be well questioned whether this proposition is true; but if we admit it, we can infer that any characteristic of the whole of the observed past is likely to apply to the future and to the unobserved past. This proposition, therefore, if it is true, will warrant the inference that causal laws probably hold at all times, future as well as past; but without this principle [the principle of induction], the observed cases of the truth of causal laws afford no presumption as to the unobserved cases, and therefore the existence of a thing not directly observed can never be validly inferred.[59]

Knowing the particular cause of a particular event is not the same as knowing that being cannot come from non-being. Russell's definition of cause roots him in the empirical camp and brings with it all the difficulties attending that viewpoint.[60] *Being* from *non-being* cannot be proven or disproven empirically. For the empiricist it remains a possibility.

Russell maintained that while it appears that the claim "there are no uncaused events" looks simple, it is in reality very complicated and can only be defended by grounding it in the principle of induction.[61] The empirical approach has already been discussed, but another aspect of analytic philosophy that contributes to its willingness to allow the possibility of uncaused events is its attempt to analyze and reduce all claims to their truth value. As was noted earlier, the claim "being from non-being" is not a formal contradiction as its stands, and so analytic philosophy has denied that it is known to be false *a priori*.[62] This approach ends in skepticism because the truth value of propositions cannot be determined apart from knowing what they mean. If "being from non-being" means "being from neither *a* nor *non-a*." What does this mean? Meaning is more basic than truth; meaning must be known before truth value can be assigned.

59. Russell, *Our Knowledge*, 225.
60. Ibid., 229.
61. Ibid., 226.
62. Ibid.

If "being from non-being" is analyzed for meaning it will be seen to be meaningless; it does not even rise to the level of "true" or "false."

9.8. ALAN GUTH, QUENTIN SMITH, AND QUANTUM PHYSICS

Alan Guth is known for his claim that the universe came into being from absolutely nothing. Guth has said: "Conceivably, *everything* can be created from nothing. And 'everything' might include a lot more than what we can see. In the context of inflationary cosmology, it is fair to say that the universe is the ultimate free lunch."[63] Upon closer inspection, "absolutely nothing" is not really nothing, but is a false vacuum, or quantum foam. These are not absolutely nothing, but are something. Whether or not his theory is true, or the ideas of a false vacuum and quantum foam make sense upon analysis, his claim that the universe came from absolutely nothing is misleading. It is not an instance of *being* from *non-being*, but *being* from *unmanifest being*. What is impressive about Guth is that he notices that there are only three options in explaining the universe: "the universe is eternal, or that it was created by some force that worked outside the restrictions of physical laws,"[64] or, as he concludes later, that there was an uncaused event. But even Guth does not actually believe that being comes from non-being. Stephen Hawking clarifies Guth's position:

> What we think of as 'empty' space cannot be completely empty because that would mean that all the fields, such as the gravitational and electromagnetic fields, would have to be exactly zero. However, the value of a field and its rate of change with time are like the position and velocity of a particle: the uncertainty principle implies that the more accurately one knows one of these quantities, the less accurately one can know the other. So in empty space it would have both a precise value (zero) and a precise rate of change (also zero). There must be a certain minimum amount of uncertainty, or quantum fluctuations, in the value or the field.[65]

Quentin Smith has used the quantum theories of physicists like Guth and Hawking to argue that the origin of the universe could have no cause, and that this disproves the existence of God. "There is sufficient

63. Guth, *The Inflationary Universe*, 15.
64. Ibid., 9.
65. Hawking, *A Brief*, 105.

evidence at present to warrant the conclusion that the universe probably began to exist over ten billion years ago, and that it began to exist without being caused to do so."[66] His approach relies on a specific quantum theory and the origin of the universe. These are not themselves empirical but are theoretical constructs involving numerous questionable presuppositions. He has been engaged at this level by others and there are articles that can be read for that purpose. Here the question is whether he has somehow proven that being can possibly come from non-being.

Smith relies on the uncertainty that quantum physics appears to reveal about causation. The best known statement of this is the Heisenberg Uncertainty Principle. This states that the speed and location of a particle cannot be known at the same time. Specifically, involving the decay of atomic particles, this is extended to argue that it cannot be known which particles will decay when, although it can be known how many particles will decay in a specified time. That this is not an instance of uncaused events, let alone being from non-being, should be clear. It is not surprising that location and speed cannot be known at the same time since to know speed one must measure a particle as it passes between multiple points which then interferes with its location, while to know location one must isolate a particle at a given point which interferes with its speed. To move from the uncertainty surrounding which particles will decay to uncaused events is a conceptual, not empirical, jump. As noted above this conceptual jump undermines intelligibility, and those who employ it must be consistent to be intellectually honest. The decay of particles might not have a *physical cause*, but this does not mean it has *no cause*.

Some in quantum physics are very explicit about uncaused events existing:

> The principle, referred to as genuine fortuitousness, implies that the basic event, a click in a counter, comes without any cause and thus as a discontinuity in space-time. From this principle, the formalism of quantum mechanics emerges with a radically new content, no longer dealing with things (atoms, particles, or fields) to be measured. Instead, quantum mechanics is recognized as the theory of distributions of uncaused clicks that form patterns laid down by space-time symmetry and is thereby revealed as a subject of unexpected simplicity and beauty. The departure from usual quantum mechanics is strikingly borne out by the absence of

66. Smith, "The Uncaused," 39.

Planck's constant from the theory. The elimination of indeterminate particles as cause for the clicks, which the principle of genuine fortuitousness implies, is analogous to the elimination of the ether implied by the principle of relativity.[67]

These physicists are also consistent in realizing that if this is the case, then the event is unanalyzable (unknowable),[68] and in connecting uncaused events to being from non-being: "a click that comes by itself as a discontinuity is not connected to a thing (object) that existed previously and thus cannot be a measurement of anything."[69] The rejection of causation is recognized to go against deeply held beliefs, but is said to be consistent with the evidence.[70] The problem with this empirical approach has already been noted: How can it be determined from experience if an event was uncaused? And to posit uncaused events conceptually (as opposed to from experience) undermines all attempts at intelligibility. Another explanation is that these "clicks" are caused but not physically caused.

Theories about the origin of the universe employed by Guth, Hawking, and Smith involve speculating about mathematical infinities and zeros. But they are not actually speaking about non-being, only unmanifest being, unknown being, non-physical being, etc. The original singularity which produces the universe involves numerous conceptual problems. It *is* something—a singularity—but it cannot be known and laws do not apply to it. As the origin of physical laws, but to which physical laws do not apply, it does not follow that it is non-being or an uncaused event. This is to assume that only physical causes are causes. Smith argues that it cannot have a divine cause because of the nature of quantum physics: If quantum physics is indeterminate, a divine cause would contradict this by determining the outcome. This is to take a specific quantum theory as decidedly true rather than highly speculative and disputed. Perhaps the truth of this quantum theory can be decided in relation to its claims about causation: Uncaused events = unintelligibility = not possibly true.

Probability is not the same as uncaused events or being from non-being. It is known how many atoms are in a given group, and how many will have decayed by time t, so the probability of any one atom decaying can

---

67. Bohr et al., "The Principle," 405.

68. Ibid., 406.

69. Ibid., 407.

70. Ibid., 415.

be specified probabilistically, *x* out of *y* will decay by *t*. Or, specific atom *a* has *x*/*y* odds of decaying by *t*. This is a way of describing a phenomenon, but has nothing to do with causation or being from non-being.

By observing specific atoms, we may determine certain probabilities to come out in specific ways. The inference is then made that in themselves, apart from observation, they do not have outcomes but are only probabilities. The inference from here to uncaused events or being from non-being is not valid. Nor is it clear what it means for things to be probabilities in themselves. To be indeterministic or probabilistic is an epistemic category, not a substantive/ontological category. Neither is the same as non-being.

Clarity about these ideas, and consistency about uncaused events and intelligibility, will reveal that quantum physics and its use to assert that the universe came from nothing is not an instance of being from non-being. Instead, the universe is said to have come from quantum foam, or a false vacuum, or some similar term. These are beings, although not material beings, and therefore if they are the source of the universe, then the universe came from *being*, not *non-being*. These are examples of the view that all being is eternal: The universe is continuous with the original quantum foam, and that had no beginning, or was the result of previous cycles extending into eternity.

9.9. EXISTENTIALISM AND POSTMODERNISM

Existentialism and Postmodernism should be studied in considering being from non-being. Must an action be uncaused to be genuine? Must my self be uncaused to be authentic? There is too much here to consider particular thinkers, although much of the above consideration can be employed to see that these thinkers are speaking loosely about being and causation. If Existentialism allows being from non-being, then it has collapsed the distinction between the two; if there is no essential difference, then it cannot be important that my self is produced by another being, or my action caused.

Jean-Paul Sartre describes himself as a materialist who gives due weight to both matter and consciousness:[71]

> Whatever object a consciousness intends, there is always a material substratum, whether it is physical or physiological, engrams in the brain, or the nebulous physical-chemical reaction that is said to

71. Barnes, "Sartre's Ontology," 17.

accompany all thinking … Consciousness is an activity dependent on molecules organized in the form of the body, but this is not to reduce it to body.[72]

In discussing consciousness as "nothingness" Sartre links it to being in a way that appears to preclude his meaning "non-being." Sartre's use of the term *non-being* is related to negative judgments such as "John is not here."[73] These judgments "have a foundation in a nonbeing that is within being and, further, that this nonbeing comes to being through the particular nonbeing that is the human consciousness."[74] The "nothingness" is the world as it is before human interpretation and search for meaning.[75] Humans are confronted with the fact of the world's existence and attempt to give it meaning, but the world responds with indifference.[76] For Sartre there is nothing besides the material world, and his phenomenology is based on an attempt to establish materialistic monism,[77] although he relies on phenomenological descriptions rather than metaphysical explanations.

The area of Sartre's thinking where actual being from non-being arises is in his thinking about free will. Sartre relies on Kant's view of free will and agency,[78] and since Kant has already been discussed that need not be repeated here. But what is different for Sartre is the idea "that the self or person enjoys a special kind of agency, wherein the ultimate determinants of its actions are its own choices, intentions, and purpose … At a certain depth, human agency is explained by itself, and no further explanation is possible."[79] Because of his phenomenological approach, Sartre's focus is on the act of interpreting the world rather than explaining the relationship between materialism, determinism, and the self, or why consciousness arose at all.[80] Even in his view of freedom it is not clear that it requires being from non-being as an uncaused event: Rather there is agent causality. The question will be, as it was for William James, whether the agent is created

---

72. Barnes, "Sartre's Ontology," 17.

73. Catalano, *A Commentary*, 51.

74. Ibid., 51.

75. Hazel, "Sartre's Ontology," 14.

76. Ibid., 14.

77. Ibid.

78. Ibid., 109.

79. Ibid.

80. Hazel, "Sartre's Ontology," 15.

by another being (God, evolution, etc.) and whether this act of creating the agent also determines what the agent will be and do. If not, then it seems that being from non-being is introduced with all the problems that follow it.

"There is nothing outside the text."[81] Jacques Derrida sought to move beyond a logos-centric model that revolves around "is" statements and the idea of being. "Deconstruction is always deeply concerned with the 'other' of language . . . The critique of logocentrism is above all else the search for the 'other' and the 'other of language.'"[82] His motivation seems to be a dissatisfaction with the state of the world and the power structures in authority: "Derrida's work is driven by a desire for momentous revolutionary change, even for 'unimaginable revolution' (SM 82). 'The world is going very badly' (SM 77–78), as he stresses throughout that 'essay in the night' called *Specters of Marx* (1993)."[83] This desire for revolution does not seem to have much relevance for the topic of being from non-being, but some have taken Derrida to affirm that the basic reality is relational. In denying being Derrida might provide a framework for uncaused events or being from non-being. But discussion of relationships, interpretation, and power structures is less basic than the distinction between being and non-being. This is a distinction between the existent and the non-existent. Either Derrida is affirming that something exists, or denying that anything exists, or remaining silent on this issue. Claims about the relational nature of existence are based on existence—they do not avoid it. To exist *is* to relate. To exist *is* to be perceived. *To be* perceived *is* to exist. Here I am not settling any debates about postmodernism, or the ancient debate about change and permanence. I am arguing that these do not challenge the distinction between being and non-being, but presuppose it and then debate about the nature of being. They are therefore not instances of being from non-being.

Derrida and others may be emphasizing the historical situatedness of all thought and the relationship between power and knowledge. Foucault may wish to expose interpretations used to justify authority structures,[84] and this may be taken as a move to skepticism that allows for the possibil-

81. Royle, *Jacques Derrida*, 62.
82. Ibid., 62.
83. Ibid., 32.
84. Rouse, "Power/Knowledge," 96.

ity of uncaused events. This is again to emphasize the relational side of existence. But it can also be to make the metaphysical claim that nothing is permanent, all is change and becoming. If this means that all events are caused by previous events which then cause the next event, but do not persist beyond that, then this is not an instance of being from non-being. But this interpretation is problematic: It seems that something is passed from the cause to the event, in which case that is what is permanent; in order to deny permanence, then, it must be denied that anything is passed from the cause to the effect—they must be radically separated. This seems to require denying causation in the sense of a being producing another being, both having a shared being. Instead, it must affirm that each instance is brought about by non-being. If this is what is meant by claiming that all is "permanence," then it is unclear how it is that this claim is different from "all is non-being" because any distinction between being and non-being is abandoned.

9.10. PHILOSOPHICAL BUDDHISM, LAO-TZU, WANG PI, AND CHUANG-TZU

Non-Western philosophy is sometimes invoked to support uncaused events or being from non-being. Buddhism, Lao-Tzu and Chuang-Tzu are the most popular examples. In Philosophical Buddhism, a radical empiricism is used to support the claim that all is impermanence—there is only the stream of consciousness:[85]

> By 'transformation' is meant that this consciousness, from time immemorial, comes into and goes out of existence every moment and changes both before and after, for while it goes out of existence as cause, it comes into existence as effect, and thus is neither permanent nor one.[86]

Each moment arises from the previous moment without having been caused by the previous moment or being substantially continuous with the previous moment. This seems to affirm uncaused events by denying that there is any causation. The denial of causation is a consistent outcome from empiricism. But this just as easily implies that empiricism should be denied as it does that causation should be denied. If consistent empiricism leads to the denial of causation, and the denial of causation leads to

85. Chan, *A Source*, 383.
86. Ibid., 382.

unintelligibility, then empiricism leads to unintelligibility. This is affirmed within those Buddhist traditions that seek to go beyond thought and understanding, and the sermons (sutras) based on silence.

Lao-Tzu affirmed that all being came from the Tao. The Tao is said to be both being and non-being. But on this point Lao-Tzu has more consistency than most moderns who attempt to make a case with quantum physics. About the Tao one must remain silent. "The Tao (Way) that can be told of is not the eternal Tao; The name that can be named is not the eternal name . . . Therefore let there always be non-being so we may see their subtlety, And let there always be being so we may see their outcome. The two are the same"[87] Being is the same as non-being. Lao-Tzu makes stronger claims than does Sextus Empiricus, but they both act consistently on the possibility of being from non-being. If this is possible, then intelligibility breaks down and silence is all that remains.

Wang Pi's formative *Commentary on the Lao Tzu* helps clarify what is meant by Lao Tzu about non-being. "All being originated from non-being. The time before physical forms and names appeared the beginning of the myriad things,"[88] this is "Mystery and more mystery" and "The door of all subtleties."[89] If the distinction between *being* and *non-being* is abandoned, then knowledge is not possible and only contradictions emerge. This is the Tao. "If we say it does not exist, the myriad things come to completion because of it. If we say it exists, we do not see its form. Therefore, it is said, 'Shape without shape. Form without objects.'"[90] Clearly this falls into the category of being as discussed here, and it has a causal relationship to the myriad of things. But it is not a physical being or a manifest being. It is called a "being which is without form and without attachment."[91] It seems either that it is a being, or it is non-being and about it nothing can be said. "Here the nameless is used to explain the beginning of all things . . . How do I know that the beginning of all things arises out of nonbeing? Through this (Tao) I know."[92] But is the Tao non-being or unmanifest being? If the latter, then this is not an instance of being from non-being. The Tao is

---

87. Lao-Tzu, in Chan 139.

88. Ibid., 2.

89. Ibid., 3.

90. Ibid., 43.

91. Ibid., 65.

92. Ibid., 68.

eternal, and cannot be named as an individual thing or physical object.[93] But it *is* eternal, and is described more as non-action or unmanifest energy/being than as absolute nothing. "All things in the world came from being, and the origin of being is based on non-being. To have being in total, it is necessary to return to non-being."[94] This is a good example of collapsing being and non-being. Either what is meant by non-being is non-action or no energy or no manifestation, or it is absolute nothing; if the latter then by blurring the distinction between being and non-being Lao-Tzu and Wang Pi also see the need for silence—nothing can be said, intelligibility is lost.

Chuang-Tzu said: "In the great beginning, there was non-being. It had neither being nor name. The One originates from it; it has oneness but not yet physical form."[95] Here again are some difficulties needing clarification. If this does mean *non-being* as discussed in this work, then the change from *non-being* to the One can occur without explanation or cause, which cannot be limited to that one instance; intelligibility is lost if this is possible at every instant. But it might also be read as Chuang-Tzu making a claim about what exists and its nature, about *being* and *unmanifest being*, rather than *non-being*. Sextus Empiricus, Lao-Tzu, and Chuang-Tzu move to silence when they are pressed further because if the distinction between *being* and *non-being* is collapsed, then no other distinction can be maintained and *nothing* can be said. This is more consistent than many moderns and postmoderns.

9.11. CONCLUSION: EMPIRICISM AND UNCAUSED EVENTS

The consistent pattern has been that if one accepts empiricism, then consistency leads to uncaused events and the denial of causation itself. This opens the possibility for being from non-being. A common method for disproving a theory is to show that it reduces to an absurdity. This can be applied to empiricism in this case.

Empirically, there is no way to know if an event was caused or uncaused. In observing an event there is no way to know, empirically, that a previous event caused it, or that no previous event caused it. Caused/uncaused becomes a distinction without a difference. Caused events cannot

93. Wang Pi, *Commentary*, 96.
94. Ibid., 123.
95. Chuang-Tzu, in Chan, 202.

be said to be those with a preceding event since both caused and un-caused would have this. They cannot be those with a local preceding event since there might be causation at a distance or non-physical causation. They cannot be those with an observed interaction with another physical object since it cannot be known if this interaction was actually the cause or accidental. The distinction has no difference. Either the empiricist's world collapses into incoherence, or the distinction collapses; to avoid incoherence we must assume causation and that there is no being from non-being. In this realization, there is a response to the critique of reason given by Hume and Kant. Reason must be able to apply to being as well as thought, and at the basic level distinctions about appearance/reality or phenomena/noumena are not applicable.

10

Conclusion: Where Do We Go from Here?

Having shown that there must be something eternal, what is the next step? That there must be something eternal is not the same as the claim that God exists. Indeed, every world religion holds that something is eternal, whether an individual being or a process of eternal return. Can Christians show that the eternal power and divine nature of God are clear, so that there is no excuse for unbelief? In this chapter we consider how this might be approached, while recognizing that there is more work to be done.

10.1. RESPONSIBILITY AT THE BASIC LEVEL

I F HUMANS ARE RESPONSIBLE for anything they must be responsible for knowing at the most basic level. The only way to avoid this responsibility is to deny clarity at the basic level. But if there is no clarity at the basic level, then there can be no clarity at less basic levels, and if nothing is clear there can be no human responsibility. This relationship is affirmed throughout academic life: If arithmetic is not clear, then calculus cannot be clear—if one cannot know arithmetic, then one cannot be held responsible for knowing calculus; if one cannot know the basic laws of physics, then one cannot be held responsible for understanding relativity theory; if one cannot read, then one cannot be held responsible for understanding Homer, Dante, or Milton. This is called *presuppositional responsibility.*

Historic Christianity maintains that humans are responsible to know God. This requires that it is clear that God exists. Being, eternal being, is a basic issue—if there is not clarity at this level, then there is not clarity at any level. It is basic in the sense that other issues presuppose it. If we

cannot know what is eternal, then we cannot know about logically de-
rivative issues such as whether all or only some is eternal. If only some is
eternal, what is temporal? If humans are created and temporal, what is the
purpose of their lives? If humans are uncreated and eternal, what is the
goal of reincarnation? Etc. Historic Christianity claims that it is clear that
only God is eternal, and that to claim anything else is eternal is inexcusable. In the previous chapters, we considered the claim that it is clear that
something must be eternal, as well as various attempts around this clarity.
If this is clear and humans have not known what is clear, then this raises
questions about the need for redemption.

10.2. IMPLICATIONS FOR SOMETHING
EXISTING FROM ETERNITY

There are important and clear implications of the claim that something is
eternal. It leaves only two possible basic beliefs: *All* is eternal or *only some*
is eternal. All discussion about origins *should* be framed within this context. Clarity about being and eternality can also bring clarity about what is
eternal. Some kinds of being cannot be eternal because they are not self-
maintaining; being that will go out of existence or end in a state of entropy
cannot be eternal because it would already have reached this point. Finite
but growing being (the self) cannot be eternal because after an eternity of
existence it would already have grown to its maximal point, or else its maximal point is not reachable (at least it would have grown further than where
it is). Both of these claims (being that is not self-maintaining is not eternal
and the finite self is not eternal) are challenged by oscillating systems or
eternal returns. If there is any accumulation through such cycles, then they
do not escape the problem outlined above, but if there is no accumulation
or change in the cycles, then all effort and choice is meaningless.

If some kinds of being are not eternal, then *only some* is eternal.
Further debate and questions about possible challenges to "only some is
eternal" or the claims about what is not eternal, should be framed within
the context of clarity about the most basic distinction (after being and
non-being) which is between eternal being and temporal being. Clarity
and responsibility are related through inexcusability. If something is clear,
then holding its contradiction is inexcusable, and one is responsible for
this. This extends to the debate about what is eternal: To hold that what

is eternal is not self-maintaining is to deny clarity; to hold that what is eternal is finite and growing is to deny clarity.

10.3. FROM THE ETERNAL TO GOD

To show that something must be eternal is not to have shown that God (of theism) exists. But the next steps are as clear as the first step *if* they are taken one at a time. These were described in chapter 8, although another book would be necessary to discuss their development and respond to objections.[1] At the beginning of chapter 8 I said that theistic arguments have failed for two reasons: They did not aim at showing clarity (the impossibility of the alternatives), and they overextended themselves. If a successful argument is to be given then it must avoid these mistakes. It must correctly identify the alternatives with the goal of showing that they are impossible, and it must argue in steps to the existence of God. To show that God exists, it must be shown that: There is something eternal, the material world exists but is not eternal, and the self exists but is not eternal. These respond to the major non-theistic positions maintained throughout history: Materialism, Hinduism, Buddhism, Dualism (Platonic, Aristotelian, Zoroastrian, Neo-Platonic), and variations based on these.

Christianity is more than theism. Christianity must also show: God acts in history—the original creation was very good, but natural evil was imposed after the Fall as a call back from moral evil, there is a need for redemption from sin through atonement, atonement can only be achieved by Christ. These respond to the major non-Christian theistic positions. Deism denies that God acts in history or that there is a need for divinely inspired redemptive revelation. Judaism and Islam deny that redemption from sin requires the atoning sacrifice of Christ.

To show that redemption from unbelief is necessary Christianity must show that unbelief is inexcusable. This requires showing that the failure to know God is inexcusable, which requires showing that alternative views of the eternal are not viable options. The claim that being can come from non-being was shown to be incoherent (and therefore inexcusable to hold) by showing that it is meaningless (being from neither *a*

---

1. A book that does this is *Surrendra Gangadean's Philosophical Foundation: A Critical Analysis of Basic Beliefs*, University Press of America, 2008.

nor *non-a*). Anyone who can think about the meaning of terms can be held responsible to know this.

To show that the material world or the finite self are not eternal is a similar process. What is eternal is unchanging, or if there is change it is a matter of an eternal cycle. Because change in the material world is undeniable, if the material world is eternal it must be self-maintaining in this change. Yet the material world is changing toward sameness. This can be seen in simple examples, like a candle burning out, or sophisticated models like the universe turning into a cold ash heap (Russell). If the universe has existed from eternity it would already have reached this point (hence the need for materialists to insist it began a finite amount of time ago from non-being—an uncaused event). Attempts to postulate an eternity of cycles run into the problem that background radiation builds up throughout each cycle—if this process has been going on from eternity this buildup would be at its maximal point already (see Hawking's *Brief History of Time*). The reality of change in the material world contradicts the nature of eternality and therefore the claim "the material world is eternal" means the same as "what is changing toward final sameness is the same as what is unchanging." This is meaningless.

That the finite self is not eternal can be established by a similar method. If the self has been growing from eternity through reincarnation (Plato, Hinduism), then it should already have reached its maximal point of knowledge/enlightenment. It at least should know more than it does know; even if it learns only one thing, or 1/10 of one thing, through each life, this would build up through eternity to an infinite amount. But it is self-evident that the self does not now have infinite knowledge. Therefore, the self cannot be eternal. The claim that the finite self is eternal means the same as "what is growing (changing) in its finitude is the same as what would have already grown beyond this point of finitude." This is meaningless.

Attempts to deny the reality of the finite self, or posit forgetfulness due to the body, become dualistic. The finite self is unreal but the ultimate self is infinite and eternal. Or, the self has infinite knowledge but forgets when placed in a body. In order to analyze these claims we must look at the relationship between the past self and the present self—if the past self is causally related to the present self, then something is passed on and after an eternality of this process I should know more than I do now. If the past self is not causally related to the present self, then the present self is new and not eternal. If the self has all knowledge it cannot be in a state of ignorance (whether about its true nature—Hinduism; or about what it knows—Platonism).

These steps are clear, but they do require reflection. They require thinking about basic concepts such as being, eternality, and change. They do not fit neatly into traditional theistic arguments, although they argue from thought to being (ontological argument) and from the reality of change to what is eternal (cosmological argument). The objection that these issues are not clear, or require technical training in philosophy, is an objection to the inexcusability of unbelief in God. The response is that if these things are not clear then nothing is clear, including what is good and how I should live my life. Good presupposes a clear distinction between good and evil, meaning and meaninglessness. If there is to be responsibility at any level, there must be clarity at the basic level, and what is clear can be known by all who can think.

Establishing that unbelief is inexcusable, that the alternatives to belief in God are not viable, brings us to the beginning of the Christian claims about sin and the need for redemption about sin and the need for redemption. What has been argued and defended here. What has been argued and defended here is that it is necessary for Christianity to show that it is clear that God exists, and there are obvious steps that can be taken to show that it is clear. The deeper one's understanding of the clarity of general revelation, the deeper will be one's understanding of the need for redemption for failing to know God. The next step for Christianity, only discussed here and not developed, is to show that God acts in history. This involves showing that the world was created very good (without evil), and that natural evil was imposed on the creation as a call back from moral evil. It involves showing that redemption is necessary and only achievable through atonement, and that Christ must be the one who gives the atoning sacrifice. Like clarity and inexcusability, these points go together as a whole and must be developed and defended together. They are a system, logically related. In doing this the process takes us to the end of the clarity of general revelation, and the beginning of the search for special revelation. This search makes sense only in the context of the inexcusability of unbelief and the clarity of God's existence.

10.4. CONCLUSION: THE PRINCIPLE OF CLARITY AND THE POSSIBILITY OF KNOWLEDGE THROUGH THE CRITICAL USE OF REASON

This work has considered a necessary presupposition behind the Historic Christian claims about redemption and the inexcusability of unbelief. This presupposition is called *the principle of clarity*. It states that for unbelief to be inexcusable God's existence must be clear (readily knowable—the opposite is impossible). A number of attempts to avoid showing the clarity of God's existence were considered and demonstrated to be insufficient to support the claim that all humans need redemption from unbelief.

Attempts to avoid giving theistic proofs were considered, and then some of the best representations of theistic arguments were analyzed. While Aquinas offered arguments, his approach undermined the claim that God's existence is clear and therefore he did not offer an adequate foundation for the claim that unbelief is inexcusable. Locke did claim that God's existence is clear but he did not offer an adequate proof (due to his empiricism) and he did not see that unbelief is inexcusable and requires redemption.

The challenges of Hume and Kant were considered in light of these shortcomings. They offered important challenges. Many abandoned Historic Christianity in light of these challenges. Some attempted to respond to the challenges and these responses were considered and seen to be inadequate.

The central features of the Hume/Kant challenge are its empirical assumptions and critique of reason. If a response is to be made, it must show that there is an ontological function to reason. It must show that reason applies to being as well as thought, that reason can be used to know God. If it can be shown that it is clear that God exists, that the alternatives are not rational, then unbelief is inexcusable. This has serious implications for most (all) people since unbelief is so widespread. The implications are that while God exists, most (all) humans are in a condition of guilt with respect to God. This guilt extends to those living within the reach of special revelation and to those outside that reach. It extends to persons living before special revelation and persons living after special revelation. The realization of guilt naturally raises the question: How can I be forgiven? This is a topic for special revelation.

As was indicated above, finding a proof to show the clarity of God's existence would imply a deepening of the understanding about the nature of sin and the need for redemption. While idolatry is generally believed to be commanded against, this brings to the surface a new level of idolatry that has not been discussed in much detail historically or currently. The failure to know God and the consequent replacement of God with some other view is idolatry. The failure to know God is culpable ignorance. This is only true if it is possible to know God, and the knowledge of God is readily available. If these are true then the need for redemption becomes all the more clear. The reality that it is clear that God exists provides a framework for establishing the seriousness of the nature of redemption; the atoning payment requires the death of Christ. The significance of this payment highlights the significance of not knowing what is clear.

On the other hand, if it can be shown that it is not clear that God exists then Historic Christianity and its exclusivist claims about redemption must be abandoned. The question is: Is there any part of Christianity that can be kept? My sense is that Bertrand Russell was right and the answer is "no!" The weak and watered down versions of Christianity contradict the claims made by Christ and the Apostles. The historic criticism of the nineteenth century might seek to winnow down the claims of Christ to one or two weak moralizing dictums. But what this leaves is pale, ghostly, and unattractive compared to the other world religions. It is not surprising that while historic criticism started by accepting most of the general claims made by Christianity it ended in unbelief. It seems that if it is not clear that God exists, Christianity has lost its viability. If it cannot maintain its central truth that ignorance of God is inexcusable what becomes of its message of redemption? Recently there have been a number of books bringing Russell's challenge into the contemporary discussion: *The End of Faith* by Sam Harris, *God is not Great* by Christopher Hitchens, and *The God Delusion* by Richard Dawkins. These are largely aimed at fideism and the failure of the traditional arguments.

These are significant implications. A person cannot avoid them. They suggest the need for significant change. And yet the principle of clarity is hardly thought about by most on either side of the theistic debate. Great effort is required, and significant difficulty faced, in trying to get this principle into focus for people. This seems to imply a continued decline of Historic Christianity. I make no prediction. The critics of Christianity have not given a rational foundation for their view either. The consequence is an age of skepticism. What is necessary to emerge from skepticism is a reaffirmation of the power of reason. Could a realization of the ontological function of reason be such a reaffirmation? Certainly. In fact, it seems impossible, after Hume and Kant, to emerge from skepticism without it. If the ontological function of reason coupled with presuppositional responsibility makes possible the ability to prove that God exists, then it opens the door to the clarity of God's existence. The clarity of God's existence and the inexcusability of unbelief become real options.

This means that the solution to skepticism and its ailments and the necessary presupposition behind the redemptive claims of Christianity are linked. They are both to be found in a reaffirmation of rationality as an essential feature of human nature and the good life. Not mere rationality but the use of reason to know what is basic, the use of reason to demonstrate what is clear. We can conclude by affirming the necessity of the principle of clarity and the possibility for knowledge through the use of reason, while admitting that much more work must be done in justifying the claim that it is clear that God exists.

Bibliography

Alton, P. William. *Perceiving God: The Epistemology of Religious Experience.* New York: Cornell University Press, 1991.

Anselm. *Monologion and Proslogion: With the Replies of Gaunilo and Anselm.* Translated by Thomas Williams. Indianapolis: Hacket Publishing, 1996.

Aquinas, Thomas. *Summa Theologica.* Great Books, edited by Mortimer J. Adler. Vol. 19. Chicago: Encyclopaedia Britannica, Incorporated, 1955.

Armogathe, Jean-Robert. "Proofs of the Existence of God." in *The Cambridge History of Seventeenth-Century Philosophy,* edited by Daniel Garber and Michael Ayers. Cambridge: Cambridge University Press, 1998.

Askew, Richard. "On Fideism and Alvin Plantinga." *International Journal for Philosophy of Religion* 23, no. 1 (1998): 3–16.

Augustine. *City of God.* Translated by Henry Bettenson. London: Penguin Books, 2003.

———. *Confessions.* Translated by Henry Chadwick. Oxford: Oxford University Press, 1991.

———. *Enchiridion.* Washington D.C.: Regnery, 1996.

Bahnsen, Greg L. *Van Til's Apologetic: Reading and Analysis.* Philipsburg: Presbyterian and Reformed Publishing, 1998.

Barnes, Hazel E. "Sartre's Ontology: The Revealing and Making of Being." in *The Cambridge Companion to Sartre,* edited by Christina Howells, 13. Cambridge: Cambridge University Press, 1992.

Barth, Karl. *The Epistle to the Romans.* Translated by E. C. Hoskyns. Oxford: Oxford University Press, 1968.

———. *Dogmatics in Outline.* New York: Harper Perennial, 1959.

Bohr, Aage, Ben R. Mottelson, and Ole Ulfbeck. "The Principle Underlying Quantum Mechanics." *Foundations of Physics* 34, no. 3 (March 2004): 404.

Brown, Peter. *Augustine of Hippo: A Biography.* Los Angeles: University of California Press, 2000.

Caldecott, Alfred. *The Philosophy of Religion in England and America.* London: Methuen and Co, 1901.

Calvin, John, Tony Lane, and Hilary Osborne, eds. *The Institutes of Christian Religion.* Abridged ed. Baker Academic, 1987.

Catalano, Joseph S. *A Commentary on Jean-Paul Sartre's 'Being and Nothingness'.* New York: Harper and Row, 1974.

Chakravartty, Anjan. "Causal Realism: Events and Processes." *Erkenntnis* no. 63 (2005): 7.

Chan, Wing-Tsit. *A Source Book in Chinese Philosophy.* Princeton: Princeton University Press, 1963.

Charnock, Stephen. *The Existence and Attributes of God.* Reprint ed. Baker Books, 1996.

Clark, Gordon. *Religion, Reason, and Revelation.* Hobbs, NM: The Trinity Foundation, 1995.

Bibliography

Clark, Kelly James. *Return to Reason: A Critique of Enlightment Evidentialism and a Defense of Reason and Belief in God*. William B. Eerdmans Publishing Company, 1990.

Clatterbaugh, Kenneth. *The Causation Debate in Modern Philosophy 1637–1739*. London: Routledge, 1999.

Copan, Paul and William Lane Craig. *Creation Out of Nothing: A Biblical, Philosophical, and Scientific Explanation*. Grand Rapids: Baker Academic, 2004.

Copleston, Frederick Charles. *A History of Philosophy, Vol. 5: Hobbes to Hume*. Search Press, Limited, 1994.

———. Frederick Charles. *A History of Philosophy, Vol. 6: Wolff to Kant*. Search Press, Limited, 1994.

Craig, William Lane. "The Classical Method." in *Five Views on Apologetics*, edited by Steven B. Cowan, 25. Grand Rapids: Zondervan Publishing House, 2000.

Craig, William Lane and Walter Sinnott-Armstrong. *God?: A Debate between a Christian and an Atheist*. Point/Counter Point, edited by James P. Sterba. Oxford: Oxford University Press.

Craig, William Lane. *Reasonable Faith: Christian Truth and Apologetics*. Revised ed. Crossway Books, 1994.

Demarest, Bruce A. *General Revelation: Historical Views and Contemporary Issues*. Grand Rapids: Zondervan Publishing House, 1982.

Diehl, David W. "Evangelicalism and General Revelation: An Unfinished Agenda." *Evangelical Theological Society Papers* Theological Research Exchange Society Network, (1987).

Feinberg, Paul D. "The Cumulative Case Method." in *Five Views on Apologetics*. Translated by CounterPoints, edited by Paul B. Cowan, 147. Grand Rapids: Zondervan Publishing House, 2000.

Feuerbach, Ludwig. *The essence of Christianity*. New York: Prometheus Books, 1989.

Frame, John. "The Presuppositional Method." in *Five Views on Apologetics*, edited by Paul B. Cowan, 207. Grand Rapids: Zondervan Publishing House, 2000.

Freud, Sigmund. *Civilization and its Discontents*. Translated by James Strachey. New York: W.W. Norton and Company, 1961.

Gale, Richard M. and Alexander R. Pruss. "A Response to Oppy, and to Davey and Clifton." *Religious Studies* 38, (2002): 89.

González, Justo L. *A History of Christian Thought*. History of Christian Thought Ser. Abingdon Press, 1987.

Guth, Alan. *The Inflationary Universe: The Quest for a New Theory of Cosmic Origins*. Reading: Helix Books, 1997.

Habermas, Gary. "The Evidential Method." in *Five Views on Apologetics*, edited by Paul B. Cowan, 91. Grand Rapids: Zondervan Publishing House, 2000.

Hart, Hendrik, Johan Van Der Hoeven, and Nicholas Wolterstorff, eds. *Rationality in the Calvinian Tradition*. Lanham, MD: University Press of America, 1983.

Hawking, Stephen W. *A Brief History of Time*. New York: Bantam Books, 1988.

Hegel, Georg Wilhelm Friedrich. *Lectures on the Philosophy of World History*. Translated by H. B. Nisbet. Cambridge: Cambridge University Press, 1975.

Henry, Carl F. H. *God, Revelation, and Authority*. Vol. 1. Crossway Books, 1999.

Hester, Marcus. *Faith, Reason and Skepticism*. Temple University Press, 1992.

Hick, John. "Religious Pluralism and the Rationality of Religious Belief." *Faith and Philosophy* 10, no. 2 (Ap, 1993): 242.

Bibliography

———. "A Philosophy of Religious Pluralism." in *Classical and Contemporary Readings in the Philosophy of Religion*, edited by John Hick. 3rd ed., 418. Uppder Saddle River: Prentice Hall, 1990.

Hodge, A. A. *The Westminster Confession: A Commentary.* Edingburgh:Banner of Truth, 2004.

Hodgson, Peter C. *Hegel and Christian Theology: A Reading of the Lectures on the Philosophy of Religion.* Oxford University Press, Incorporated, 2005.

Hume, David. *Hume's Enquiries*, edited by L.A. Selby-Bigge. New York: The Clarendon Press, 1966.

———. *Dialogues Concerning Natural Religion.* New York: Hafner Publishing Company, 1955.

James, William. *The Varieties of Religious Experience.* New York: Routledge, 2002.

———. "The Dilemma of Determinism." Rutgers University.http://rci.rutgers.edu/~stich/104_Master_File/104_Readings/James/James_DILEMMA_OF_DETERMINISM.pdf (accessed March 1, 2007).

Jopling, David A. "Sartre's Moral Psychology." in *The Cambridge Companion to Sartre*, edited by Christina Howells, 103. Cambridge: Cambridge University Press, 1992.

Kant, Immanuel. *Critique of Pure Reason* . Translated by Norman Kemp Smith. New York: Palgrave Macmillan, 2003.

Karkkainen, Veli-Matti. *An Introduction to the Theology of Religions: Biblical, Historical and Contemporary Perspectives.* Downers Grove: InterVarsity Press, 2003.

Kierkegaard, Søren.Soren, *Concluding Unscientific Postscript.* Translated by Howard V. Hong and Edna H. Hong, edited by Howard V. Hong, Edna V. Hong. Princeton: Princeton University Press, 1992.

———. *Philosophical Fragments.* Princeton: Princeton University Press, 1992.

King, James T. "Fideism and Rationality." *New Scholasticism* Autumn, no. 49 (1975): 431.

Kung, Hans. *Does God Exist?: An Answer for Today.* Crossroad Publishing Company, 1994.

Leibniz, G. W. *New Essays on Human Understanding.* Translated by Peter Remnant and Jonathan Bennett. Cambridge: Cambridge University Press, 1996.

Livingston, James C. *Modern Christian Thought: The Enlightenment and the Nineteenth Century, Vol. I.* 2nd ed. Prentice Hall PTR, 1996.

Locke, John. *An Essay Concerning Human Understanding*, edited by Peter H. Nidditch. Oxford: Clarendon Press, 1979.

McGuckin, John Anthony. *The Westminster Handbook to Patristic Theology.* The Westminster Handbooks to Christian Theology. Westminster John Knox Press, 2004.

McLeod, Mark S. *Rationality and Theistic Belief: An Essay on Reformed Epistemology.* Cornell Studies in the Philosophy of Religion. Cornell University Press, 1993.

Mill, John Stuart. *A System of Logic: Ratiocinative and Inductive.* Honolulu: University Press of the Pacific, 2002.

Neiman, Susan. *Evil in Modern Thought: An Alternative History of Philosophy.* Princeton: Princeton University Press, 2002.

Nietzsche, Friedrich. *Beyond Good and Evil: Prelude to a Philosophy of the Future.* Translated by Walter Kaufmann. Vintage, 1989.

Oppy, Graham. *Arguing about Gods.* New York: Cambridge University Press, 2006.

Packer, J. I. *Concise Theology: A Guide to Historic Christian Belief.* Carol Stream: Tyndale House Publishers, 2001.

Bibliography

Plantinga, Alvin. "On Taking Belief in God as Basic." in *Religious Experience and Religious Belief*, edited by Joseph Runzo and Craig K. Ihara. Lanham: University Press of America, 1981.

——. *The Nature of Necessity*. Oxford: Clarendon Press, 1974.

——. Alvin. *Warranted Christian Belief*. Oxford University Press, Incorporated, 2000.

Pojman, Louis. "Rationality and Religious Belief." *Religious Studies* 15, (Je, 1979): 159–72.

Rouse, Joseph. "Power/Knowledge." in *The Cambridge Companion to Foucault*, edited by Gary Gutting. 2nd ed., 95. Cambridge: Cambridge University Press, 2003.

Royle, Nicholas. *Jacques Derrida*. Routledge Critical Thinkers. New York: Routledge, 2003.

Russell, Bertrand. *Why I Am Not A Christian*. New York: Simon and Schuster, 1957.

Sankey, Howard, ed. *Causation and Laws of Nature*. London: Kluwer Academic Publishers, 1999.

Schleiermacher, Friedrich. *On Religion: Speeches to its Cultured Despisers*. Translated by John Oman. Louisville: Westminster/John Knox Press, 1994.

Sell, Alan P. F. *Philosophy, Dissent and Nonconformity, 1689–1920*. James Clarke Company, Limited, 2004.

Sextus Empiricus. *Scepticism, Man, and God: Selections from the Major Writings of Sextus Empiricus*. Translated by Sanford G. Etheridge, edited by Philip P. Hallie. Middletown: Wesleyan University Press, 1964.

Smart, J. J. C. "Laws and Cosmology." in *Causation and Laws of Nature*,161. London: Kluwer Academic Publishers, 1999.

Smith, Norman Kemp. *A Commentary to Kant's 'Critique of Pure Reason*. New York: Humanities Press, 1962.

Smith, Quentin. "The Uncaused Beginning of the Universe." *Philosophy of Science* 55, no. 1 (1988): 39.

Spencer, Stephen R. "Fideism and Presuppositionalism." *Grace Theological Journal* 8, no. 1 (Spr, 1987): 89.

Sproul, Robert Charles, John H. Gerstner, and Arthur W. Lindsley. *Classical Apologetics: A Rational Defense of the Christian Faith and a Critique of Presuppositional Apologetics*. Zondervan, 1984.

Talbot, Mark. "Is it Natural to Believe in God?" *Faith and Philosophy* 6, no. Ap (1989): 155–71.

Tertullian. "The Prescription Against Heretics." in *Ante-Nicene Fathers*. Translated by Rev. Peter Holmes. Vol. 3. Peabody, Mass: Hendrickson Publishers, 2004.

Vos, Johannes Geerhardus and G. I. Williamson, eds. *The Westminster Larger Catechism: A Commentary*. P & R Publishing, 2002.

Wang Pi. *Commentary on the Lao Tzu*. Translated by Ariane Rump and Wing-Tsit Chan. Hawaii: University Press of Hawaii, 1979.

Warfield, Benjamin B., E. D. Warfield, W. P. Armstrong, and C. W. Hodge, eds. *The Works of Benjamin B. Warfield*. Reprint ed. Baker Books, 1992.

——. "Introduction." in *Apologetics or the Rational Vindication of Christianity* by Beattie R. Francis. The Presbyterian Committee of Publication, 1903.

Williamson, G. I. *The Westminster Confession of Faith: For Study Classes*. 2, illustrated ed. P & R Publishing, 2003.

Wolterstorff, Nicholas. "Introduction," *Rationality in the Calvinian Tradition*. Toronto: University Press of America, 1983.